*Paul McCartney*

Printed in the United Kingdom by MPG Books, Bodmin

Published by Sanctuary Publishing Limited, Sanctuary House,
45–53 Sinclair Road, London W14 0NS, United Kingdom

www.sanctuarypublishing.com

Distributed in the US by Publishers Group West

ISBN: 1-86074-486-9

# Paul McCartney

*Alan Clayson*

**Sanctuary**

# Contents

| | | |
|---|---|---|
| *About The Author* | | 8 |
| *Prologue: "Till There Was You"* | | 11 |
| *1* | *"Que Sera Sera"* | 16 |
| *2* | *"That'll Be The Day"* | 33 |
| *3* | *"It's Now Or Never"* | 42 |
| *4* | *"What'd I Say?"* | 54 |
| *5* | *"Over The Rainbow"* | 65 |
| *6* | *"Some Other Guy"* | 75 |
| *7* | *"Don't You Dig This Kind Of Beat?"* | 86 |
| *8* | *"Nobody I Know"* | 95 |
| *9* | *"I'm The Urban Spaceman"* | 109 |
| *10* | *"Goodbye"* | 124 |
| *11* | *"Wedding Bells"* | 133 |
| *12* | *"Love Is Strange"* | 136 |
| *13* | *"Mary Had A Little Lamb"* | 154 |
| *14* | *"Crossroads"* | 164 |
| *15* | *"Japanese Tears"* | 184 |
| *16* | *"(Just Like) Starting Over"* | 198 |

17  "Don't Get Around Much Anymore"          215
18  "Come Together"                          228
19  "My Dark Hour"                           245
20  "She Said Yeah"                          257
Epilogue: "Besame Mucho"                     280

Notes                                        284
Index                                        293

*To Garry Jones, singer, composer, bass guitarist and all he should have been*

# About The Author

Born in Dover, England in 1951, Alan Clayson lives near Henley-on-Thames with his wife Inese and sons, Jack and Harry.

A portrayal of Alan Clayson by the *Western Morning News* as the "AJP Taylor of the pop world" is supported by *Q*'s "his knowledge of the period is unparalleled and he's always unerringly accurate." He has penned many books on music – including the bestsellers *Backbeat*, subject of a major film, and *The Yardbirds* – and has written for journals as diverse as *The Guardian, Record Collector, Mojo, The Times, Mediaeval World, Eastern Eye, Folk Roots, Guitar, Hello!, The Independent, Ugly Things* and, as a teenager, the notorious *Schoolkids Oz*. He has also been engaged to perform and lecture on both sides of the Atlantic – as well as broadcast on national TV and radio.

From 1975 to 1985, Alan led the legendary Clayson and the Argonauts, and was thrust to "a premier position on rock's Lunatic Fringe" (*Melody Maker*). As shown by the formation of a US fan club – dating from an 1992 *soirée* in Chicago – Alan Clayson's following has continued to grow as well as demand for his talents as a record producer, and the number of versions of his compositions by such diverse acts as Dave Berry – in whose Cruisers he played keyboards in the mid-1980s – and New Age outfit, Stairway. He has worked too with The Portsmouth Sinfonia, Wreckless Eric, Twinkle, The Yardbirds, The Pretty Things and the late Screaming Lord Sutch among others. While his stage act defies succinct description, he is spearheading an English form of *chanson*. Moreover, his latest single, 'The Moonlight Skater', may stand as Alan Clayson's artistic apotheosis were it not for a promise of surprises yet to come.

Further information is obtainable from www.alanclayson.com.

*"Wings are what The Beatles could have been."*
  *– Alan Partridge, Travel Tavern, Norwich, 1997*

# Prologue
## "Till There Was You"

"The number of things that The Beatles are doing gets less and less as the years go on."
              – *Editor Johnny Dean when* Beatles Monthly
                          *ceased publication in* 2002[1]

I've never been able to like Paul McCartney. However, he's not one of myriad pop stars I love to hate either, and I recognise that he's realized some extraordinary visions, whether as a rough-and-ready rock-a-balladeer or as a purveyor of cultured "contemporary" pop. Furthermore, having glided for so long on pop's strongest winds, he's become a past master at pulling unexpected strokes – often just after critics had written him off. He can also be forgiven almost anything for his stand on animal rights.

Perhaps one of the reasons why I'm not his greatest fan is because, of all The Beatles, he was the one I most minded girlfriends fancying. John was married, George was the quiet one and Ringo didn't enter the equation. Paul also took charge of 'Till There Was You', 'And I Love Her' and most of the pretty-but-nothings that sent frissons through female nervous systems. The most cloyingly showbiz of the four, he scored too with his boyish grin, doe-eyes and stronger commitment to public relations than rough old John.

Yet I will not indulge in too many cheap laughs at Paul's expense because, within my limitations, I am a principled wordsmith. As disgruntled record reissue specialists who have commissioned me to pen eulogistic sleeve notes will tell you, I never write anything

I don't mean. Moreover, I have to have enough empathy with the artist concerned to even begin any heart-searching contractual arithmetic. As such, Paul McCartney passes muster. If I don't consider him the colossal talent that others make him out to be, I understand that he isn't entirely to blame for being so overrated, and agree with Nick Garvey, bass player on one of the post-Wings albums, that Paul was "more driven than George or Ringo".

Needless to say, this isn't the first literary excavation of McCartney or, indeed, my debut as a chronicler of Beatle-associated matters. For instance, Clayson accounts of George Harrison and Ringo Starr – the "other two" – were completed for another publisher over a decade ago – though they have been thoroughly updated for subsequent editions by Sanctuary.

I have altered my literary approach for the more celebrated McCartney, partly because of too many dissolving outlines and mergers of contents between his tale and those of George and Ringo – as well as that of John Lennon. Rather than dwelling on a straightforward life story and details that every Beatlemaniac or McCartney crackpot knows already, I've focussed on aspects about him that interested me, and attempted to place him in the context of the social, political, cultural and environmental undercurrents that formed him and that he had a hand in changing.

Nevertheless, I am aware that there has developed a too-analytical if respectable form of pop journalism that intellectualises the unintellectual, turns perfume back into a rotten egg, and tells you what Greil Marcus thinks about *Band On The Run* and what Simon Frith thinks he means. Why should I be any different by not dismantling Paul McCartney and sticking him back together again? Yet I wouldn't have embarked on this project if I didn't feel that it was a worthwhile historical exercise, a way of trying to convince people that I'm clever or, as the more cynical amongst you may assume, so I will be paid the remainder of my advance.

I'll shoot myself metaphorically in the foot further by saying that any serious student of McCartney ought to go first and last to Bill Harry's *Paul McCartney Encyclopaedia*[2] that, for raw fact, deals with the bloke as adequately and as accurately as anyone might reasonably expect. Moreover, if you're after constructive analysis of his post-Beatles music, try John Blaney's *Paul McCartney: The Songs He Was Singing*[3].

However, as Horace cautions us, "*quandoque bonus dormitat Homerus*", which loosely translated means "even the cleverest can make mistakes" – even Barry Miles, author of McCartney's official biography, *Many Years From Now*[4], with, say, his propagation of the myth that The Beatles and other Merseybeat groups had the edge over those in other areas because they acquired the discs from which they drew their repertoire from "Cunard Yanks" rather than buying them from local record shops. "Everyone knew someone with a brother, a cousin or a father on the boats," Barry assures us, "and when they returned, they brought with them [hitherto unheard] rock 'n' roll records."

While one of my intentions is to fine-tune, correct and debunk, I want more than this to recreate a feeling of being there – though, ultimately, the litmus test of any musical biography is to compel you to rise from the armchair to check out the records. Whether I succeed in this or not, I hope that I shall utilise your time intriguingly – but remember, however elaborately I dress it up, these are only my opinions – and not always subjective ones either – about items of merchandise available to all. Your thoughts about 'I Saw Her Standing There', 'Give Ireland Back To The Irish', *Liverpool Oratorio* and all the rest of them are as pertinent as mine – and, beyond either of us, the only true approbation an artist needs is from those who buy the albums and pay admission to the shows.

My principal perspective is that of a recording artist, composer, stage performer and writer on musical subjects for more than 30 years. During this period too, I discovered that the music industry, national and beyond, is not so much a small world as a parochial one, which has brought me into contact with many who, however cognisant they were of it, provided relevant information and insight.

Here's an example. You may think I'm making it up, but Denny Laine, awaiting his destiny as Paul's second-in-command in Wings, signed the back of a Lord John boutique card after I'd spotted him emerging from a Carnaby Street tobacconist's in spring half-term 1965, just as his Moody Blues's 'Go Now' was slipping from the charts. I came up to his shoulders then, but he came up to mine when next we met at a charity concert near Farnham on a February afternoon in 1996.

'Go Now' was a highlight of a set that spanned every familiar avenue of a professional career that has switchbacked to the very peaks of pop and down to its most desperate backwaters. Much of this was – and still is – dictated by Denny's restless nature. "That's what I tend to do," he reflected, "get into a band, and then it gets busy, and all of a sudden you want to get away from it all again. That's what happened with the Moodies and Wings with me. Enough was enough. I like to try my hand at other things – things you can't do when you're in a band."

I am grateful to Denny – and also to Cliff Bennett, Rod Davis, Bill Harry, Neil Innes, John Duff Lowe, Gerry Marsden, Ruth McCartney, Tony Sheridan and the late Vivian Stanshall for conversations and interviews that took place before this project was commissioned.

Please put your hands together too for Iain McGregor, Michelle Knight, Laura Brudenell, Chris Bradford, Chris Harvey, Alan Heal, Anna Osborn and the rest of the team at Sanctuary, who went far beyond the call of duty from this biography's genesis to its final publication.

Now let's have a round of applause for these musicians: Frank Allen, Don Andrew, Roger Barnes, Alan Barwise, Dave Berry, Barry Booth, Tony Crane, the late Lonnie Donegan, Nick Garvey, "Wreckless" Eric Goulden, Rick Hardy, Mike Hart, Brian Hinton, Tony Jackson, Garry Jones, Billy Kinsley, Billy J Kramer, Phil May, Jim McCarty, Henry McCullough, Mike Pender, Larry Smith, Norman Smith, Mike and Anja Stax, the late Lord David Sutch,

Dick Taylor, John Townsend, Paul Tucker, Fran Wood and Twinkle. As invaluable were the archives and intelligent argument of my principal researcher, Ian Drummond.

It may be obvious to the reader that I have received much information from sources that prefer not to be mentioned. Nevertheless, I wish to thank them – as well as B and T Typewriters, Robert Bartel, Bemish Business Machines, Stuart and Kathryn Booth, Maryann Borgon, Eva Marie Brunner, Jennie Chamberlain, the late Ray Coleman, Kevin Delaney, Peter Doggett, Katy Foster-Moore, Ann Freer, Gary Gold, Louise Harrison, Michael Heatley, Dr Robert Hieronymous, Dave Humphreys, Robb Johnson, Rob Johnstone, Allan Jones, Barb Jungr, Graham Larkbey, Mark Lapidos, Spencer Leigh, Martin Lewis, Russell Newmark, Mike Ober, Mike Robinson, Jim Simpson, Mark Stokes, Michael Towers, Angela Williams and Ted Woodings – plus Inese, Jack and computer expert Harry Clayson for talking me down from the precipice.

*Alan Clayson*
*May 2003*

# 1 *"Que Sera Sera"*

"There's nothing new – only a new way of doing it."
– *Johnnie Ray on Elvis Presley*[1]

When, in the first flush of their stardom, The Beatles made their stage debut in Ireland – at Dublin's Adelphi Cinema on 7 November 1963 – Paul McCartney announced that "It's great to be home!". Liverpool, see, is known facetiously as "the capital of Ireland" – and three of the Moptopped Mersey Marvels had more than a splash of the Auld Sod in their veins.

Most of Paul's was inherited from mother Mary, whose maiden name was Mohin. Almost as a matter of course, she was devoutly Roman Catholic. Nevertheless, the issue of religion did not label a citizen of mid-20th-century Liverpool politically as much as it had over in Ireland since the Sinn Fein hostilities disturbed the War Office's conduct of The Great War, and led to the secession of all but the affluent north of the country from the United Kingdom in 1921. Mary, therefore, did not take to heart the Catholic Information Centre's boxed warnings in the *Liverpool Echo*'s classified section about the inherent dangers of mixed marriages. Furthermore, while Mary kept the pledge required of the Catholic party in such a union to have any offspring baptised into the faith, her two sons – James Paul and Peter Michael – were not to be educated in Roman Catholic schools or to attend any of the Roman Catholic churches that stood in Merseyside suburbs, but were becoming lost in an encroaching urban sprawl that had spread from central Liverpool since the turn of the century.

Yet the area may be comparable now to Gauguin's South Sea islands or Byron's Italy in its potential to inspire greatness or at least accommodate it. Nonetheless, as far as making headway in showbusiness was concerned, this was nowhere as obvious as it was eastwards to Manchester, which, with its radio and television stations was "Entertainment Capital Of The North", or half a world away in the opposite direction where many of Liverpool's exports (of labour as well as goods) were directed: North America, which Hollywood movies would have you believe was a new-old wonderland of Coca-Cola and the Wild West.

Before the Great Depression, which saw the collapse of all sizes and manner of international business enterprises with attendant multitudes suddenly unemployed, the Mersey had been aswarm with ships bound, however indirectly, for the "land of opportunity". Their voyages had been motivated by the slave trade and then cotton – and it had been during World War I that the 14-year-old Jim McCartney had entered the world of work on the ground floor at a dockside cotton merchants. He had risen to the high office of salesman there by the start of the next global conflict when, as an infinitesimal cog provisioning the bloodshed afar, he did his bit in a local munitions factory. Then, following Hitler's suicide, Jim passed a written test for eligibility to work for Liverpool Corporation.

During those distracted times, he wondered whether his late '30s wasn't a suitable age to look for a wife. He wasn't a bad-looking fellow, was he? He stood straight as a lance and looked over 6ft (180cm) tall in the bowler hat worn when those of his generation walked out with a lady. He was introduced to Mary Mohin by one of his sisters and married her in 1941.

Just over a year later, the remarkable James Paul was born on 18 June 1942, a dry Thursday with alternate warm and cool spells, in Liverpool's Walton Hospital, the nearest maternity ward to the furnished rooms in Anfield where Jim and Mary lived in a forlorn cluster of Coronation Streets.

The "James" was both after his father and in respect of the scriptures, but, from the cradle, the boy was called by his middle name, just as his brother – who arrived two years later – was to be.

From Anfield, the family moved to the south of Liverpool, settling eventually in 20 Forthlin Road, a semi-detached on a new estate in Allerton, ten minutes dawdle from the river, and more convenient for Mrs McCartney in her capacity as health visitor and then a district midwife.

In the living room of this house stood an upright piano. Whilst it suffered the investigative pounding of the infant Paul and Mike's plump fists, it also tinkled beneath the self-taught hands of their father who, to put it simply, loved music. He immersed himself in it as other dads might in do-it-yourself, photography or being so unswervingly faithful to a chosen soccer team that a home game is never missed. As well as listening to artefacts from an impressive sheet music and record collection, McCartney *père* was able to speak with authority about all kinds of elements in North America's musical melting pot, particularly jazz – and his own musical aptitude was judged to be exceptional.

In the 1920s Jim had had no qualms about performing in public, whether extrapolating often witty incidental music as silent movies flickered in city cinemas or performing at parochial entertainments on the 88s – and, for a while, trumpet – with his Jim Mac's Jazz Band. Though still in its infancy, "jazz" had been elevated from slang on 6 March 1913 via its use in a San Francisco Bulletin in a feature concerning Al Jolson, whose 78rpm recording of 'The Spaniard That Blighted My Life' had been released that week. Jim McCartney understood jazz then to embrace both Dixieland and semi-classical items like *Rhapsody In Blue* from George Gershwin, lumped together derisively as "swing" by those who'd automatically switch it off the wireless.

Dapper in immaculately stiff evening dress, Jim Mac's Jazz Band took their places on a palais bandstand to begin the night's selection of dances. In the more unrefined venues, apart from when the high C notes from the trumpet stabbed the air, there was often an underlying noise of boozy chatter until, in the hullabaloo, someone would catch a jazzed-up fragment of melody and an ale-choked mouth would trigger unison singalongs from barrack-room ditties to sentimental ballads about my blue heaven and Ida, sweet as apple cider.

Obliged by economic necessity to focus more exclusively on his day job, Jim cut back on the extra-curricular Charlestons, finally breaking up the band in around 1927. Nevertheless, he continued to play for his own amusement and compose too, though the only extant Jim McCartney opus seems to be 'Walking In The Park With Eloise', an instrumental. He was also the principal accompanist during those "musical evenings" that were a frequent occurrence in many working class households before television became an indispensable domestic fixture.

The sounds that emanated from the McCartneys' front room ranged from sonorous renderings of selections from the latest film musicals like *South Pacific* and *Oklahoma!* to a hymn, nursery rhyme or popular song in an uncertain treble from a child who might have been been led forth, glistening with embarrassment, to the centre of the room to pipe it out prior to being packed off to bed.

Sensibly, while Jim was only too willing to impart hard-won knowledge, neither he nor Mary goaded their lads to over-formalise what were assumed to be innate musical strengths. Of the two, Paul seemed keenest and, from being a fascinated listener whenever Dad was seated at the piano, he progressed at his own speed on the instrument, acquiring the rudiments of harmony, and adding to a repertoire that embraced tunes from cross-legged primary school assemblies and – then quite a new idea – traditional songs from *Singing Together* and other BBC Home Service radio broadcasts to schools.

Three decades before 'Baa Baa Black Sheep' was banned in a London corporation kindergarten, no one had batted an eyelid when the *Singing Together* pupils' handbook required you to sing "mah" for "my" and "wid" for "with" on the few "coon songs" included.[2] Neither were token West Indians or Asians present on the covers of the standard *Oxford School Music Book*, which was distributed to most British primary schools. Preference was given instead to a blazered boy in National Health spectacles trumping a euphonium, a girl attentive and beribboned on triangle, a choir in kilts and rows of young violinists and recorder players in pleated skirts or flannel shorts – all under the baton of a bespectacled teacher.

More exciting than the Home Service's dashing white sergeants, drunken sailors, Li'l Liza Janes and John Barleycorniness was the Light Programme, which interspersed the likes of Educating Archie – comic goings-on of a ventriloquist's dummy (on the radio!) – and *Workers' Playtime* with approved items from the newly established *New Musical Express* record sales "hit parade". Though Sunday lunch has never been the same since the departure of *The Billy Cotton Band Show*, most of the music on the wireless – as in the *NME* charts – before about 1955 was aimed at grown-ups.

Otherwise, there was *Housewives Choice* and *Children's Favourites* – record requests aired by "Uncle Mac" – though Lonnie Donegan, who was to loom large in The Beatles' legend, was to aver, "I first heard blues on *Radio Rhythm Club* on the BBC every Friday night. There'd be one folk song per programme. Sometimes, it was a blues." Generally speaking, however, in between Patti Page's 'How Much Is That Doggie In The Window' – covered by Liverpool's very own Lita Roza – and adult-themed 'Finger Of Suspicion' from Dickie Valentine, there was no middle ground beyond 'Davy Crockett' novelties and lewd outrages like 'Such A Night' by Johnnie Ray, "the Prince of Wails". As in the 1940s, you jumped from nursery rhymes to Perry Como as if the intervening years had been spent in a coma.

This was reflected in the easy-listening permanency of music heard in Britain's dance palais. In Liverpool, however, there appeared to be a more pronounced element of check-shirted country-and-western, ranging from maudlin "sincerity" to clippety-clop propulsion; from stirring songs forged in the cow camps, wagon trains and shotgun shacks of the old frontier to enduring Tin Pan Alley crossovers by the likes of Vaughn "Ghost Riders In The Sky" Monroe, Frankie Laine, Tennessee Ernie Ford, Guy Mitchell and whip-crack-away Doris Day as "Calamity Jane". As the 1950s wore on, Jim Reeves became a name that abided above all these.

"Featured popular vocalists" were brought forward to either specialise in areas thought unsuitable for the usual singer or simply to let them knock back a swift half-pint of beer. A spirit of appeasement might permit maybe two current smashes, including one dip into a new strain of teenage nonsense per night – because, as well as customary demands for 'The Anniversary Waltz' and 'Que Sera Sera', there was always some young smart alec during these days who wanted dance bands – spiritual descendants of Jim Mac-type outfits – to give 'em 'Rock Around The Clock', 'Blue Suede Shoes' or some other "rock 'n' roll" number. What with Kay Starr's crafty 'Rock And Roll Waltz' topping the hit parade, it was going stronger than previous crazes, such as the Jitterbug and the Creep. What were Bill Haley And The Comets after all? They were a dance band like any other middle-aged dance band, except they'd got lucky with this 'Rock Around The Clock' detritus and would have been stupid not to have cashed in quickly.

Now and then, some vocalist or other onstage in a British dance hall would be permitted to gyrate, snarl and roll on his back as if he had a wasp in his pants. Not letting personal dislike of the style stop them either, better-known jazz and dance band musicians also clung onto rock 'n' roll's coat tails. The first record release by Ronnie Scott's former vocalist Art Baxter was 'Jingle Bell Rock'. As a gen-u-ine North American rocker, Chuck Berry was seen derisively duck-walking with his red guitar in *Jazz On A Summer's Day*, a US film documentary. Britain struck back with The Kirchin Band – whose sixth 78rpm single was 'Rockin' And Rollin' Thru' The Darktown Strutters' Ball', for a jazz extravaganza at Butlin's Clacton holiday camp.

As puerile in their way were the twirling sticks of US swing band drummer Lionel Hampton, whose raucous nod to rock 'n' roll during a 1955 concert at the Royal Festival Hall prompted jazz purist Johnny Dankworth to voice his disgust from the audience. Dankworth must have felt like King Canute when England's oldest jazz club, Studio 51, closed to reopen as the 51 Club. Its new policy enabled rock 'n' roll and jazz bands to share the same bill. Well, you have to move with the times – as did *Housewives' Choice* idol Lee Laurence, a trained opera tenor, with his spoof 'Rock 'N' Roll Opera' that same year.

Like all but the most stuffy adolescents of the 1950s, Paul McCartney would have been thrilled by 'Rock Around The Clock' whenever it intruded upon Uncle Mac's jingle bells and winter wonderlands as 1955 drew to a close. "The first time I really ever felt a tingle up my spine," he gasped, "was when I saw Bill Haley And The Comets on the telly."[3]

Now a loose-lipped and rather chubby youth, Paul had left Joseph Williams Primary School, a "bus ride away from Forthlin Road", after passing the Eleven-Plus examination – as would brother Mike – to gain a place at Liverpool Institute, which was located within the clang of bells from both the Roman Catholic and Anglican cathedrals, along with most of the city centre's other seats of learning, including the university – opened in 1978 on the site of the old lunatic asylum – and the Regional College of Art.

Thus far, Paul had proved sound enough, even very able, in most subjects. He had a particular flair and liking for creative writing because as well as submitting homework, he would tinker with fragments of verse and prose for a purpose unknown apart from articulating the inner space of some private cosmos.

It goes without saying that he shone during music lessons too. Indeed, while he'd never be able to sight-read faster than the most funereal pace, he became as well known for his musical skills as the school bully and football captain were in their chosen spheres. However, an attempt to master a second-hand trumpet his father had given him was, let's say, an "incomplete success", put off as he was by the unpredictable harmonics, which jarred his teeth during his first shaky sessions in front of a prescribed manual. "Guitars hadn't come in yet," he'd recall. "Trumpeters were the big heroes then"[3] – even if in Liverpool, you were most likely to be blowing one in a public park or Remembrance Day procession in one of the brass bands that were more prevalent in the north than anywhere else in Britain.

Nevertheless, if Blackpool hosted the Mineworker's National Brass Band Contest every November, Eddie Calvert, Britain's foremost pop trumpeter, was from Preston in the same neck of the woods. If well into his 30s, he'd shown what was possible by scoring a 1954 Number One in the *New Musical Express*'s chart with sentimental 'Oh Mein Papa', recorded at EMI's studio complex along Abbey Road, a stone's throw from Lord's Cricket Ground in London.

Eddie's renown was to infiltrate a Giles cartoon in the *Daily Express* in which an elderly classical musician with a trumpet under his arm is mobbed for autographs by teenagers at the Edinburgh Festival. Three other members of the orchestra watch the frenzy ill-humouredly. "How does he do it?" rhetoricates a cellist. "Signs himself Eddie Calvert. That's how he does it."[4]

How could any British musician become more famous than to be the inspiration for Carl Giles? Young Paul McCartney was impressed, "but I couldn't sing with a trumpet, and I wanted to sing."[5] This wish was granted after a fashion because Paul's musical genesis was ecclesiastic as well as academic, and his then unbroken soprano was put to use in the choir at St Barnabas Church, off Penny Lane, common ground between the raw red council houses of Allerton and, half a class up, the mock-Tudor thoroughfares of Woolton, a suburb that regarded itself as more "county" than "city".

In cassock, ruff and surplice, Paul and Mike cantillated at three services every Sunday and, when required, at weddings and in St Cecilia's Day oratorios. Before his voice deepened, Paul was appointed head chorister. As befitted this office, he was privileged to bear the processional cross as priest and choir filed to and from the vestry. He also doused the altar candles after the General Confession during Matins. Yet the holy sounds he sang every Sunday were novel and intelligible at nine, over-familiar and rote-learnt by thirteen. As it is with every intelligent adolescent, he questioned the motive of adult communicants. Were the rafter-raising votes of confidence and thanks to the Lord once a week to assuage His inferiority complex, to quench His restless thirst for applause or a stockpiling of spiritual ammunition for the defence when the worshippers' cases came up in the afterlife?

Nevertheless, in 1953, with hardly a murmur, Paul had gone along with his father's advice to try for Liverpool's Anglican Cathedral choir. Another supplicant was John Charles Duff Lowe, a boy who was to be in the same class as Paul at the Institute. In middle life, Lowe came upon "a photograph taken when Paul and I both auditioned for the Liverpool Cathedral choir when we were ten, just before we went to the Institute. We both failed on that occasion. I got in six months later – and so, incidentally, did Stuart Slater, later of The Mojos – but Paul never tried again. I think he was recorded as saying he'd tried to make his voice break because he didn't really want to do it. If he had, he'd have got the same musical training that I got: music theory pumped into you every evening and weekends, and services on top of that. As a result, you tended to grow up apart from your mates where you lived. However, in 1958, my voice broke, and I stopped going straight from school to the Cathedral every night."

Whatever Jim's thwarted aspirations for Paul as perhaps a round-vowelled solo tenor setting the Cathedral walls a-tremble with one of Handel's biblical arias, his wife imagined Paul as either a teacher or a doctor. She was, however, never to see either of her children grown to man's estate because, during the summer of 1955, 47-year-old Mary had the removed look of a dying woman – which she was. What she may have self-diagnosed as stomach acidity and non-related chest pains turned out to be terminal cancer.

A photograph on the mantelpiece was to prompt opaque memories of life before the end came on 31 October 1956 – though, in many respects, Mary continued to govern family behaviour patterns from the grave, especially those rooted in appreciation of the value of money, and the notion that hard work and tenacity are principal keys to achievement.

Life without a wife wasn't easy for Jim at first. For a northern male, he was obliged to become unusually attentive to household tasks, particularly cooking. With assistance from relations and neighbours, however, he ensured that his – thankfully, healthy – offspring were as comfortable and contented as his new station as a single parent would allow.

Paul and Mike helped according to their capabilities with jobs on the rotas their father would pin up in the kitchen. Yet though the situation nurtured self-reliance, Paul's childhood was shorter than it needed to be, even though he stayed on at school beyond the statutory age, raised recently to 16. He was a likeable and seemingly unassuming pupil, who walked a tightrope between teacher's pet and the source of illicit and entertaining distraction as some withered pedagogue droned like a bluebottle in a dusty classroom. "Paul was a very amusing cartoonist," laughed John Duff Lowe, "His drawings – maybe one of the master taking the lesson – would appear under your desk, and you'd pass it on."

Before entering the sixth form, Paul had been securely in the "A" stream throughout his sojourn at the Institute, even winning a school prize for an essay. As it was with future Beatle colleagues, Pete Best and Stuart Sutcliffe, distinguishing themselves likewise at Liverpool Collegiate and Prescot Grammar respectively, teacher training college, rather than medical school, was looming larger as the summer examinations crept closer. Paul, however, wasn't keen, half-fancying the idea of being some sort of bohemian artist. One of the two GCE "A" levels he was expected to pass was actually in Art, a subject that – like music – the ordinary working man from the northwest, whether navvy or ledger clerk, saw as having doubtful practical value, an avenue for humorous scepticism as exemplified when an abstract by Arthur Ballard, a Liverpool painter, was exhibited upside-down.

Though Merseysiders might feel quiet pride from personal familiarity with the likes of Ballard, art was less precious a commodity, and its executants were treated less deferentially than in London. As late as 1960, no artist based in Liverpool had been able to rely solely on his work for a reasonable income, owing mainly to the dearth of effective commercial and promotional outlets within the region.

Musicians were in the same boat. If on a business trip to Manchester, moguls from EMI or the kingdom's other three major record companies rarely seized the chance to sound out talent in Macclesfield, Preston, Liverpool or other conurbations within easy reach. In the realm of popular music, it had been necessary for Eddie Calvert as well as Lita Roza and fellow Liverpudlians Frankie Vaughan and Michael Holliday to go to the capital in order to Make It.

Sport too was regarded as a legitimate means of escape from provincial Britain's overall drabness, and dwelling until the grave in the same socially immobile situation as your older relations.

Staring glumly through the lace curtains of the front room, Paul McCartney would have wondered if that was all there was. There was nothing on the horizon to indicate openings other than in secure but dead-end jobs with a gold watch on retirement to tick away the seconds before you went underground.

The view from the city's first tower block – in Huyton – was even more depressing, if perversely spellbinding: the creeping smog, the sulphuric light, the miles and miles of Coronation Streets that multiplied by the year. Looking west, you could just about make out the stadium of a football team stuck halfway down the Second Division.

Yet the city had forged tangible opportunities for cultural development matching those of any in London. It benefitted from the bequeathment of private artistic purchases by John Rankin, James Smith and other enlightened industrialists in its close-knit business community. Such gifts were manifest in all manner of public galleries; some of them purpose-built by the givers. Works could be hung and mounted in the Walker, the Bluecoat, the Academy, the Williamson and in the University. Otherwise, they could be seen in the less rarified atmosphere of arty coffee bars like the Blue Angel, Streate's, the Zodiac and the Jacaranda.

The Jacaranda was a watch repair shop prior to its transformation in 1957 via newly painted walls, bench seats and a dropped trellis-work ceiling with dangling fishnets and coloured balls. A conveniently short stroll from the art college, it had become a rendezvous for its students and staff as well as those with business at the nearby labour exchange. You could sit in the Jacaranda for hours on end for the price of a transparent cup of frothy coffee. Entertainment was usually coin-operated but, as a change from the juke box, musicians were hired to play evening sessions on the minuscule dance floor in the basement.

After its opening in 1959, tutors and students alike could also hold court in the cellar bar of Hope Hall (later, the Everyman). As well as exhibitions of local art, "the Hope" hosted poetry recitals and the kind of films that, having faded from general circulation, were watched as an intellectual duty.

Cinema proprietor Leslie Blond had financed the building of Hope Hall, but the city's most famous commercial patriarch was the late John Moores, instigator of the Littlewoods "football pools" in 1934. Labour party leader Ramsey McDonald had denounced it as "a disease" as it spread across the nation; countless heads of families filling in the weekly coupon that might win them a fortune. By the 1950s, Moores, an adventurous if old-fashioned businessman, controlled a retailing empire that employed 10,000 on Merseyside alone.

The paternalistic firm's art society, 70-strong choir and similar recreational facilities were inspired by the boss himself. Nevertheless, Moores the man was a self-effacing fellow with a harelip and spectacles, who shunned publicity. Yet, in other respects, he might be seen now as a role model for a Paul McCartney in later life, because, if parsimonious in small matters, Moores lent generous support to charities, and was a painter himself on the quiet as well as a collector and connoisseur of modern British art. Indeed, a portion of his millions was tithed to the fostering of art in Liverpool via scholarships and, in conjunction with the Walker Gallery, in 1957 he inaugurated the biennial John Moores Exhibition Of Contemporary Art, one of few British arts institutions known simply by its benefactor's name. Its declared purpose was "to encourage living artists, particularly the young and progressive", justified when the winning of a John Moores prize became one of the proudest boasts a British artist could make.

Quite a few of the artists shown came from Merseyside itself, and noisy argument about the merits of their entries and further aspects of art resounded in Ye Cracke, the pub that was frequented by denizens of the art college – as they did in the Jacaranda outside licensing hours, though the café also attracted the type blamed for what moral crusaders had lately coined "the generation gap".

Yet these youths were fundamentally no different from an archetype that has surfaced in every branch of society down the ages: a "fast boy" oozing sullen introspection, despised by your parents for coming from the wrong side of town. On uncovering your sister's illicit trysts with him, a responsible father would order her to never see him again.

Flighty girls revelled in their disobedience. In the 1950s, they tried either combining child-like naivety and *décolleté* eroticism like Brigitte Bardot, Gallic cinema's "answer" to Marilyn Monroe

– or aligned themselves to Juliette Greco, the Thinking Man's French actress, whose pioneering of white lipstick, coupled with black mascara, tent-like sweater and trousers, made her the vesperal heroine of intellectual adolescent females in dim-lit middle-class bedrooms.

The effect wasn't the same in a Scouse accent – as it wasn't either when the secondary modern yobs who, unlike Paul and Mike McCartney, weren't shackled to homework in the evenings, tried to copy James Dean, the rock 'n' roll rebel prototype who left this vale of misery in his Silver Porsche Spyder at 138kph (86mph) on 30 September 1955. Of Dean's three movies, the posthumously released *Giant* was one of the highest grossing of all time – merely because he was in it for 40 minutes.

1955's *Rebel Without A Cause*, however, remains an all-time favourite – partly through its illustration that you don't have to come from a rough district to qualify as a charismatic wrong 'un. On Merseyside, even boys from Allerton and Woolton mooched down to corner shops with hunched shoulders, hands rammed in pockets and chewing gum in a James Dean half-sneer.

If the attitude was derived from Dean, the appearance of the most menacing teenage cult of the 1950s was almost entirely British. Garbed approximately as Edwardian gentlemen, "Teddy Boys" went around in packs to, say, wreck a Church youth club, snarling with laughter as a with-it vicar in a cardigan pleaded ineffectually. A meek if vulgar reproof – "you flash cunt" – by the victim had sparked off the first Teddy Boy murder in 1954. After that, there'd been questions in Parliament, hellfire sermons, plays like Bruce Walker's *Cosh Boy* – that suggested flogging was the only answer – and films such as *Violent Playground* and 1957's *These Dangerous Years*, both set in Liverpool.

*These Dangerous Years* – about a teenage troublemaker reformed by a spell in the army – had a title song performed by Frankie Vaughan who, in 1958, had become a bigger pop star than even Eddie Calvert, rivalling Dickie Valentine as Ireland's most beloved male vocalist. There were, nonetheless, perceptible signs of danger for Frankie after the coming of ITV's *Oh Boy!*, a series pitched directly at teenagers, and unmarred by its BBC predecessor, *Six-Five Special*'s frightened dilution of the rock 'n' roll elixir with string quartets, traditional jazz and features on sport and hobbies.

*Oh Boy!* arrived a year after Bill Haley's first European tour – the first by any US rock 'n' roller. "The ticket was 24 shillings," remembered Paul McCartney, "and I was the only one of my mates who could go as no one else had been able to save up that amount – but I was single-minded about it, having got that tingle up my spine. I knew there was something going on here."[3]

Described by *Melody Maker* as resembling a "genial butcher"[5], Haley was an ultimate disappointment at the Liverpool Empire and virtually everywhere else, though he paved the way for more genuine articles.

Paul McCartney had been approaching his 14th birthday when he first caught Elvis Presley's 'Heartbreak Hotel' on the Light Programme. In a then-unimaginable future, he was to own the double-bass thrummed on this 78rpm single. However, in 1956 he was just one of countless British youths who'd been so instantly "gone" on 'Heartbreak Hotel' that all he could think was that its maker was surely the greatest man ever to have walked the planet.

Listening to this and consequent Presley hits either sent McCartney into a reverie that no one could penetrate or brought on an onset of high spirits that drew in Mike and even a bemused Jim. It was to be the same when Paul discovered Little Richard. In a typically succinct foreword to Richard's 1984 biography, Paul would recollect, "The first song I ever sang in public was 'Long Tall Sally' in a Butlin's holiday camp talent competition when I was 14."[6]

So "gone" was he this time that he started buying Little Richard discs without first listening to them – as you could in those days – in the shop, thus bringing upon himself angered dismay when

"I found this Little Richard album that I'd never seen before. When I played it, I found there were only two tracks by Little Richard. The rest was by Buck Ram and his Orchestra. You needed a magnifying glass to find that out from the sleeve. It's rotten, that kind of thing."[7]

It was, indeed. Yet, having invested an amount of cash that was the equivalent of three week's paper round earnings, Paul intended to spin that long-player (LP) – well, the Little Richard numbers anyway – to dust, sometimes concentrating on maybe only the piano or bass, then just the lyrics. He was determined to get his money's worth. "I didn't have much," he'd affirm, "not enough to chuck about anyway – but most Saturdays, I'd got enough saved to buy a record. It was, like, the highspot of the week, that record. I couldn't wait to get home and play it."[7]

Neither Richard nor Elvis were to visit Britain until they'd shed the qualificative bulk of their respective artistic loads, but a singing guitarist named Buddy Holly did, leaving a lasting and beneficial impression upon one who was to be his greatest champion. Visually, Holly, unlike Presley, was no romantic lead from a Hollywood flick, recast as a rock 'n' roller. To offset an underfed gawkiness, Buddy wore a huge pair of black hornrims. Until he and his accompanying Crickets – guitar, bass and drums – played Liverpool's Philharmonic Hall on 20 March 1958, Paul McCartney had been attracted by "really good-looking performers like Elvis. Any fellow with glasses always took them off to play, but after Buddy, anyone who really needed glasses could then come out of the closet."[8]

Yet it was still a magazine picture of a smouldering Elvis on the bedroom wall that greeted Paul when he first opened his eyes in the pallor of dawn. Presley was also hovering metaphorically in the background during Paul's maiden attempts to make romantic contact with girls who, in the years before the contraceptive pill, had been brought up to discourage completion of sexual pilgrimages until their wedding nights.

McCartney, however, was to enjoy more such conquests than most, his appeal emphasised by paternity allegations after The Beatles left the runway. Among forums for initiating carnal adventures were coffee bars like the Jacaranda where, according to a regular customer named Rod Jones, "there used to be office girls who'd go up there to get laid because all the art students used to hang around there."[9]

# 2 "That'll Be The Day"

"You've got to want to try; win, lose or draw."
– *Clint Eastwood as "Rowdy Yates" in
"Incident Of The Day Of The Dead",
an episode of* Rawhide[1]

Paul knew Rod Jones, but not as well as he did one who'd started his art college course a year earlier in 1957. How had Paul classified John Lennon during the first days of their acquaintance? Was he a friend?

To all intents and purposes, Lennon – nearly two years older than McCartney – had lived with his aunt in well-to-do Woolton from infancy. Soon to die, his mother dwelt nearby with his half-siblings and her boyfriend. After she'd gone, John was not to understand the profundity of the less absolute loss of his father until much later.

The situation with his parents was a handy peg on which to hang all sorts of frustrations. Life had long ceased to make sense for a very mixed-up kid with a huge chip on his shoulder. At Quarry Bank, a grammar school not as liberal as the Institute, he'd undergone often exultant application of corporal punishment for the mischief he made and because he was less an overt bully than something of an emotional fascist as he experimented how far beyond permissible small atrocities he could take mostly non-physical pain and terror with regard to weaker pupils and vulnerable figures of authority. At college, he was loud-mouthed, argumentative and given to bouts of sulking. From breakfast to bedtime, he projected himself as being hard as nails, as hard as his hardened heart.

Despite everything, Paul – like so many others – couldn't help liking John Lennon. For a start, he was hilarious. His calculated brutishness never quite overshadowed a grace-saving, if sometimes casually shocking, wit as well as a disarming absence of a sense of embarrassment, a selective affability and a fierce loyalty towards those few he'd accepted as intimates.

Something else that interested Paul about John was that he was leader of a "skiffle" group called The Quarry Men. He sang and was one of too many rudimentary guitarists. A chap named Rod Davis picked at a banjo, while the rest used instruments manufactured from household implements.

The skiffle craze had followed a hunt for an innocuous British riposte to Elvis Presley. The job had gone to Tommy Steele, a former merchant seaman, but his first chart strike, 'Rock With The Cavemen', had been shut down in 1956's autumn Top 20 by 'Dead Or Alive' from Lonnie Donegan – 'The King of Skiffle', a form born of the rent parties, speakeasies and Dust Bowl jug bands of the US Depression. In Lonnie's lordly opinion then, "rock 'n' roll has no musical value, no variety in sound, nondescript lyrics and a rhythmical beat about as subtle as that of a piledriver. A section of the public likes it – but it's only the youngsters who have to be 'in the swim'. You know, when marbles are the craze, they all play marbles – and rock 'n' roll just about comes into the marbles category. I'm a folk singer, and I intend to stay that way; no rock 'n' roll gimmicks for me!"[2]

When I challenged him about this shortly before his death in 2002, Lonnie Donegan sidestepped by contemplating, "What is 'pure' rock 'n' roll? Its whole essence is that it's impure. It's worse than skiffle to try and pin down as a *mélange* of influences and styles. Rock 'n' roll when she was originally spoke was rhythm and blues, and God knows what that was either. Country blues brought to the city and put through an amplifier?"

Whatever it was, Donegan's first single, 'Rock Island Line' – from the catalogue of walking musical archive Leadbelly – also penetrated a US Top 40 upon which UK acts had rarely encroached. Another was 'Freight Train' by The Chas McDevitt Skiffle Group – with Nancy Whiskey, a Glaswegian lass on lead vocals. It too took coals to Newcastle in that it was an upbeat arrangement that belied the gloomy lyrical content of a 1905 composition by black gospel singer Elizabeth Cotton.

Conversely, Johnny Duncan, a Tennesseean, came to Britain with the US army, but, awaiting demobilisation, stayed on to cause Lonnie Donegan some nervous backward glances during skiffle's 1957 prime. Johnny drew from the same repertory sources as everyone else – blues, gospel, rockabilly, country *et al* – but, being a bona fide Yank, he had an edge over the plummy gentility of most native would-be Donegans.

Yet it was Lonnie rather than Johnny who was the dominant precursor of the 1960s beat boom, given those future stars who mastered their assorted crafts in amateur outfits that followed his example. As well as Cliff Richard, Marty Wilde, Adam Faith and others who received more immediate acclaim, Paul McCartney too had taken on skiffle after buying himself an acoustic guitar. Encouraged as always by his father, he'd taught himself to play after an initial setback on discovering that he needed to restring it to hold down chords commensurate with his left-handedness.

Paul had absorbed pop like blotting paper, and was making what he hoped was a pleasant row on his new acquisition, but Jim would remind him that perhaps it was time to cast aside adolescent follies. He might think that this rock 'n' roll was the most enthralling music ever, but he'd grow out of it. There was no reason why it should last much longer than previous short-lived fads. It just happened to be going a bit stronger than hula-hoops and the cha-cha-cha. Hadn't Paul read in *Melody Maker* that many skiffle musicians were switching their allegiance to less-than-pure traditional jazz, the next big thing, so they said? Unlike skiffle, anyone couldn't do it.

Liverpool's principal bastions of "trad" were contained mainly within the lofty ravines of warehouses round Whitechapel. These included the Cavern, the Temple and – with "no Weirdies, Beatniks or Teddy Boys admitted" – the Storyville (later, the Iron Door). Student union dances at the art college too were generally headlined by a trad band.

Yet no "dads" from Liverpool were to join Acker Bilk, Chris Barber and Kenny Ball in the Top 20 when British trad touched its commercial zenith in 1961 with million-sellers by trumpeter Ball ('Midnight In Moscow') and clarinetist Bilk ('Stranger On The Shore'). See, it wasn't how good you were, it was being in the right place – London or maybe Manchester – at the right time. More than that, it was who you knew.

Paul McCartney didn't know anyone apart from Lennon's Quarry Men and a couple of Institute skiffle combos that trod warily amidst official disapproval. All pop musicians took drugs and had sex, didn't they? In truth, the only stimulant available was in local pubs, where skifflers might be allowed to perform as a change from providing interval music at school and college shindigs.

Feeling the chill of reality, Paul sat his GCE "O" levels – two a year early, the remainder during 1958's rainy June. Two months later, the results alighted on the Forthlin Road doormat. Having passed enough to enter the sixth form, he was able to keep that most noxious of human phenomena, a decision about the future, at arm's length for a while longer, enabling the growth of an *idée fixe* that if he kept at it, he might make a reasonable living as a musician.

He didn't know how Jim was going to take any suggestions about a profession that tended to be treated with amused contempt, unless you'd been born to it – as epitomised by a Mancunian youth named Malcolm Roberts, whose showbiz parents had enrolled him at the Manchester School of Music and Drama. His immediate post-graduate career was multi-faceted. As well as blowing trumpet in the National Youth Orchestra, he also made inroads as an actor, notably via a bit-part in *Coronation Street*. Soon after, he landed leading roles in the West End musical *Maggie May* and a touring production of *West Side Story*.

Paul could have been Malcolm under the same circumstances. That said, it was feasible to climb such an Olympus without coming from a family like Malcolm's, prime examples being Frank Sinatra and our own Matt Monro – who Sinatra was to compliment with "He sounds like me on a good day – or after an early night."[3] A "singer's singer", Monro was appreciated too by the diverse likes of Bing Crosby – and Paul McCartney.

Like McCartney, Matt – born Terry Parsons in 1930 – came from a humble background and had lost a parent (his father) at a young age. When his mother became ill, he spent a year in an orphanage. However, US crooner Perry Como's early records on the Light Programme spurred the starry-eyed Terry's desire to be a singer too. In a voice that would never drop below a strong but soothing light baritone, he started by apeing Como in local concerts where the discovery that responsible adults are actually listening to you singing can create false impressions of personal abilities in an immature mind. Therefore, with more confidence and hope than he could possibly justify, Terry told his mum of a hitherto unspoken intention to make a go of it eventually as an entertainer.

However, though less so than Liverpool, the distance from the Parsons' home, where London bleeds into Hertfordshire, to the storm centre of the British music industry in the West End might as well have been measured in years rather than miles. So it was that Terry Parsons' working life began in a tobacco factory; an unfortunate legacy of which was an inability to stop smoking.

Ten years younger than Terry, Cliff Bennett's background was as lugubrious. He lived along Maxwell Road deep in the heart of West Drayton in outer London suburbia. On leaving school, he commenced an apprenticeship at his father's foundry, "but I didn't enjoy the job and, most of the time, I just listened to music."

Record sessions evolved into attempts at reproducing the unsettling new rock 'n' roll noises, and a 17-year-old Cliff sang in public for the first time at The Ostrich Inn in Colnbrook, Middlesex, accompanying himself on a cheap guitar. Other bookings followed, and if you closed your eyes, with delicate suspension of logic, you could believe that this unlikely looking local herbert had truly got the blues from the Mississippi delta or the ghettos of southside Chicago.

Bennett and Matt Monro were each to have a bearing on Paul McCartney's life years later, but nowhere near as much as Denny Laine, a youth as steeped in showbusiness as Malcolm Roberts. His maternal grandfather had been a music hall trouper, and his elder sister was already preparing for a career as a dancer when Denny was born Brian Frederick Hines during an air-raid on the Birmingham district of Tyseley on 29 October 1944.

As a young teenager, Denny/Brian endured the Draconian rigours of Yardley Grammar School. As he seemed disinterested in academic subjects, Mr Hines enrolled his son in one of the Second City's stage schools, which provided *in situ* training with public presentations such as pantomimes and cabaret at works parties. "I never went in for acting so much," remembered Denny, "the music sort of took over." At the age of 12, he'd already developed into a sufficiently skilled acoustic guitarist to fill intermissions with "Django Reinhardt gypsy-jazz stuff", but an appearance at a prestigious local festival had him singing the skiffle standard, 'Does Your Chewing Gum Lose Its Flavour On The Bedpost Over Night?'.

Like Denny, the rising sap of puberty found Paul McCartney seeking openings among suburban music-makers. That's how he'd come to hear of The Quarry Men during the hiatus between "O" and "A" levels. Prospects didn't seem all that bright for them. Engagements beyond Liverpool were unknown, and the line-up was mutable in state, and yet drawn from the same pool of faces. Neither had The Quarry Men yet received actual money for playing when McCartney saw them for the first time at a church fête in Woolton on Saturday, 6 July 1957.

"I noticed this fellow singing with his guitar," said Paul, smiling at the memory, "and he was playing bum chords, and singing 'Come Go With Me' by The Del-Vikings. I realised he was changing the words into folk song and chain gang words, a clever bit of ingenuity. That was Johnny [sic] Lennon. My mate Ivan knew them, so we went backstage, and after a couple of drinks, we were around the piano singing songs to each other. Later, they sort of approached me on a bike somewhere, and said, 'You want to join?' We used to go around the record shops, listen to the record in the booth and then not buy it. They used to get very annoyed with us, but we had the words by then."[4]

From his first date as a Quarry Man – reckoned to be at a Conservative Club functions room on 18 October 1957 – Paul rose quickly through the ranks, coming to rest as Lennon's lieutenant, and in a position to foist revolutionary doctrines, namely the songs he'd started to write, onto the status quo. The affront to the older boy's superiority was such that Lennon contemplated starting again with new personnel before deciding to try this composing lark himself, and then joining forces with McCartney in what neither of them could even have daydreamed then was to evolve into one of the most outrageously successful songwriting partnerships of all time.

There was no indication of that in 1957. Few, if any, Lennon–McCartney efforts were dared on the boards – probably none at all during slots of three numbers at most in talent contests advertised in the *Echo*, where they'd be up against comedy impressionists, knife-throwers, Shirley Temples and "this woman who played the spoons," glared Paul. "We reckoned we were never going to beat this little old lady as she wiped the floor with us every time. That's when we decided to knock talent contests on the head."[4]

It cost just a little ego-massaging to hire The Quarry Men to do a turn at wedding receptions, youth clubs, parties and "Teenage

Shows" offered by cinema proprietors on Saturday mornings – so that Lennon and McCartney could enjoy fleeting moments of make-believing they were Donegan or Presley.

As well as a singing voice that was on a par with Lennon's, that McCartney had taken more trouble than the others to learn guitar properly made him one of the group's two natural focal points. Lennon got by less on orthodox ability than force of personality. Moreover, unlike everyone but Paul, he wasn't in it for the sake of his health, but as a purposeful means to make his way as a professional musician.

Not exactly the attraction of opposites as some biographers would have it, John and Paul's liaison was now based as much on amity as shared ambition. Nevertheless, they began weeding out those personnel who either regarded The Quarry Men as no more than a hobby or were just barely proficient passengers who made you flinch whenever you heard a difficult bit coming up in a given song.

Those who got by on home-made instruments were the first to go. Among replacements was John Duff Lowe, now a competent rock 'n' roll pianist. Even so, he was subjected to McCartney's quality control. "He asked me to play the introduction to Jerry Lee Lewis's 'Mean Woman Blues'," grinned Lowe. "I did so to his satisfaction, so he invited me to his house in Allerton to meet John Lennon. By then, the repertoire was all Gene Vincent, Buddy Holly, Chuck Berry and so on."

Lowe was present on the day The Quarry Men went to a recording studio in June 1958. They came away from this suburban Aladdin's cave of reel-to-reel tape machines, editing blocks and jack-to-jack leads with a now-legendary acetate that coupled a pointless replica of 'That'll Be The Day' by Holly's Crickets with 'In Spite Of All The Danger', an original by Paul and 15-year-old lead guitarist George Harrison, as new a recruit as John Lowe, who affirms that McCartney was the main writer, qualifying this with "Some say that he was inspired by a favourite record of his, 'Tryin' To Get To You' by Elvis Presley, which, when Paul went to Boy Scout camp in 1957, was Number 15 in the UK charts."

The disc was in John Lowe's possession when The Quarry Men faded away sometime in 1959 – though he'd hear that "John and Paul got together again – and George was playing with other groups." As for Lowe himself, "I joined Hobo Rick and his City Slickers, a country-and-western band. I've got a feeling that George played with us on one occasion. It never occurred to me to become a professional musician – though most evenings, I'd be in either a club called the Lowlands or down the Casbah, Pete Best's mother's place."

# 3  "It's Now Or Never"

"I don't remember him – or George – being anything special.
They were just mates from school."

*– John Duff Lowe*

Apart from a smattering of offstage lines many acts later, John Duff Lowe's part in the play was over, but, as the world knows, George Harrison was there for the duration. He'd been in the year below Lowe and McCartney at the Institute, but he owned an electric guitar and amplifier, and his fretboard skills had been the most advanced of any Quarry Man – "though that isn't saying very much," qualified Paul, "as we were raw beginners ourselves."[1] Yet, even before McCartney's sponsorship had brought Harrison to the group, the idea of an Everly Brothers-type duo with George may have crossed Paul's mind – and, before teaming up with John, a McCartney–Harrison songwriting liaison had borne half-serious fruit.

Overtures from other combos for George's services had been among factors that had led to the unnoticed dissolution of The Quarry Men, but, for reasons he couldn't articulate, Harrison was to commit himself exclusively to not so much a working group as a creative entity whose principal audience was a tape recorder in the living room at 20 Forthlin Road.

After Paul had fiddled with microphone positioning the valves warmed up to this or that new composition, attributed to him and John regardless of who'd actually written it. Of these works, all that remain are mostly just titles – 'That's My Woman', 'Just Fun',

'Looking Glass', 'Winston's Walk', anyone? One that survived, Paul's 'Cayenne', was, like a lot of the others, an instrumental that took up the slack of The Shadows, very much the men of the moment in early 1960. If backing group to Cliff Richard, a more comfortable British Elvis than Tommy Steele had been, they'd just scored the first of many smashes in their own right.

Perhaps when they'd acquired a more professional veneer (and a drummer) accompanying a Cliff Richard sort was the way forward for Paul, George, John – and Stuart Sutcliffe, an art student who Lennon had stampeded into hire-purchasing an electric bass guitar (a magnificent Hofner "President") for what it looked like rather than its sound.

Michael Cox, a lanky youth Stuart had known at Prescot Grammar, had sung a bit, and his sisters had written on his behalf to an intrigued Jack Good, producer of *Oh Boy!* and later pop showcases on TV such as *Boy Meets Girls* and *Wham!* – on which a majority of male solo vocalists followed each other so quickly that the screaming studio audiences scarcely had pause to draw breath. Thanks to Cox's regular plugs on these transmissions, his third single, 'Angela Jones', was poised to slip into the Top Ten.

It was a shame, thought Paul and George, that Stuart was no longer in touch with Cox. Sutcliffe's arrival in their midst had followed Lennon's proposal that Harrison switch to bass. This had had as much effect as if he'd suggested an Indian sitar. John didn't even bother sounding out McCartney for whom "bass was the instrument you got lumbered with. You didn't know a famous bass player. They were just background people, so none of us was prepared to spend money on something like that."[1]

Paul would maintain that Sutcliffe "was kind of a part-time member because he'd have to do his painting, and we'd all hang out, and Stu would come in on the gigs." Stuart was a gifted painter, then in the style of Britain's post-war "Angry Young Men". Titles from the movement's books, plays and films – *Billy Liar, Look Back In Anger, Room At The Top et al* – are more familiar now than *The Toilet, Milk Bottles, Back Garden* and further in-yer-face executions in oils by such as Edward Middleditch, David Bomberg, Derrick Greaves and John Bratby. Vigour not subtlety was the name of the game. Like Van Gogh, brushwork was conspicuous, and impasto slapped on so aggressively that it stood out in lumps. The subject matters for which these "kitchen sink" artists are most remembered are domestic squalor and sordid scenarios from the inner city – just the thing that you would nail over your mantelpiece.

Yet Bratby in particular was much admired by Sutcliffe – and McCartney, then about to take his Art "A" level. His sole quote in Bratby's biography[2] was to caption its back cover. Inside, there was a 1967 portrait of Paul among those of other celebrities by this self-fixated and faintly unpleasant talent who pioneered an art form that caught a mood of cultural radicalism that would first climax in the Swinging Sixties.

Bratby bypassed Pop Art, predicted as the coming trend, but scorned by the establishment as a novelty. Its British pioneers included Peter Blake, Richard Hamilton and Edinburgh-born Eduardo Paolozzi. Pre-empting Warhol's soup cans, the aim was to bring humour and topicality back into painting via the paradox of earnest fascination with the brashest of junk culture, a mannered revelling in hard-sell advertising hoardings; magazines such as *True Confessions, Tit-Bits* and *Everybody's Weekly* and escapist horror flicks about outer space "Things". Like artefacts of a Coca-Cola century, these were usually disparaged as silly, vulgar and fake for their custard-yellows and tomato-reds. In the interests of research, nascent pop artists listened avidly to Top 40 radio, clogged as it was in the early 1960s with one-shot gimmicks, dance crazes and – just arrived this minute – the well-scrubbed and all-American catchiness of Bobby Vee, Bobby Rydell, Bobby Vinton, Bobby this and Bobby that.

The other horn on the same goat – and one more acutely felt in Art circles on Merseyside – was the beatniks. They tended to consume specific paperback books rather than records. Though not even a pretend beatnik himself, Paul McCartney was caught in the general drift, but actually read some of the literature bought merely for display by others.

Sometimes he got stuck as his brow furrowed over Søren Kierkegaard, the Danish mystic, and his existentialist descendants, chiefly Jean-Paul Sartre. Because their work contained more dialogue, Paul was far keener on Kerouac and Burroughs, foremost prose writers of the "Beat Generation" as well as associated bards such as Corso, Ginsberg and Ferlinghetti. Now a television scriptwriter, Johnny Byrne, one of Merseyside's arch-beatniks, went further: "I fell in with a group of people who, like me, were absolutely crazy about books by the beats. We were turning out our own little magazines. In a very short time, we were into jazz, poetry – straight out of the beatniks – and all around us were the incredible beginnings of the Liverpool scene.'[3]

While this was to become homogeneously Liverpudlian in outlook, beatnik culture in general was as North American as the pop charts. Moreover, in most cases, it was intrinsically as shallow in the sense that it wasn't so much about being anarchistic, free-loving and pacifist as being seen to sound and look as if you were. With practice, you would insert "man" into every sentence, and drop buzz-words like "warmonger", "Zen", "Monk", "Stockhausen", "Greco", "Bird", "Leadbelly" and "Brubeck" into conversations without too much affectation.

A further "sign of maturity" was an apparent "appreciation" of either traditional or modern jazz, but the nearest McCartney, Sutcliffe, Lennon, Harrison and the tape recorder got to it was black, blind and heroin-mainlining Ray Charles who, as "the twisted voice of the underdog", caused the likes of Kerouac and Ginsberg to get "gone" on 'Hallelujah I Love Her So', 'Don't Let The Sun Catch You Cryin'" and the "heys" and "yeahs" he traded with his vocal trio, The Raelettes, during 1959's 'What'd I Say', with all the exhorter-congregation interplay of an evangelist tent meeting. Jerry Lee Lewis and Little Richard were products of the same equation, but they didn't punctuate their catalogues of vocal smashes with instrumental albums and collaborations with such as Count Basie and Milt Jackson of The Modern Jazz Quartet.

Through John and Stuart, midday assaults on the works of Charles and other favoured pop entertainers were heard in the life room at the art college. Another place to rehearse was the flat Stuart shared in Hillary Mansions along Gambier Terrace within the college's environs. A large curtainless window, dim with grime, opened onto a small balcony and a view of not social realist gasworks, but the vast Anglican cathedral. As bare as the 60-watt bulb above, the floorboards were pocked with oil paint from the half-used tubes on the mantelpiece. Like farms always smelt of manure, so Sutcliffe and Co's bedroom-cum-studio did of the turpentine necessary for cleaning the brushes and pallet-knives. Canvasses leaned against walls on which charcoal sketches and the odd picture scissored from some periodical or other were pinned.

For a while, John dwelt there as well before returning to Woolton. It went without saying, however, that he and his ensemble could still use Gambier Terrace, said Rod Jones, another tenant, "to make a hell of a lot of noise" to the exasperation of two middle-aged ladies on the ground floor.

It also reached the ears of Johnny Byrne, one of the organisers of poetry readings accompanied by local jazz musicians at Streate's. Further jazz-poetry fusions took place at the Crane Theatre. One presentation there was at the behest of Michael Horovitz who launched 1959's *New Departures*, a counterculture poetry magazine: "At the party afterwards, Adrian Henri, who was the host, said, 'Oh, this poetry stuff is all right, I think I'm going to start doing it.' Roger McGough had read with us in Edinburgh – and Brian Patten, who'd sat in the front row of the Crane gig trying to hide his school cap, was this marvellous boy who came up and read rather different, passionate, romantic poems."[3]

While they weren't exactly "jazz", Lennon, Sutcliffe and their two pals from the Institute framed the declamations of Brighton's *vers libre* bard Royston Ellis in the Jacaranda's bottle-and-candle cellar. Afterwards, he introduced them and other interested parties in the Gambier Terrace fraternity to a particularly tacky way of getting "high" with the aid of a Vick nose-inhaler from the chemists. You isolated the part of it that contained a stimulant called benzadrine. This, you then ate.

While each tried not to put his foot in it with some inane remark that that showed his age, Paul and George went along with this and other bohemian practices of the big boys from the college – even though, apart from an interest in art, McCartney and Sutcliffe especially "hadn't much in common, and there was always jealousy within the group as to who would be John's friend. He was the guy you aspired to. Like, you got an Oscar if you were John's friend."

Lennon's personal bond with his college chum was tighter than that with McCartney: "John and Stuart went to this sort of grown-up thing together. George and I were school kids. We were younger – so I think age was something to do with it. The girls at the college were objects of desire etc etc, and they could talk about that. I'm totally guessing now – but I think John was a little bit political, and he might have felt that to let one of us in would be bestowing too many favours – so that Stu might have been a little more neutral than choosing George or me. There was a little separation by the fact that he was John's mate."[1]

Their wonderment at Lennon caused McCartney and Harrison to cut classes for not only rehearsals but simply to sit at one of the kidney-shaped tables in the Jacaranda, proudly familiar as he held court. Revelling in their wickedness, they'd flash packets of Woodbines or a loose handful of a more sophisticated brand filched, perhaps, from parents' walnut cases. The pair pitched in too when proprietor Allan Williams, the latest in a series of Dutch uncles that Stuart would always have, required the painting of murals in the basement.

Services rendered to Williams were in exchange for his acting in a quasi-managerial capacity for Sutcliffe, Lennon *et al* who, observed Colin Manley, guitarist with The Remo Four, "never intended to have ordinary jobs. They just wanted to play music."[4] Though the Four were recognised as Liverpool's top instrumental act, Manley was not prepared then to give up his post with the National Assistance Board for the treachery of full-time showbusiness. Most other local musicians were similarly cautious.

Now calling themselves The Silver Beatles, the more ambitious amalgam of art students and schoolboys were freer than the likes of The Remo Four to accept virtually any engagement offered. Venues ranged from novelist Beryl Bainbridge's house party, which could be heard in all the surrounding streets in an age before phrases like "noise pollution" and "environmental health" were in common use, to a fly-by-night jive hive in Upper Parliament Street where they did battle with a public address system centred on a solitary microphone tied to a broom handle.

The two most willing to picket for more bookings were Paul and, perhaps to mitigate his musical shortcomings, Stuart. With silver-tongued guile, they'd lay on their "professionalism" with a hyperbolic trowel, either face-to-face or in letters when negotiating with this quizzical pub landlord or that disinterested social secretary. To this end, while they spurned the synchronised footwork with which The Shadows iced their presentations, The Silver Beatles were at one with an ancient *New Musical Express* dictum concerning "visual effect". "Some sort of uniform is a great help," it ran, "though ordinary casual clothes are perhaps the best as long as you all wear exactly the same."[5]

On settling for black shirts, dark blue jeans and two-tone plimsolls – strictly off-the-peg chic – all they needed now was the drummer they'd lacked since they were Quarry Men. They secured one of uncertain allegiance in Tommy Moore, a forklift truck driver at Garston Bottle Works. Tommy's frequent night shifts and a very possessive girlfriend bridled him from the outset. At Gambier Terrace rehearsals, "he used to turn up to do the odd thing in the back room," said Rod Murray, another resident, "and he'd disappear early, thank God, because his drums shook the floor."[1] Significantly, the first legal machinations to get the bohemian element out of the flats dated from Moore's recruitment.

Tommy – impossibly ancient at 26 – would suffice until the arrival of someone more compatible with young "arty" types like The Silver Beatles and their coterie with their long words and weaving of names like Modigliani and Kierkegaard into conversations that would lapse into student vernacular. Not over-friendly, Moore preferred the no-nonsense society of Cass and his Cassanovas, Gerry And The Pacemakers and other workmanlike semi-professionals who derided The Silver Beatles as "posers".

To an extent, John, Stuart and, most palpably, Paul played up to the image. The title of 'Cayenne' had been derived from Magritte's surreal 'Daybreak In Cayenne', and, whilst acknowledging that Sutcliffe "contributed an intellectual spirit that we were all kind of happy to pick up on", McCartney was at the forefront of a dressing room incident when someone in another group barged in on a seemingly po-faced reading of Russian poetry: "It was all very beatnik of us. I can't remember any of it now, but it was [gravely] 'Yea, morning shall not be so bright, lest ye look over the...' – and I'm doing this seriously. The rest of the group's like Rodin's *Thinker*. They're all going, 'Ummmm, ummm, yeah, ummmm' – and this sax player starts creeping around unpacking his sax, and whispering 'Sorry to interrupt you.' We could put people on like that."[1]

McCartney and Lennon's pretensions as composers also caused comment when reputations were made much more easily by churning out rock 'n' roll standards and current hits. One of 1960's summer chart-toppers was 'Three Steps To Heaven' by Eddie Cochran, a US classic rock latecomer, whose long-awaited tour of Britain's "scream circuit" was freighted with an indigenous supporting programme made up mostly of clients on the books of Larry Parnes, one of Britain's most colourful pop managers.

On the bill too was Tony Sheridan, a 19-year-old singing

guitarist from Norwich. After the final date in Bristol on 17 April 1960, Sheridan had been "stranded alone in the dressing room when everyone else had gone. For the first and last time in my life, I'd bought myself a bottle of whiskey, and was trying to vent my frustration at being an inferior British musician by getting sloshed. In the end, I smashed the bottle against the wall – but the next day, I was alive and well."

Cochran, however, wasn't, having perished when his taxi swerved into a lamp-post whilst tearing through a Wiltshire town in the small hours. "Sympathy sales" assisted the passage of 'Three Steps To Heaven' to Number One, just as they had 'It Doesn't Matter Any More' by Buddy Holly – snuffed out in an air crash – the previous year. Like Holly too, Cochran was more popular in Europe than on his own soil. In the same boat was one of Eddie's fellow passengers on that fatal journey, Gene Vincent, who paid respects with a heavy-hearted 'Over The Rainbow' when, on 3 May, he headlined a three-hour spectacular at a 6,000-capacity sports arena in Liverpool, supported by an assortment of Larry Parnes ciphers and some first-division Scouse groups procured by Allan Williams.

When the show was over, "Mister Parnes Shillings And Pence" had charged Williams with finding an all-purpose backing outfit for use by certain of his singers for some imminent runs of one-nighters in Scotland. Among those who auditioned successfully the following week were a Silver Beatles that Allan agreed had much improved. He hadn't actually been there, but it had been reported that they'd worked up a wild response from a full house of 300 at the Casbah, a basement club in leafy Hayman's Green, run by a Mrs Mona Best, mother of the drummer in the house band, The Blackjacks.

Therefore, within three weeks of the Gene Vincent extravaganza, The Silver Beatles were north of the border for eight days in the employ of a vocalist with the stage alias "Johnny Gentle".

To use an expression peculiar to the north, Jim McCartney had "looked long bacon" when his son had announced that he was interrupting "A" level revision to go on the road with John Lennon's gang and this risible Gentle man. Like the younger Silver Beatles, Paul was even going to give himself a stage name too – "Paul Ramon", for heaven's sake. All that could be hoped was that the trip would flush this Silver Beatles nonsense out of him.

In the no-star hotels where The Silver Beatles would repair each night, Paul, like all the others, "wanted to be in a room with John"[1]. The week also coincided with Sutcliffe being temporarily *persona non grata* with the mercurial Lennon. Going with the flow, McCartney no longer had to contain his pent-up resentment of Stuart. Teasing became open harangues that were to increase in frequency throughout the tour and beyond.

Spiking it with the diplomacy that would always come naturally to him, Paul would "remember one source of annoyance. This was, I think, the first argument we really had, because we generally got on well, but there were moments when it was definitely me and Stu. We came down to breakfast one morning, and we were all having cornflakes and sort of trying to wake up. Stu wanted to smoke a cigarette, and I think we made him sit at the next table: 'Oh bloody hell, Stu, come on, man! You know we're having cornflakes. Do us a favour.' The joke was that his sign was Cancer. That just happened one morning, and there was a sort of a flare up, but, you know, we soon got back together. There was never anything crazy, and we got on fine."[1]

Tommy Moore, however, had had more than enough of being a Silver Beatle. His resignation after the expedition put paid to the group next going to Scotland to work with Dickie Pride, a diminutive Londoner whose trademark convulsions onstage had earned him the sub-title "The Sheik Of Shake".

Back on the trivial round of suburban dance halls, Paul volunteered to beat the skins before and after the loss of Moore's successor, a picture-framer named Norman Chapman, after only three weeks. Despite hardly ever sitting behind a kit before,

McCartney was quite an adroit sticksman. He would also pound available yellow-keyed upright pianos, amplified by simply shoving a microphone through a rip in the backcloth.

While he was one rhythm guitarist too many as well, his and John's respective tenor and baritone were the voices heard most during any given evening. Paul was genuinely surprised when his singing of ballads caused some of the sillier girls beyond the footlights – if there were any – to make unladylike attempts to grab his attention.

He wasn't impervious to their coltish charms, far from it, but was, nonetheless, aware of how brittle such adoration could be. Symptomatic of the new pestilence now ravaging the record-buying public, a TV series entitled *Trad Tavern* filled the 30 minutes once occupied by *Boy Meets Girls*.

A sure sign of stagnation in pop is adults liking the same music as teenagers. *Trad Tavern* appealed to both – and, while they might not have bought their records, grandmothers warmed to Ronnie Carroll, Mark Wynter, Craig Douglas and others from a mess of UK heart-throbs in the early 1960s who took their lightweight cue from the States. Some breached the Top Ten, but hovering between 20 and 40 was more their mark.

Amidst all the trad and Bobby candyfloss were the kind of big-voiced ballads and singers that had preceded 'Rock Around The Clock'. As much a culmination of all that had gone before as a starting point for what followed (as The Beatles would be), even Elvis succumbed in 1960 with 'It's Now Or Never', an adaptation of 'O Sole Mio', a schmaltzy Italian job from the 1900s – and his biggest hit thus far.

1960 also bracketed Top Ten debuts by Roy Orbison ('Only The Lonely'), Liverpool comedian Ken Dodd (in "serious" mode with 'Love Is Like A Violin') and Matt Monro, whose 'Portrait Of My Love' had been made under the supervision of George Martin, recording manager of Parlophone, an EMI subsidiary, which usually traded in comedy and variety rather than outright pop. "I was convinced that it was the most uncommercial number I had ever heard," Monro would recall, "but within two weeks, it was in the charts and stayed there for months."[6] After falling from its peak of Number Three, it was voted "Record Of The Year" by readers in *Melody Maker*'s annual popularity poll.

Monro, Ken Dodd and Roy Orbison were exceptions, but it was a sweeping adult generalisation that the common-or-garden pop singer "couldn't sing". That was the main reason why they loathed another hit parade newcomer, Adam Faith, the most singular of our brightest post-skiffle stars. Yet his verbal contortions and less contrived wobbly pitch had enough going for it to lend period charm to his 'What Do You Want?' breakthrough and even 'Lonely Pup In A Christmas Shop' – "a ridiculous, stupid thing to do," he'd shrug in his 1996 life story[7], but still a Top Ten entry.

Such was the state of pop affairs when, shortly after the Johnny Gentle jaunt, The Silver Beatles hacked the adjective from their name, and wondered what to do next.

# 4 *"What'd I Say?"*

"It was one of those constellations at the right time, the right people, the right situation. There was no accident or coincidence to it. The nearest German word for it is *Zufall* – which means literally 'to fall to one'. That's how The Beatles happened as far as I'm concerned: the pieces 'fell' into place."

– *Tony Sheridan*

Trad bands were everywhere, as were places they could play in. With this stylistic stranglehold on many venues, it was small wonder that groups keeping the rock 'n' roll faith were open to offers from abroad – particularly West Germany. In 1959, Mr Acker Bilk's Paramount Jazz Band had been well primed to capitalise on the trad boom after six weeks in a Dusseldorf hostelry where "you just blew and blew and blew," exhaled Acker, "and had 20 minutes off for a drink, and then you were back blowing again."[1] Within a year, however, bastions of Teutonic trad – from Cologne's Storyville to Kiel's Star Palast – had converted to rock 'n' roll *bierkellers*, complete with the coin-operated sounds of Elvis, Gene, Cliff, Adam and the others.

Among difficulties encountered by the Fatherland's club owners was that of "live" entertainment. Patrons were often affronted by native bands who invested the expected duplications of US and British hits with complacent exactitude, a neo-military beat and an unnatural gravity born of singing in a foreign tongue.

Moreover, five years behind the times, German-language chart strikes were principally for middle-of-the-road consumers. There was no plausible domestic "answer" to Elvis or even Cliff Richard – but there were plenty of Dickie Valentines and Frankie Vaughans. Among them were Freddy Quinn, a former deckhand, whose first major hit was with a translation of Dean Martin's jog-along 'Memories Are Made Of This'; Udo Jurgens, omnipresent at every European song festival on the calendar; and Fred Bertelmann, "The Laughing Vagabond". Each one of them was the stock "pop singer who can really sing", and looked about as sexy as your favourite uncle.

Back in Britain, Cliff Richard, Marty Wilde, Dickie Pride and nearly everyone else who'd driven 'em wild on *Oh Boy!* had gone smooth as epitomised by wholesome film musicals from Cliff (once damned in the *NME* for "the most crude exhibitionism ever seen on TV"[2]). Marty was jubilant in his newly married state, and Dickie's 1960 album, *Pride Without Prejudice*, was full of Tin Pan Alley chestnuts with Ted Heath's orchestra in accord with a lodged convention of British pop management that it was OK to make initial impact with rock 'n' roll or whatever the latest craze was, but then you had to ditch it quickly and get on with "quality" stuff so that your flop singles could be excused as being "too good for the charts".

Yet if the average teenager was faced with a choice between Dickie Pride-as-third-rate-Sinatra's 'Bye Bye Blackbird' and Screaming Lord Sutch's 'Jack The Ripper' – "nauseating trash", sniffed *Melody Maker*[3] – it'd be his Lordship every time. The most famous pop star who never had a hit, Sutch and his backing Savages were among few of their sort assured of plenty of work, with or without hits – or trad – and so were Johnny Kidd And The Pirates. The focal point of each was a blood-and-thunder stage act with the performances of Kidd and Sutch themselves as fervently loyal to classic rock as Lonnie Donegan was to skiffle.

The Beatles were more Johnny Kidd than Cliff Richard. Paul McCartney drew the short straw if ever they responded to a request for 'Voice In The Wilderness', 'Please Don't Tease' and other of Cliff's recent chartbusters, but Paul left a deeper wound with Kidd's

'Shakin' All Over' and party pieces like 'What'd I Say?' as a window-rattling, extrapolated finale in which he'd enhance his vocals with knee-drops, scissor kicks and general tumbling about during George's solos. Then about to form The Merseybeats in The Beatles' image, Tony Crane would recall, "McCartney had a guitar that he didn't play slung around his neck. They finished with 'What'd I Say?', and he was madder than any time I've seen Mick Jagger. He danced all over the place. It was marvellous."[4]

This was part of a transformation wrought by a 1960 season in Hamburg's cobbled Grosse Freiheit, a prominent red-light district just beyond the labyrinthian waterfront of the Elbe. A soft "Want business, love?" from a prostitute in Nottingham or Portsmouth might secure a chilled, empty tryst in a darkened doorway, but over the North Sea, bartering in sex was never so furtive. Gartered erotica was openly displayed on the billboards of striptease palaces, and tearsheets exhibited their seamy charms in the perfumed flesh from windows of whorehouses that were to certain Teutonic cities as steel was to Sheffield.

Germany had also clasped British pop to its bosom as a robust bawd would some young dingbat not sure if he was quite ready to lose his virginity. Making tentative enquiries elsewhere, the more out-of-touch impressarios had stretched their eyes at the seemingly extortionate fees for this Presley *schmuck* that all the Fräuleins were talking about. What was the problem? He was actually in the country just then as a soldier in the US Occupation Forces, wasn't he? However, until a cabal of wealthy German promoters commenced, around 1962, a ruthless and costly campaign for US idols to fill spaces in their European tours with engagements in the more capacious clubs, "it was easy," explained the leader of Salisbury's Dave Dee And The Bostons, "to bring British bands in and work them to death, doing two- to three-month stints."[5]

As late as 1968, sending a group over for residencies in German night spots was, reckoned Jim Simpson, a noted West Midlands agent, "rather like training a 1,000m (1,100 yards) sprinter by making him run 5,000m (5,500 yards) courses." Two Birmingham outfits, The Rockin' Berries and Carl Wayne And The Vikings were among those that would make the Storyville and associated Rhineland venues in Heidelberg and Frankfurt thrive again, just after Georgie And The International Monarchs, a Belfast showband, had worked similar magic on the same network.

On the Grosse Freiheit, a haunt called the Kaiserkeller had struck first in June 1960 by enticing some unemployed London musicians across the North Sea to mount its ricketty stage as "The Jets". Their number included Tony Sheridan – with whom The Beatles were to begin their commercial discography.

That lay a year in a future, which Paul, John, Stuart and George couldn't imagine during an endless search for work in and around Liverpool. Then, to cut a long story short, an offer came via Allan Williams of a residency in the Indra, a companion club to the Kaiserkeller, commencing in August 1960. A stipulation about a drummer was satisfied because, at the Casbah, The Blackjacks were about to disband, and, when asked, Pete Best was quite amenable to becoming a Beatle – even if, said McCartney, "he just wasn't the same kind of black humour that we were. He was not quite as Artsy [sic] as certainly John and Stu were."[6]

As Paul had finished his "A" levels, his father supposed it was all right for him to go gallivanting off to Germany like other sixth formers might go back-packing in Thailand. Thus he and the rest boarded Allan Williams's overloaded mini-bus outside the Jacaranda, bound for the night ferry from Harwich to the Hook of Holland.

Hot-eyed with sleeplessness, the Liverpudlians passed through the concrete desolation of the Dutch customs area the next morning. McCartney awoke from one of several brief slumbers with the road buzzing in his ears. As they crossed the German border, quips about spy novels and fake passports ignited nonstop rumbustious banter – with Lennon the central figure – while the bus hurtled through the inky firs of Lower Saxony. Villagers peered incuriously as the elated young Merseysiders wound down the side-windows and shouted insults about *krauts* or thumped out a beat on the bus roof.

Their exuberance died down a little on the outskirts of Hamburg, and had expired completely as they struggled with the first armfuls of careworn equipment into the Indra, pungent still with a flat essence of yesterday's tobacco, food and alcohol intake. With a face like a bag of screwdrivers, Bruno Koschmider, the proprietor, wasn't exactly Uncle Cuddles – but if his manner was cold, he did not seem ill-disposed towards The Beatles. It wasn't in his interest to be. An antagonised group might take it out on the customers.

The Beatles did not complain of any shortage of romantic squalor – well, squalor anyway – after Herr Koschmider had conducted them to three tiny rooms adjoining a lavatory in the Art Deco Bambi-Filmkunsttheater cinema over the road from the Indra. While there weren't enough musty camp beds or frayed old sofas to go round, this was where they could sleep. Like the foul coffee served – as they were to discover – behind the facade of the local police station, it would have sickened pigs, but another Liverpool outfit, Derry And The Seniors, seemed to be making do in two similarly poky holes at the back of the Kaiserkeller.

That evening, the border of light bulbs (not all of them working) round the stage were switched on, and a tired Beatles gave their first ever performance outside the United Kingdom. To their costumes, they'd added houndstooth check jackets, and replaced the plimsolls with winkle-pickers – all except for Pete who hadn't had time to buy the right gear. His gradual isolation from the others had started before they'd even reached Harwich.

After a slow start, Paul had unzipped his toothpaste smile, John's runaway tongue had unfurled and one or two of the glum old men waiting in vain for the usual Grosse Freiheit fare of stripteasers allowed themselves to be jollied along. A more transient clientele of sailors, gangsters, prostitutes and inquisitive youths laughed with them and even took a chance on the dance floor as they got used to the newcomers' endearing glottal intonations and ragged dissimilarity to the contrived splendour of television pop stars.

This was all very well, but, during wakeful periods after they'd retired, the full horror of The Beatles' filthy accommodation reared up in the encircling gloom. Daylight could not pierce it after Paul was jerked from the doze that precipitates consciousness by John breaking wind before rising to shampoo his hair in a washbasin in the movie-goers' toilets.

Up and about by mid-afternoon, The Beatles were recognised occasionally in the immediate vicinity of the Grosse Freiheit. Further afield, they were just anonymous wanderers of the Hanseatic city, one of the oldest municipal republics in Europe and, though 95km (60 miles) from the sea, then the world's third largest port. Its recreational facilities included the Alster yachting lake and promenade; a museum containing the largest model railway ever constructed; a zoo; the mammoth Dom funfair – and, of course, the fun to be had in the Grosse Freiheit mire.

When the '60s started swinging, one of Paul McCartney's paternity suits emanated from the Grosse Freiheit where the night's love life could be sorted out during the first beer break. On initiating conversations with Paul, fancy-free and affectionate females were delighted that he wasn't one to deny himself casual sexual exploits. Though he had a steady girlfriend back home – Dorothy Rhone, a bank clerk – he was perpetually on the lookout for an unsteady one. And if it's salaciousness you're after, Paul and his fellow Liverpudlians' unchallenging appropriation of sexual intimacies was brought to public notice in the first of Pete Best's three autobiographies[7] with its illustrative encounter between the group and no less than eight nubile fräuleins in the murk of the Bambi-Filmkunsttheater quarters. The next day, the five didn't even remember what their faces looked like, let alone their names.

Advisedly, shadowy thighs and lewd sniggering did not leap out of the pages of Paul's letters home during four months away that saw a transfer from the Indra to the plusher Kaiserkeller, where an abiding memory of Horst Fascher, Koschmider's indomitable chief of staff, was of Sutcliffe sketching secretively in a remote corner of the club, and McCartney and Lennon composing in the bandroom where, elucidated Paul, "the only things we write down are lyrics on the backs of envelopes to save forgetting them, but the tunes, rhythms and chords we memorise."[8]

Creative advances did not correlate with personal relationships within The Beatles. John was still prone to antagonising his best friend just to see his hackles rise, but his inner ear ignored the stark truth that Stuart's playing hadn't progressed after all these months. Had Paul expressed a recent willingness to take over on bass before the trip, the group wouldn't have been cluttered still with an unnecessary rhythm guitarist, no matter how contrasting McCartney and Lennon's chord shapes could be. If Stuart hadn't been around, Paul wouldn't have felt so redundant, just singing and gyrating around with an unplugged guitar or impersonating Little Richard at the worn-out Kaiserkeller piano, from which aggravating Sutcliffe would snip wires to replace broken bass strings.

There was no let-up in the tension-charged ugliness, visible and invisible, back in the Bambi-Filmkunsttheater, more loathsome than ever with its improvised receptacles for junk food leavings, empty liquor bottles, overflowing cigarette ash, used rubber "johnnies" and dried vomit.

Yet Germany changed The Beatles and many other British acts forever. Much of it was down to the harsh working conditions. "We started performing every night at 7pm," groaned Bev Bevan, one of Carl Wayne's Vikings, "and did seven 45 minute spots with 15 minute breaks until two in the morning. Each weekend, there were three hour matinees too. Any hopeful beliefs I might have had that pop could earn me easy money were swept away in those weeks in Cologne."[9]

Some were destroyed by the experience. For Twinkle, fresh from a Europe-wide hit with the death-disc 'Terry', "it was a nightmare – mainly because I thought I'd only have to do one set. I did several, doing the same numbers and wearing the same stage outfit. I gave up performing then and there – at the age of 17."

It all but finished The Beatles too when they hadn't even the decency to lie to Bruno Koschmider about spending their rest periods in a more uptown rival establishment, the Top Ten. He was furious to learn that its manager intended to lure them away with better pay and conditions as soon as their extended contract with the Kaiserkeller expired in December. Rather than racketeers and ruffians, the Top Ten attracted young "Mittelstand" adults – a couple of social rungs higher than "youths" – whose liberal-minded parents might drop them off in estate cars. Most of these would be collected just before midnight, owing to the curfew that forbade those under 18 from frequenting Grosse Freiheit clubs past their bedtimes.

The German administration was conscientious too about protecting minors from temptation – though it was too often the case that *Polizei* couldn't be bothered with the paperwork after catching young aliens like George Harrison, only weeks away from his 18th birthday, flaunting the law. However, an ireful Koschmider's string-pulling ensured more intense official interest, and George was sent home before November was out.

The Beatles seemed quite prepared to carry on without him, but the Top Ten was obliged to replace them with Gerry And The Pacemakers (straight from the civil service and British Rail rather than art college and grammar schools) after McCartney and Best were deported too – on Bruno's trumped-up charge of arson.

Though tarred with the same brush, Stuart and John had been free to go after signing a statement in German that satisfied the Polizei that they knew nothing about Exhibit A: the charred rag that constituted Herr Koschmider's accusation that The Beatles had all conspired to burn down the hated Bambi-Filmkunsttheater.

Lennon followed the others back to Liverpool, but Sutcliffe stayed on, moving in with Astrid Kirchherr, a German photographer to whom he was unofficially engaged. She was a leading light of Hamburg's "existentialists" – the "Exis" – whose look anticipated the "Gothic" style prevalent in the late 1970s. Always black with maybe white collars or ruffs like 18th-century dandies, it was predominantly unisex with suede and velvet the dominant fabrics – though you could get by with jeans, windcheater and polo-neck pullover. Exi girls wishing to look more feminine walked the line with ballet slippers, fishnet stockings and short leather skirts. Exi haircuts were *pilzen kopf* – "mushroom head". Though commonplace in Germany, a male so greaselessly coiffured in Britain would be branded a "nancy boy", even if Adam Faith was the darling of the ladies with a similar brushed-forward cut.

Astrid's circle – mostly undergraduates – was a variant of the Parisian existentialists who, since the 1950s, had been stereotyped by period film directors as one of two types of pretentious middle class beatnik: "hot" (incessant rapid-fire talking and pseudo-mad stares) and "cool" (mute, immobile and unapproachable). Both were present at demi-monde parties where table lamps were dimmed with headscarves, and Man Ray hung on the walls. The musical entertainment was scat-singing, bongo-tapping or a saxophone honking inanely. The eyelids of cross-legged listeners stayed closed in ecstasy. With a nod towards the censor, the stimulants and pansexual undercurrents were played down. These weirdos were "good kids" at heart.

"Why kill time when you can kill yourself?" asks a spectral Greco-like woman in 1960's *The Rebel*[10], a Tony Hancock vehicle set in bohemian Paris – all berets, ten-day beards and holey sweaters. *The Rebel* might have been less resolutely banal and probably funnier had the great comedian's flight from respectability taken him to either of the demi-mondes of Hamburg or Liverpool.

It is tempting to imply that the Exis fell for The Beatles like the "Parisian set" in *The Rebel* did for the verbose but artistically cack-handed Hancock. Yet it was more likely that the Hamburg students were tacitly bored with the "coolness" of Dave Brubeck, Stan Getz, The Modern Jazz Quartet and other "hip" music-makers whose LP covers were artlessly strewn about their "pads".

"We had been Dixieland or [modern] jazz fans," explained Jurgen Vollmer, another high-ranking Exi, "and ever since then, we really got into rock and roll, and we never went to the jazz clubs anymore. Our interest developed after we had heard The Beatles, and not only The Beatles but also the other British rock and roll groups – but The Beatles were always our favourite, right from the start."[6]

In content alone, The Beatles were uncannily like all the other groups who could claim *droit de seigneur* over the principally US rock 'n' roll mother-lode. However, Sutcliffe, McCartney and Lennon were all great talkers, using the same reference points as the Exis. "Up north, we'd be reading Kerouac, and they'd be reading Kerouac," affirmed Paul. "We'd be looking at the same kind of things."[11]

The Beatles got to be quite addictive. Exis would neglect their studies, art and day jobs to be near them throughout the watches of the night. "Their natural energy, good humour and wit were seductive," confirmed Vollmer. "We felt at times that we had to force ourselves not to go. Astrid and I went to the movies instead – but we had such an urge to return to The Beatles that we let ourselves go into the doorway of the room, way in the back of the dance floor. The Beatles saw us, and, as soon as they finished the number, broke immediately into 'Stay'[12]. They sang to us."[6]

Of individual Beatles, Pete was a strong-but-silent type in contrast to winsome Paul who, so Horst Fascher would insist, was the "sunny boy"[13] of the group as he scuttled to and from microphones or lilted 'Besame Mucho', one of those sensuous Latin-flavoured ballads that, like 'Begin The Beguine', 'Sway' and 'Perfidia', never seem to go away. Generally, only the title was sung in Spanish when 'Besame Mucho', a frequent *wunche* (request) from the ladies – transported you for a few minutes from the shimmering sea of bobbing heads in the Kaiserkeller to warm latitudes and dreamy sighs – and then the squiggle of lead guitar that kicked off 'Too Much Monkey Business' would jolt you back to reality – either that or Stuart's fluffed run-down into 'It's So Easy'.

A little of Stuart's singing went a long way too, and as an instrumentalist, he was as good as he'd ever get – and that wasn't good enough. Privately, he admitted as much to Astrid, adding that he had only came along for the laugh and because he was John's friend. Whatever was left for Stuart to enjoy about playing with The Beatles was for the wrong reasons. For devilment, he'd deliberately pluck sickeningly off-key notes. If Paul – and George too – thought he was the group's biggest liability, then he'd amuse himself being it. They could get John to sack him for all he cared, even if they'd slain a fire regulation-breaking audience on the last night at the Kaiserkeller.

# 5  "Over The Rainbow"

"Before Paul McCartney gave the bass credibility, the instrument was usually given to the fat boy, who stood at the back and stayed out of sight."

*– Donald Hirst of The Spinning Wheels*[1]

Before they'd departed from Hamburg so ignominiously, Paul had evolved into an outstanding showman, possessed of that indefinable something else – the "common touch" maybe – that enabled him, via a wink and a broad grin diffused to the general populace, to make any watching individual feel – for a split-second anyway – like the only person that mattered to him and his Beatles in the entire city.

Offstage too, he produced the same effect when someone waved at him from across the street, and he creased his face into a bashful half-smile and waved back. There was, nonetheless, a crouched restlessness about Paul, and, however much he might have gainsaid it, he was looking out for any signpost that pointed in the direction of fame.

He was even willing, so he'd intimated already to John, to play bass, even though it was a presence rather than a sound on the vinyl that crackled on the Forthlin Road gramophone, and its executants overshadowed by the higher octaves available to lead and rhythm guitarists.

Such a sacrifice would be to The Beatles' general good because, if Lennon might be closing his ears still, McCartney and Harrison had gauged Stuart Sutcliffe's limitations and could hear what was

technically askew – and always would be. They were running out
of patience. "We can't go on like this," Gary Bakewell-as-Paul
McCartney protests in the 1994 bio-pic, *Backbeat*. "The joke's
over. Half the time, he doesn't show up. When he does, he's in the
Fifth Dimension. I'm not having it!"

Sutcliffe had become almost literally The Beatles' sleeping
partner. Onstage at the Kaiserkeller, he'd been as nonchalantly
gum-chewing as ever, but usually miles away mentally. More than
ever before, he was physically elsewhere too – so much so that it
had been necessary to line up an understudy in Colin Millander,
a former Jet who had stayed on as part of a duo in a nearby
restaurant. Though three years Stuart's junior – when such a
difference mattered – George's exasperation that "he was in the
band because John conned him into buying a bass"[2] had shown
itself in desultory sabre-rattling with Sutcliffe in safe assurance
that Paul would support him when John intervened.

Paul, see, was Stuart's truer enemy. Their animosity boiled
over after the latter lost his temper when McCartney, seated at
the piano, made some remark about Astrid. Flinging down his
bass, Sutcliffe bounded across the boards, mad fury in his eyes,
to knock the detested Paul off his perch. Manfully, the others
kept the song going as the pair tumbled wrestling to the floor.
Used to The Beatles' excesses on the boards, the audience emitted
whoops of drunken encouragement and bellowed instruction as
the number finished and the irresolute fight ebbed away to a
slanging match and the combatants glowering at each other from
opposite ends of a huffy dressing room.

Characteristically, Paul would laugh off this proclamation of
an open state of warfare as a bit of a lark in retrospective:
"Occasionally, we would have our set-to's, not too many really –
but the major one was a fight onstage. The great thing about it
was it wasn't actually a fight because neither of us were good
fighters – so it was a grope! We just grappled each other, and I
remember thinking, 'Well, he's littler than me. I'll easily be able to

fight him.' But, of course, the strength of ten men this guy had – and we were locked. All the gangsters were laughing at us, and me and Stu are up by the bloody piano, locked in this sort of death embrace. All the gangsters were going, 'Come on! Hit him!' to either of us, and we couldn't do anything."[2]

As events were to demonstrate, McCartney might not have been so jocular had he managed to strike a blow to Stuart's head. Indeed, he might have ended up on a charge of murder before a German judge and jury tacitly prejudiced by his nationality and hirsute appearance. The next day, however, Paul was Mr Nice Guy again, but neither he nor Stuart would forget, and, for weeks afterwards, Paul found himself casting an odd thoughtful glance at Stuart sweating over the bass when Lennon was hogging the main microphone. Who'd have thought it – Stuart sticking up for himself without John protecting him?

Yet almost all the cards were on the table when four-fifths of The Beatles reassembled back in Liverpool – "and then the thing was, 'Well, who's going to play bass?'" asked Paul.[1] As he'd rattled the traps in the absence of Tommy Moore, so McCartney had adapted likewise to bass whenever Colin Millander or Stuart had been indisposed at the Kaiserkeller, but for their first four post-Hamburg engagements, another ex-Blackjack, Chas Newby, was roped in.

Chas was there when The Beatles were a last minute addition to a bill at Litherland Town Hall the day after Boxing Day. A lot of groups would sell their souls for a career, however it ended, that had had a night like that in it. You couldn't refute their impact on a crowd who'd been spellbound from the 'Long Tall Sally' opening until the last major sixth of the final encore. Along the way, The Beatles had stoked up the first scattered screams that had ever reverberated for them.

While there were concessions to the passing joys of the hit parade, they still fell back on olde tyme rock 'n' roll whenever a show dragged – though the catalogue had also been injected with a massive shot of rhythm-and-blues – R&B – via overhauls of The Isley Brothers' 'Shout', 'Money (That's What I Want)' by Barrett Strong, 'Shop Around' from The Miracles and other discs of a kind that would become known as "soul" music (perhaps the most abused term in pop).

Drinking from the same pool were Gerry, The Big Three, Kingsize Taylor, Rory Storm and other personalities who were as much stars on Merseyside as Cliff Richard And The Shadows were nationally. While an element of repertory overlap was expected when, say, The Beatles, Rory and Gerry appeared at the same venue on the same evening, "we took to looking for B-sides, songs that were a little more obscure," recalled McCartney, "in the hope that the other acts wouldn't play them." He contended too that "that is the reason why John and I began writing our own songs. There was no other reason for that other than you knew then that other bands couldn't access your stuff. That's the truth: John and I never sat down and decided we must become composers. We just wrote because it was the only way of saving our act."[3]

Suddenly, there'd been a lot of competition. When Stuart Sutcliffe returned home in mid-January, he was astonished too at how many substitute Beatles, Rories and Gerries had crawled out of the sub-cultural woodwork since he'd been away. From Bootle's Billy Kramer And The Coasters to The Pathfinders in Birkenhead, each district seemed to have an outfit enjoying local celebrity. Even one of Stuart's Prescot Grammar classmates, Neil Foster, was blowing sax with The Delacardoes, who held northeast Liverpool.

Many of these emerging groups had got off the ground by begging elderly promoters for intermission spots to the big bands and jazz combos from which many of their older members had sprung. If allowed, they played between nine o' clock and just after the pubs closed. Then the rock 'n' roll temperature would be lowered for the influx of grown-ups and an interrelated bringing of the evening to a close in squarely "professional" manner. Both the newly arrived revellers and the older musicians fancied that the muck to which their children had been cavorting earlier would fade and die so that "decent" entertainment could reign once more.

Yet the swing towards compact vocal-instrumental (or "beat") groups was unstoppable, and an increasing number of suburban and out-of-town venues were becoming their strongholds. In the city centre too, the Iron Door and the Cavern were no longer prohibiting pop from defiling their hallowed boards.

The Beatles were to become a fixture at the Cavern, making their debut in February 1961 during one of the newly established lunchtime sessions. This was to be Stuart Sutcliffe's only performance at what was destined to become as famous a Liverpool landmark as the Pier Head. Its idiosyncratic reek of disinfectant, mould and cheap perfume was still on his clothes 24 hours later – as it was on those of Colin Manley, among the audience for what must have been an off-day for The Beatles who "still had Stuart with them, and they really weren't very good."[4]

Lennon had been pleased to see Sutcliffe, but to the others their errant bass guitarist's reappearance was like that of the proverbial bad penny now that they'd experienced Chas Newby and then Paul's – and, on one occasion, Johnny Gustafson of The Big Three's – more agile playing. Neither Paul, George or Pete knew how they were supposed to feel when Stuart kept his options open by applying immediately for both a visa to re-enter Germany and for a place on a one-year Art Teacher's Diploma (ATD) course back at the college. Each represented an attempt to "settle down". Either way, it would not bode well for The Beatles.

After he failed to get on the course, Stuart was back in Hamburg by March, but an official colour was given to this by The Beatles, who were pencilled in for a four-month Top Ten season commencing on April Fools' Day. Stuart was to be on hand in negotiations between the club, the West German Immigration Office and Herr Knoop, Hamburg's chief of police. Crucially, he had to support Mona Best's badgering and Allan Williams's assurances that The Beatles were reformed characters, especially fire-bugs Pete and Paul.

While Stuart had proved useful as a mediator, "I believe to this day that he would eventually have been thrown out," said Rod Jones, expressing a commonly held view, "as soon as there was some sort of future. I'm actually surprised that he didn't go before."[2]

Just as it was a case of when rather than if Stuart left the group, the band did not replace him, opting instead for the simpler expedient of transferring McCartney permanently to bass. Years later, Paul would be profoundly disturbed by a suggestion from one Beatles' biographer that his machinations to play bass had effectively squeezed Stuart out: "I thought, 'God, this is a long time ago. This guy might be right.' I mean, he wasn't but you can't help wondering. I rang up George Harrison and I said, 'George, do you remember how I got on bass?', and he said, 'Yeah, we lumbered you with it.' I said, 'Thanks for saying that, because there's this guy who says otherwise.' That was it anyway. It was basically that. Stu lent me his bass, and so we obviously liked each other well enough."[2]

Paul's low-fretted cohesion with Pete's drumming was a subliminal element of The Beatles' intensifying local popularity as word got round, and it became customary for the Cavern to fill long before they followed the trad band or whatever else was in support, to invoke a mood of a kind of committed gaiety, often with cramped onlookers assuming the dual role of accompanying choir and augmenting the rhythm section.

While The Beatles' rowdy style was now not only acceptable but demanded at the Cavern and other recurring engagements, the going was erratic elsewhere, partly because certain parochial agents had no qualms about marrying a loud R&B outfit with, say, the ubiquitous trad band, the C&W (country-and-western) of Hank Walters and his Dusty Road Ramblers and the monologues of comedian Ken Dodd – as took place at a Sunday matinee in a cinema in Maghull, more Lancashire than Liverpool.

The Beatles would arrive too in Birkenhead, Seaforth or – for one fabled night only – Aldershot, over the edge of the world in distant Hampshire, where the cissy *pilzen kopfs* that George, Paul and John would be sporting by the end of 1961 were sometimes a red rag to those for whom an Elvis quiff was not yet a symbol of masculinity.

When Lennon and McCartney had blown a coming-of-age cheque that came from one of the former's well-heeled aunts on a holiday in Paris, Jurgen Vollmer had been there too, and, after getting him, said Paul "to try and cut our hair like his,"[2] the two chief Beatles came back with a heavily fringed variant – almost down to the eyebrows – on not so much Adam Faith as The Kaye Sisters, a corny vocal trio forever on British television variety shows. Nonetheless, while Pete demurred, George steeled himself to do likewise.

A lesser provocation in more unrefined venues was some bruiser's girlfriend's eye being caught by the corporate all-leather uniform in force since the Kaiserkeller stint – particularly the form-fitting trousers, just like the ones Gene and Eddie had worn on that fateful tour.

Apart from a handful cowering near the sanctuary of the stage, The Beatles were, therefore, confronted now and then with a crowd determined to hate them. Within a minute of the first item, a crewcut roughneck, bold with beer, might have to be restrained from being a lion of justice by charging on to strike a blow for decent entertainment for decent folk. Others in the audience, however, confined themselves to howls of derision, sporadic barracking and outbreaks of slow handclapping – though there were instances of grudging applause by those gawping antagonists who tuned into the group's unflagging dedication to their music, and the circumstance's awry absurdity – of which The Beatles themselves seemed be cognisant too.

On the firmer turf of the Liverpool jive-hives where they were rebooked into the foreseeable future, other groups would be copying The Beatles' stagecraft and repertoire, including 'I Saw Her Standing There', an original that had dripped mostly from the pen of McCartney.

Other than that terrible journey to Aldershot, however, campaigns for UK engagements beyond Merseyside yielded next to nothing. So inward-looking was provincial pop that there seemed to be few realistic halfway points between obscurity and the Big Time – and a policy of territorial defence was epitomised by a closed shop of venues in England's westward regions where, visitors of hit parade eminence notwithstanding, work tended to be given only to groups from the area such as The Betterdays, an R&B quintet who were to Plymouth's Guildhall what The Beatles were to the Cavern. The sentiment was why book a group from Liverpool when our own boys can do the job just as well for a fraction of the cost?

A quantum jump could be managed by sending a tape that might prompt someone important from the Promised Land to steer The Beatles to stardom. That was how Cliff Richard had got going. Since him, Shane Fenton And The Fentones from the wilds of Mansfield had mailed a recording of one of their local recitals to the Light Programme and hooked a regular spot on *Saturday Club*, the Light Programme's main pop showcase. Then it was onwards and upwards to a deal with Parlophone and a few modest chart strikes. The combination of a demo and grassroots petitioning had forced a Fontana recording manager to at least listen to The Betterdays.

Paul was keenly aware that his group's present state of marking time was prodding nerves at home, especially as he was still embroiled in hire-purchase payments for his equipment, and income from The Beatles was far less than Mike's as a hairdresser.

Not helping either was the cost of a Hofner "violin" bass that Paul had bought from a Grosse Freiheit shop. This didn't leave much change from his earnings at the Top Ten, which were "OK by English standards," agreed Ian "Tich" Amey of Dave Dee's Bostons, "but didn't go a long way in Germany".

Among The Beatles' duties there was backing Tony Sheridan both onstage – and in the studio after he was offered a recording contract by Bert Kaempfert, a power on Polydor, a division of Deutsche Grammophon, Germany's equivalent of EMI.

As a composer, 36-year-old Bert had contributed to 'Wooden Heart', Elvis Presley's European spin-off 45 from the movie soundtrack of *GI Blues*, a fictionalisation of his military service in Germany. The King acknowledged the melodic debt 'Wooden Heart' owed to the traditional 'Muss I Denn Zum Stadtele Naus', by breaking into German for a couple of verses.

Like nearly everybody else, The Beatles inserted a token song in German into the proceedings in Hamburg. The line of least resistance in this respect was for Paul to sing 'Wooden Heart', but more erudite was his 'Falling In Love Again' from the 1943 Marlene Dietrich movie vehicle, *The Blue Angel*. McCartney excerpts from stage and film musicals also impinged on otherwise frenetic hours on the boards. 'Summertime' (from *Porgy And Bess*) and, when that was dropped, 'Till There Was You' (*The Music Man*) and 'Over The Rainbow' could silence the most rumbustious crowd like a mass bell in Madrid. Inverting the principle that a drop of black makes white paint whiter, neither had The Beatles – and Sheridan – any inhibitions about making a run of the most frantic rock and R&B numbers all the more piquant by hanging fire midway and inserting one deadpanned selection from the perverse and antique likes of 'Beautiful Dreamer', 'You Make Me Feel So Young' and 'We'll Take Manhattan'.

A few Lennon–McCartney efforts were unveiled publicly – two in as many hours by late 1962 – but though 'I Saw Her Standing There' became something of a fixture during The Beatles' later Hamburg seasons, it hadn't the immediacy of 'Twist And Shout' – another from The Isley Brothers – or 'Shimmy Shimmy' by The Orlons, and other more ardently anticipated crowd-pleasers.

Where did songwriting get you anyway? No one paid attention to a home-made song, least of all Bert Kaempfert on the prowl on behalf of Polydor for a bargain-basement "Beat Gruppa" rather than the preferred orchestra for Tony Sheridan's first single.

Bert put his head round the door at the Top Ten during one of many transcendental moments that could not be recreated, that would look impossible if transcribed on manuscript paper. By today's standards, the sound *per se* was puny yet harsh and atrociously distorted as Tony and The Beatles battled with amplifiers of 30-watts maximum that were sent through speakers known to tear, explode and even catch fire because of power surges and the mismatch of British and German ohms. McCartney would recall that, "If we had troubles with our overworked amplifiers – we had to plug two guitars into the same one – I'd just chuck it all in and start leaping all round the stage or rushing over to the piano and playing a few chords."[2]

Despite off-putting technical problems, Sheridan was to remember that "Bert Kaempfert came for several nights. He was impressed by what he thought was our authenticity – which, of course, was second-hand American music infused with elements of our own that were authentic. Afterwards, we discussed with Bert what we ought to record. I'd heard Gene Vincent do 'My Bonnie' – very differently – and later on, a Ray Charles version. Long before we'd even thought about recording it ourselves, we'd done a sort of Jerry Lee Lewis-type arrangement on stage, but without piano. The B-side was the signature tune of my Norwich skiffle group, The Saints."

Tony Sheridan's was the name on the orange Polydor label when these rocked-up versions of 'My Bonnie Lies Over The Ocean' and 'When The Saints Go Marching In' were issued as a single in October 1961. So began Paul McCartney's recording career – helping Tony, Pete, John and George make the best of a couple of so-so numbers intended purely for Germany. It looked like being the only disc on which he'd ever be heard too.

# 6 *"Some Other Guy"*

"Pete gave Paul competition in the pretty face department."
*– John Lennon*[1]

As things turned out, 'My Bonnie' wasn't to be the only disc Paul and The Beatles would make. The Tony Sheridan single sold sufficiently to warrant an album containing some other tracks with the group. There was also to be an associated extended-play (EP) disc, also entitled *My Bonnie*.

Import copies were spun by Bob Wooler, one of the disc jockeys at the Cavern, and these consolidated The Beatles' regional fame within a radius of about 25km (15 miles). Now they'd rid themselves of Stuart Sutcliffe, the group epitomised the two guitars-bass-drums archetype of what would go down in cultural history as 1963's Merseybeat explosion. "They improved when Stuart left," noticed The Remo Four's Don Andrew, "but it was a long time before I appreciated what they were doing."[2] There were, however, local music lovers several steps ahead of Don. They were of such a multitude that 'I Saw Her Standing There' occasionally went down as well as some of the non-original ravers. Almost fully mobilised now, The Beatles were at the top of the first division of Liverpool popularity, having won in January 1962 the first readers' poll in a new fortnightly journal, *Mersey Beat*.

They also moved up a further rung or two through their acquisition just before Christmas 1961 of a manager in 27-year-old Brian Epstein, a sales manager at his grandfather's central Liverpool department store, which contained what could be deservedly advertised in *Mersey Beat* as "The Finest Record Selection In The North". Until then, The Beatles had made do with Mona Best, who was efficient enough, but, as she herself realised, didn't have the entrepreneurial contacts and know-how to remove The Beatles from the Liverpool–Hamburg grindstone.

With the advent of Epstein, her say in the group's affairs was diminished to the point of eventual silence, despite vainglorious efforts for it to be otherwise, especially as her handsome Pete was, Mona believed – with much justification – the most effusive fount of the group's teen appeal. Because Mrs Best was of far less use to them now, "John, Paul and George resented her interference," said Bill Harry, editor of *Mersey Beat*. Why couldn't all Beatle women be more like Paul's uncomplaining Dorothy Rhone, who supplied occasional passive glamour when he made her sit on a bar-stool in the midst of The Beatles? Yet for all her apparent acquiescence, it had still been necessary for Paul to suspend his routine philanderings when she and John's future wife, Cynthia Powell, visited Hamburg during the months at the Top Ten.

It was John and Paul, rather than John and Stuart nowadays as, with their girlfriends, they went on picnic excursions by train on hot afternoons to seaside resorts like Ostsee where they would recharge their batteries for the labours of the night. If there was no work that evening, they'd travel further to Timmendorf Strand where it was sometimes mild enough to sleep on the beach.

At the water's edge in hazy sunshine, Paul, Dorothy, John and Cynthia were like children, splashing and yelling in the freezing North Sea surf. Hands dripping sand, they'd direct their artistic endeavours towards the low-tide construction of a tottering castle sinister – all Transylvanian spires, battlements and moat.

The waves had not yet started gnawing at its foundations, and the dying sun was like a lone orange as they simmered down on the empty shoreline to a driftwood campfire and guitar singsongs.

Because there's no Top Ten that evening the idyll slips into a woodsmoke-smelling night of whispered sweet nothings and rhythmic movement beneath blankets and the pale moonlight. The sea sucks at the castle, and it crumbles and falls.

Serenities like this would be few and far between after McCartney and Lennon – and Harrison – could no longer venture into a public place without the pestering of fans and reporters. In unconscious preparation, they took in their stride Brian Epstein's moulding of them into entertainers destined ideally to emerge from provincial oblivion. The Germans have a word for what Brian was doing: *verharmlosen*, to render harmless.

By March 1962, the black leathers – aggressively redolent of Nazi officer trench-coats or motor-bike hoodlums – had been superseded by tweed suits of nondescript design. These, however, were a holding operation for the following year's epauletted jackets with no lapels, which buttoned up to the throat and had no unsightly bulges in the high-waisted trousers owing to the absence of pockets around tight hips. While the basic pattern had been taken from a blue-brushed denim get-up sold in the Hamburg branch of C&A's, that The Beatles had consented to wear it was down to the fastidious Epstein assuring them that it was for the best.

Wisely, however extensive his re-inventions of their visual image, Brian chose not to get very involved in the musical activities of his charges. Unlike Andrew Loog Oldham, soon to be The Rolling Stones' flamboyant man-of-affairs, he would never, for instance, presume to be more than an *éminence grise* behind publicity and further merchandising ballyhoo – or insist on producing their records.

In any case, relaxing in the privacy of his own home, Brian, for all his knowledge and interest in pop, was more inclined to tune into a classical concert on the BBC's Third Programme (later, Radio Three) than the Light Programme's *Pick Of The Pops*. Yet, convinced of something incredible taking place at the Cavern, Epstein had wanted to believe it even if he didn't understand what it actually was any more than his 1970s counterpart would be when looking for a New Sex Pistols. All he knew was that the club was packed, there was an infectious atmosphere and the phenomenon hinged on the enigma of untouchable boys-next-door.

For reasons that included erotic attraction and frustrated aspirations to be a performer himself, he'd made investigative forays into the world of pop long before encountering The Beatles, once worming his way backstage during the interval of a Larry Parnes presentation at the Liverpool Empire. A hall like that with its grand proscenium, velvet curtains and tiers of high-backed chairs, could give you big ideas.

"He remarked on the unusual lighting," Larry would recall, "the pace, individual artists' performances and their clothes. I was extremely flattered"[3] – so flattered that Parnes considered taking Brian on as an assistant. The younger man elected instead to go it alone and he decided that the next titans of teen were as likely to be The Beatles as any other in this new breed of guitar outfits.

If he'd found time to scan *Mersey Beat* and amble over to some of the other clubs, he may have discovered that there were equally capable beat groups in the vicinity. Instead, he persuaded himself that he'd struck luckiest with The Beatles, having stood himself amongst the battalions of iron-bladdered girls positioned stage-front at the Cavern to better gawk at Pete and the other three.

The Beatles had also risen to the challenge of the ballroom circuit, becoming a reliable draw as, courtesy of Brian's persistence via telephone and post, their booking spectrum broadened intermittently to Yorkshire, Wales and as far south as Swindon. As for Hamburg, they were back again in April 1962 to wow 'em at the new Star-Club, which had given no quarter during a ruthless campaign to outflank the Top Ten as the Grosse Freiheit's premier night spot.

Epstein had also signed up Gerry And The Pacemakers, second in the *Mersey Beat* poll. McCartney would "remember all too well sweating the outcome, hoping we could scrape together the necessary points to beat Gerry's band. That's how close it was."[4]

Anyone with the means and tenacity to research Britain's local pop scene then would have discovered that everywhere else had boss groups too. As The Betterdays did Plymouth, Kerry Rapid and his Blue Stars ruled Aldershot (and were playing a rival palais when The Beatles made their solitary foray there). Likewise, Ricky Ford And The Cyclones were supreme in Weston-super-Mare as The Golden Crusaders were in Belfast, The Viceroys in Llanriddod Wells, The Poor Souls in Dundee and Dave Berry And The Cruisers in Sheffield – while in Kidderminster, Shades Five were to weather an intrusion into the town's Playhouse by Birmingham's Denny Laine And The Diplomats.

Before adopting his *nom de théâtre* – "something to do with Cleo Laine and Johnny Dankworth" – Brian Hines had been one of Johnny And The Dominators in which "Johnny could have been anyone because they kept changing the singers". The outfit's Buddy Holly specialist, Brian was also moonlighting as juvenile attraction in a palais big band before leading The Diplomats which, in 1962, also contained Bev Bevan – who was to beat a gradually more splendid drum kit with Carl Wayne And The Vikings, The Move and The Electric Light Orchestra. Among "featured vocalists" that passed through the ranks was Tipton's Nicky James, who'd defied all comers in an "Elvis of the Midlands" contest.

Though the group's catchment area stretched as far away as Oxford, efforts to infiltrate certain territories met organised opposition. Worcester's Lansdowne Agency was, noted regional pop gazette *Midland Beat*, "formed with the sole intention of stopping Brum bands playing at local venues"[5] – an embargo, however, that did not prevent Denny's diplomatic Sunday show at Kidderminster Playhouse in October 1963.

The group were, nonetheless, not in an immediate position to forsake their day jobs like Brian/Denny's as a trainee in the electrical goods section of a department store not unlike I Epstein & Sons. It wasn't exactly showbusiness, but it proved instructive as he was required to both sell and requisition records and musical instruments. He recalled: "I actually got them to buy guitars; they didn't originally."

When Laine And The Diplomats turned fully professional after a year, they sought attention initially by wearing matching suits, peroxiding their hair and making out that they were two pairs of brothers. The repertoire was mostly the current Top 20 and what had become R&B standards like 'Money' and 'Love Potion Number Nine'. "A lot of the bands in Birmingham had the same repertoire as those in Liverpool," noted Denny, "I had a friend called Danny [of Danny King and the Mayfair Set] who had a great collection. He used to put stickers over record labels so that rival groups like us wouldn't know what they were."

The Laine outfit was among a handful in Birmingham that tried self-composed items – though, as everyone knew, these usually caused dancers to sit them out. However, some were more intrigued than the musicians thought. "John Bonham [later of Led Zeppelin] used to watch me and The Diplomats at the Wednesbury Youth Centre," recounted Denny, "Years later, he stayed at my house, and, though I couldn't remember any of the original material the Diplomats did to save my life, he could. We got a bit drunk, and he started singing 'Why Cry', 'A Piece of Your Mind' and others we did. He knew all the words and everything. Unbelievable!"

Rather than any idiosyncracies in their music, it was because the group toed an orthodox line that they made a television debut on topical *Midlands At Six*. As *Saturday Club* – and ITV's *Thank Your Lucky Stars* – were recorded in Birmingham, Denny Laine And The Diplomats were well placed to be booked too for two sub-*Thank Your Lucky Stars* shows – *For Teenagers Only* and *Pop Shop* – and as token pop act on *Lunch Box*, a light entertainment series, built round the personality of Noele Gordon prior to her *grande dame* part in ITV's long-running soap opera, *Crossroads*. Yet, though they also got as far as taping several demos for EMI, The Diplomats and Denny had reached much the same impasse as The Beatles before Brian Epstein had entered the picture.

Thanks to Epstein's dogged prodding of Polydor's UK outlet, 'My Bonnie' by Tony Sheridan and The Beatles was released in Britain on 5 January 1962. *NME* reviewer Keith Fordyce was generous – "both sides are worth a listen for the above-average ideas"[6] – but, unaired on either the Light Programme or Radio Luxembourg, the disc sank without trace.

In June, the same was in store for 'You Got What I Like' by Cliff Bennett And The Rebel Rousers, but Parlophone seemed to regard the group as a long-term investment because it was prepared to risk another six singles before reaping the harvest of its faith in X-factor Bennett, highly regarded as a bandleader, and one of few Britons who imagined that they had a black soul within a white skin that could actually take on black pop without losing the overriding passion.

Yet chart recognition seemed a far-fetched afterthought to Cliff when he and his Rebel Rousers were on the wrong side of the North Sea, putting on the agony night after night at the Star-Club where Paul and John of The Beatles promised to give him a leg up by writing him a song if their group got famous before his did.

Both the Middlesex and Merseyside factions at the Star-Club were mixing socially with Little Richard and Gene Vincent as each disturbed Tony Sheridan's reign as incumbent rock 'n' roll king of the Grosse Freiheit. "I remember how excited The Beatles were to meet Richard," enthused Billy Preston, the Georgia Peach's 16-year-old organist. "In Hamburg, they'd always be with him, asking him about America, the cities, the stars, the movies, Elvis and all that."[7]

Since the most culturally important chapter of his life had closed, Little Richard had recorded little but sacred material following his enrolment in a theological college. In 1961, he'd commenced a gospel tour of the world, but by the time it reached Germany, Richard was giving 'em 'Tutti Frutti', 'Long Tall Sally' and hardly anything else that hadn't been a massive hit for him before he'd got religion.

The billowing drapes of old had been mothballed, and the overhanging pompadour abbreviated severely, but Paul McCartney was still awestruck by the soberly attired, bristle-scalped exquisite he met in the dressing room, and later saw onstage, shrieking his head off and hammering the ivories, just like he had in *The Girl Can't Help It* when it had reached Merseyside cinemas in 1957.

Richard himself would inform his biographer, Charles White, that "Paul [McCartney] would just look at me. Like, he wouldn't move his eyes – and he'd say: 'Oh Richard, you're my idol. Let me touch you.' He wanted to learn my little holler, so we sat at the piano going 'Oooooooh! Oooooooh!' until he got it."[7]

Like Caesar deified by the Gallic peasants, Richard would offend none by refusing gifts pressed upon him – like one of Paul's best shirts after "I developed a specially close relationship with Paul, but me and John couldn't make it. John had a nasty personality."[7]

By the middle of the decade, Richard was to have cause to be grateful to The Beatles when they revived 'Long Tall Sally' on disc. In 1962, however, while he continued to feed off a more glorious past, they could only carry the torch of classic rock – well, their take on it – back to the confines of Liverpool.

Yet more than mere Merseybeat was unravelling there now. Following a lucrative London exhibition, sculptor Arthur Dooley had become a professional Scouser, often on BBC television's early evening magazine, *Tonight*. A protégé of Pop Art pioneer Richard Hamilton, Adrian Henri had reached beyond slapping oil on canvas to performance art and, as he had promised Michael Horovitz, poetry. Other bards and *nouvelle vague* artists of the same vintage included Roger McGough, Brian Patten, John Gorman, Alun Owen (who was to write the script of *A Hard Day's Night*, The Beatles' first feature film), Mike Evans – and Mike McCartney who, with Gorman and McGough, had formed Scaffold, an ensemble that mingled poetry and satirical sketches during the audio-visual and literary events that, walking a tightrope between near magical inspiration and pseudo-intellectual ramblings, were springing up as alternatives to doing the 'Hippy Hippy Shake' with all o' your might down the Iron Door.

The gifted Mike was to adopt the stage surname "McGear" to stay accusations of boarding his more famous brother's bandwagon though, in 1962, the two were on terms of fluctuating equality in their respective spheres. Scaffold were leading what the economist would call a "full life" with regular bookings at Streate's, the Everyman and the Blue Angel, while The Beatles were to be flown, not driven, to Hamburg for a penultimate spell at the Star-Club in November.

While the previous season had been a professional triumph, it had been blighted by the cerebral haemorrhage that had killed Stuart Sutcliffe the afternoon before their arrival. An advance party of Paul, Pete and John hadn't heard the news when they'd taken off from Liverpool. In the skies, they'd been shrill with their first BBC radio broadcast (*Teenagers' Turn* from Manchester's Playhouse) the previous weekend – and in then-unknowing empathy with 'Homesick For St Pauli', the Freddy Quinn million-seller that German milkmen were whistling that spring.

Still raring to go as the aeroplane descended, the three came down with a bump when Astrid Kirchherr, drained of her usual sparkle, met them after their passports had been checked. Paul was at a loss for words. Anything he said or did then wouldn't ring true somehow: "It affected John the most because he'd been closest to him. John was most disturbed by it. For me, it was a distant thing. I can't remember doing or thinking anything – but the main thing for me, that I remember feeling bad about was that he died of a brain thing. It struck me as all being Van Gogh and sort of a wild artistic thing, but I think by then, I'd got a little hardened to people dying. It wasn't like Stu was with us. We'd got used to not being with Stu – but it was a shock."[8]

That night, Paul and Pete grizzled into their beer for a boy they hadn't understood but had liked because, outside the context of all the in-fighting, he'd come to like them. If neither had been over-complimentary about his musicianship, they had to admit that

The Beatles were a better group for Stuart's creative instincts, even if his talents and appetites had proved too much at odds with theirs.

Their eyes were still sore the next day when they went with John and Astrid to greet Brian, George and Stuart's distraught mother at the airport. A few hours later, however, The Beatles were pitching into their opening number with all their customary verve.

They were still at the Star-Club on Maundy Thursday, 19 April when Stuart was interred in Huyton's Blue Bell Lane cemetery. "It was all happening when Stu died," gloomed Paul, "and we were caught up in a sort of whirlwind. John was able to pause in that whirlwind and say, 'Jesus Christ, Stu's died!' – but when you were back in that whirlwind, I don't think we were able to spend much time on it – probably a good thing too."[8]

The next to go – albeit in less absolute terms than Stuart – was Pete Best after the group and manager had netted a hard-won recording contract with Parlophone, having been turned down by virtually every other UK company that mattered. The first session took place on 6 June in the EMI complex along Abbey Road. Like every consequent visit, it was supervised by no less than the head of Parlophone himself, George Martin, who preferred to tape pop groups in cavernous Studio Two where he'd vetoed freshening up the paintwork in case it affected the acoustics that had spiced up the chart entries of such as Eddie Calvert and Shane Fenton.

Martin's only reservations about The Beatles that first day was that he'd heard no unmistakable smash hit within their cache of Lennon–McCartney originals, and that the drummer's lack of studio experience was more pronounced than that of the guitarists. A hireling would have to ghost him when The Beatles returned to record 'Love Me Do', a McCartney opus that, for want of anything better, had been picked as the first A-side.

BBC Radio Merseyside presenter and pop historian Spencer Leigh was to devote an entire book to chronicling the saga of Pete Best's subsequent sacking.[9] One of the lengthier chapters explores divergent theories as to why he was replaced by Ringo Starr, one of Rory Storm's Hurricanes, two months after that initial trip to Abbey Road. One of these suggests that a green-eyed monster had whispered to the other three – particularly McCartney – that Best was the fairest of them all. This was exacerbated by *Mersey Beat*'s report that, during the *Teenagers' Turn* showcase, "John, Paul and George made their entrance on stage to cheers and applause, but when Pete walked on, the fans went wild. The girls screamed! In Manchester, his popularity was assured by his looks alone."[10]

At the stage door afterwards, Pete was almost killed with kindness by over-attentive females from the 400-strong audience while Paul, John and George were allowed to board a ticking-over charabanc after signing some autographs. Jim McCartney was on the periphery of this incident, and admonished the sweat-smeared drummer: "Why did you have to attract all the attention? Why didn't you call the other lads back? I think that was very selfish of you."[11]

Did Mr McCartney have an indirect hand in Pete's dismissal? To what extent did his unfair reprimand – and interrelated exchanges at Forthlin Road – make dark nights of the ego darker still? He rubbed salt into the wound on observing the dismissed Best in the Cavern shadows when a Beatles bash was being documented for the ITV series, *Know The North*. "Great, isn't it!" he crowed. "They're on TV!"[11] Pete bit his tongue and left quietly.

Jim's glee had to be contained as edited footage – of Paul, John, George and the new member doing 'Slow Down' and 'Some Other Guy' – wasn't screened until it had gained historical importance, and the concept of a Beatles without Ringo had become as unthinkable to the world as one without Pete had once been in Liverpool.

"I was a better player than him," protested Starr 30 years later. "That's how I got the job. It wasn't on no personality [sic]."[12] Nevertheless, a session drummer had been on clock-watching stand-by for the recording of 'Love Me Do', but Ringo kept his peace just as Paul did when directed by George Martin to extend the sung hook-line, radically altering the embedded arrangement of the humble little ditty that changed everything.

# 7 *"Don't You Dig This Kind Of Beat?"*

"It was fairly innocent then, a bit of a cottage industry. We thought we'd last maybe two or three years."
– *Dick Taylor of The Pretty Things*

The release of 'Love Me Do' in October 1962 meant that The Beatles could be billed as "EMI Recording Artists", and that the glory and the stupidity of being in a 1960s pop group now necessitated being shoulder-to-shoulder in a van for hours on end during a staggered procession of one-nighters that were often truly hellish in an age when England's only motorway terminated in Birmingham.

While local engagements were becoming less frequent, the single shifted plenty in loyal Liverpool, and eventually touched the national Top 20 – just. This followed on from ITV's *Tuesday Rendezvous* on 4 December 1962, which was the first we southerners at large ever saw of The Beatles.

The follow-up, 'Please Please Me', gave more cause to hold on hoping as, before slipping in mid-March, it lingered in a Top Ten in which Frankie Vaughan, Cliff Richard, Bobby Vee and Kenny Ball were also vying to topple Frank Ifield who was at Number One with 'The Wayward Wind'.

If still revolving round clubs and ballrooms, there were even more dates booked than The Beatles could possibly keep. Most burdensome were contracts finalised when the Local Boys Made Good had been only one of many – though the backstage lionising was often quite satisfying: I always knew you'd make it, lads.

Two hits in a row was sufficient to justify a long-player – which The Beatles and George Martin were expected to complete in an allotted 12-hour day with Musicians Union-regulated tea and lunch breaks during conventional London office times and an evening period with a jobsworth locking-up well before midnight.

After Gerry And The Pacemakers, The Big Three, Billy J Kramer, The Searchers, The Merseybeats and The Fourmost notched up respectable chart entries too before 1963's cool, wet summer was out, what was deemed by the media to be a "Mersey Sound" or "Liverpool Beat" gave way to a more generalised group boom, the Big Beat, also spearheaded by John, Paul, George and Ringo – the "Fab Four" – which finished off chart careers of soloists like Mark Wynter. *In extremis*, he was to resort to a Beatles' ballad ('And I Love Her') as a 1964 A-side. After a disturbing hat-trick of comparative misses, Adam Faith took more pragmatic heed of the Big Beat by hiring Chris Andrews, a tunesmith who'd fronted the obscure Chris Ravel And The Ravers but had, nevertheless, put in much hard graft in Hamburg to provide made-to-measure smashes, and The Roulettes, one of the more able also-ran outfits of the mid-1960s, to accompany him. Both on stage and on vinyl, Adam's new repertoire was either derived from Andrews' prolific portfolio, whether both sides of the Ravers' only 45, 'Don't You Dig This Kind of Beat?' and 'I Do' on a 1964 LP, or from plunderings that included a confident 'I Wanna Be Your Man' on the album yet to come.

This, however, was not the way of he who was The Silver Beatles' front man for their 1960 expedition to Scotland. Without a recording contract by 1963, Johnny Gentle joined The Viscounts, a dated harmony trio who popped up on ITV's prime-time *Sunday Night At The London Palladium* emasculating a mildly choreographed 'I Saw Her Standing There'.

They raised a few screams by association. Yet, by 1964, The Viscounts couldn't get arrested, together with The Brook Brothers – self-proclaimed "Britain's ace vocal group" – as well as The King Brothers, The Avons, The Kestrels, The Kaye Sisters, The

Dowlands and similarly dapper non-beat groups who, previously, had buttressed certain wrong-headed music industry moguls' theories that outfits with electric guitars were behind the times. We know these things, Mr Epstein.

Some tried to adjust, usually without getting the point – as did The Kestrels with a xerox of 'There's A Place' from The Beatles' first album. However, The Dowlands' disinclined cover of 'All My Loving' (which, like 'I Wanna Be Your Man', was from the second, *With The Beatles*) was to spend seven weeks in the domestic Top 50 in early 1964, though their 'Wishin' And Hopin'' and 'Don't Make Me Over' were vanquished by The Merseybeats' and Swinging Blue Jeans's respective versions.

If Liverpool had an "answer" to anachronisms like The Viscounts, Dowlands *et al*, it was the all-black Chants, who had been backed onstage by the pre-'Love Me Do' Beatles among others. In 1963, their 'Come Go With Me', the number John Lennon had been singing when Paul McCartney first heard The Quarry Men, surfaced on disc as merely the B-side of a debut 45 – an odd executive decision that kept what might have been a surefire hit from the ears of UK radio listeners.

Adhering closer to the two-guitars-bass-drums Merseybeat archetype, the test case of The Trends made a more obvious attempt to cash in with fleeting changes of name – The Beachcombers, The Beatcombers and The Mersey Men – before their 'All My Loving' lost a Top 40 bout against The Dowlands. The Trends had been as much a fixture at Kirby's Westvale Youth Club as The Beatles at the Cavern – and The Undertakers at Orrell Park ballroom. Among the all-out ravers in The Undertakers' repertoire were 'Mashed Potatoes' and 'Money' but, as it was with The Chants, these tracks were buried on B-sides. Nevertheless, 'If You Don't Come Back', a tale of lovesick insanity, was a "turntable hit" following a plug on *Thank Your Lucky Stars*, which obliged the group to mothball the black crêped top hats and other macabre props and abbreviate their name to "The 'Takers".

Most Liverpool acts who'd breathed the air round The Beatles came within at least a rumour's distance of a qualified fame after convincing this record label or that London impresario that their bass player had sat next to John at infant school, that the drummer had been in the same Boy Scout troop as Paul or that the lead guitarist had danced with a man who'd danced with a girl who'd danced with George. That's not all that much of an exaggeration.

Decca, Pye, Oriele and the other companies who'd turned their noses up at The Beatles in 1962 had read *NME* and *Melody Maker* despatches about the group's first national tours with heart-sinking fascination. Ostensibly second-billed, the four had upstaged Helen Shapiro – Britain's biggest female pop attraction in 1963 – and then Tommy Roe and Chris Montez, North American Bobbies with hits fresh in consumers' minds, who headlined a "scream circuit" package for the first night only.

The next such jaunt was in May 1963 with Roy Orbison – who, bar the remote Elvis Presley, was to command the most devoted British following of any US pop star – plus Gerry And The Pacemakers and various small fry. The Beatles' third single, 'From Me To You', would be a Number One fixture for the entire tour. Shrieking pandemonium and chants of "We want The Beatles!" would greet even compère Tony Marsh's attempts to keep order.

The Beatles' domination of an edition of *Sunday Night At The London Palladium* drew out the agony for Decca *et al*. Worse was to come when they all but stole the *Royal Variety Show* at the Prince of Wales Theatre on 4 November 1963 when, with McCartney's pretty 'Till There Was You' oiling the wheels, the general feeling among adults and others who hadn't wanted to like them, was that John, Paul, George and Ringo were the stock Nice Lads When You Get To Know Them. Ireland's Bachelors – more Viscounts than Beatles – were even nicer lads who, as token pop group in the next year's *Royal Variety Show*, had faced the Royal Box for an amended opening line – "*we* wouldn't change *you* for the wurrrrld!" – of their most recent Top Ten strike.

If The Bachelors and The Beatles put themselves in the way of potentially damaging publicity – like one Bachelor's extra-marital amour with a a well-known female vocalist or a Liverpool woman's imputation of her baby's irregular kinship to Paul McCartney – their respective managers would ensure that no nicotine-stained fingers would type out lurid coverage of it for the following Sunday's *News Of The World*. Besides, even if it was true, nothing too sordid was likely to be yet brought to public notice about The Beatles, Gerry, Billy J, The Fourmost and other ostensibly wholesome groups by a scum press who judged any besmirching of cheeky but innocent personas as untimely: save the scandal for The Rolling Stones, who, seized by Decca, were to be a closer second to The Beatles than earlier pretenders like Gerry and his Pacemakers, The Searchers and, in early 1964, The Dave Clark Five.

Perhaps with the Five's – and The Bachelors' – clean-cut, amiable precedent in mind, the Stones' then co-manager Eric Easton had tried and failed to spruce them up with uniform slim-jim ties and waistcoats. While he'd got them to capitulate to photo sessions in which they'd affect what were intended to be smiles, certain Stones would sign autographs with bad grace or refuse altogether. To no avail, Easton would stress the importance of making themselves pleasant to reporters and fans. If a stranger came up to guitarist Keith Richards and said, "Hello Keith. How is your brother Cliff?", Eric – and Decca – would rather a polite lie along the lines of "Fine, thanks. He's keeping well" than Keith telling the enquirer to fuck off. Finally, Easton gave up, deciding instead to leave personal management to his younger sidekick, Andrew Loog Oldham.

As anti-Beatles, the Stones cut appositely sullen figures on the front photograph of an eponymous debut long-player – though anyone awaiting seething musical outrage were disappointed because its content didn't ring many changes. Almost as weighty with R&B standards as the first LPs by The Animals, The Yardbirds, The Kinks, The Downliners Sect, Them, The Pretty Things and

The Spencer Davis Group, it even contained 'Route 66', a set-work that any self-respecting R&B aficionado now heard no more than a mariner hears the sea.

The rise of such groups – principally Londoners – was indicative of the decline of Liverpool as a pop Eldorado by the close of 1963. Too rapid turnovers of personnel within The Merseybeats and The Big Three didn't help either at a time when teenagers needed to identify clearly with a favoured group to the extent that, ideally, the drummer toiling over his kit was as much its public face as the lead singer.

Striking while the iron was lukewarm, all manner of German labels were still rushing out as much associated product as the traffic would allow. Most of it was pressed onto cheap compilations such as 1964's *Liverpool Beat*, an album featuring both Kingsize Taylor And The Dominoes and the more versatile Bobby Patrick Big Six – from Glasgow! – who were to be taken on semi-permanently to back Tony Sheridan. Some were immortalised *au naturel* at the Star-Club, while others were hastened to a studio as soon as the final major sixth of the shift had reverberated so that their adrenalin could be pumped onto a spool of tape.

On the rebound from a night on stage, Kingsize Taylor and his boys thought nothing of banging out an entire LP in four hours from plug-in to final mix. Certainly, they came closest here to capturing the scintillatingly slipshod power forged unknowingly from the Star-Club fracas, day after day, week upon week.

As Taylor did, Cliff Bennett could have continued making a good living in Germany, but he preferred to take his chances at home where he and The Rebel Rousers aroused the interest of Brian Epstein who, encouraged by his runaway success with the cream of Liverpudlia, was eager to diversify. With this entrepreneurial muscle behind them, Cliff's seventh single, a tougher Anglicised copy of The Drifters' 'One Way Love', tore into the Top Ten in autumn 1964, but a second bite at that particular cherry wouldn't present itself for another two years.

Denny Laine went off the boil too after striking even harder a few weeks later. In a last-ditch attempt to shake off provincial fetters, he'd left his Diplomats to fend for themselves in April 1964, the month that Solihull's Applejacks entered the Top Ten. When The Rockin' Berries did likewise that summer, *Midland Beat*'s editorial judgement that "Liverpool started the ball rolling. Now the Midlands is ready to take over"[1] seemed to be proving correct. This first flush of "Brumbeat" peaked when both the Berries and Denny Laine's new group, The Moody Blues, were seen on the same January 1965 edition of *Ready Steady Go*, that most atmospheric of televised pop series of the Swinging Sixties.

If The Moody Blues's name was chosen in vain hopes of sponsorship from Mitchell and Butler, a local brewery, there was also an instrumental by urban bluesman Slim Harpo entitled 'Moody Blue'. "I pushed the group in the direction of the blues- and jazz-based London bands," maintained Denny. "Also, we'd gone to see The Spencer Davis Group, and I was knocked out by them. I thought that if they could get away with it, we could – and that convinced the other lads."

As The Moody Blues had rejected the assembly-line pop otherwise vital for survival in the ballrooms, they came to be appreciated as a "group's group" by the students and bohemians that patronised rhythm-and-blues evenings in, say, the Golden Eagle on Hill Street, or, less regularly, in the nearby Birmingham Town Hall where, on 11 September 1964, ravers could twist the night away to Blue Sounds from Leeds, the jazzy Sheffields and Alexis Korner's Blues Incorporated. Representing the Second City itself were The Spencer Davis Group – and, wrote *Midland Beat*, "the much-improved Moody Blues Five [sic]"[2].

The quintet continued to do so well that they acquired the services of manager Tony Secunda and producer Denny Cordell, who, if Londoners, will be remembered as the Tweedledum and Tweedledee of Brumbeat after they ministered to later Second City acts – including the Move (and died within days of each other in

February 1995). "They were a good team," commented Laine, "who made sure that The Moody Blues didn't do the wrong things."

In the first instance, Secunda negotiated a season of Monday nights at London's Marquee club for the group. From this fêted showcase, they speedily landed a deal with Decca. Despite a *Ready Steady Go* plug and a stunning version of Bobby Parker's 'Steal Your Heart Away' as B-side, the maiden Moody Blues 45, 'Lose Your Money' – penned by Denny and pianist Mike Pinder – did just that.

There were, however, no grumbles from their investors about sales for an overhaul of US soul star Bessie Banks's 'Go Now' – though its abrupt fade provokes visions of Laine being suddenly hooked offstage like a vaudeville warbler getting the bird. "We knew a public schoolboy called James Hamilton," said Denny, "who had a fantastic record collection, and knew a New York disc jockey, B Mitchell Reed. Through them, we got a lot of material that nobody else was doing – like 'Steal Your Heart Away'. 'Go Now' was another one. Bessie Banks did a great slow version, and we bopped it up, put harmonies on it it, made it sort of gospel in our limited way."

Corroboration of this British Number One suffered a setback when 'I Don't Want To Go On Without You' barely rippled the Top 40, dogged as it was by simultaneous covers from The Searchers and The Escorts. Moreover, between session and pressing plant, a flute solo vanished from the master tape. In addition, The Moody Blues looked a motley crew, what with Laine hogging the singing and guitar spotlights on 'Go Now' while general factotum Ray Thomas merely bashed the tambourine and went "aaaaaah" into a microphone.

Ray was allowed one lead vocal on *The Magnificent Moody Blues*, an LP padded with The Hit and stand-bys from the stage act like James Brown's 'I'll Go Crazy' and a fast treatment of Sonny Boy Williamson's 'Bye Bye Bird'. There were also four originals including 'Stop!', flatteringly covered by a singer named Julie Grant. "I formed a writing duo with Mike Pinder because it was an easier way of disciplining yourself," reckoned Denny, "by having another person involved – but Mike didn't really write a lot. He would help me put them together. I would write a song and go to him and ask how we were going to do it with the band, and he'd develop it."

Pinder and Laine's 'From The Bottom Of My Heart' was, perhaps, the most exquisite track any incarnation of The Moody Blues ever made. Laine certainly discharged a remarkable vocal from preludial muttering to a howled, wordless coda as if what was being expressed was too intense for normal verbal articulation.

'From The Bottom Of My Heart' was two months away from release when The Moody Blues secured a slot at the "*NME* Pollwinners' Concert" at Wembley Empire Pool. The predominantly female audience went as indiscriminately crazy over them as it did over all male performers on a bill that embraced what was then the very upper crust of British pop – including The Rolling Stones, The Kinks, Twinkle, The Animals, Them, The Searchers, Georgie Fame, Tom Jones, Wayne Fontana And The Mindbenders, The Moody Blues, Donovan, Herman's Hermits, Dusty Springfield, Freddie And The Dreamers, Cilla Black – and, of course, The Beatles who closed the show.

This afternoon extravaganza on 11 April 1965 encapsulated, I suppose, the beat boom at its hysterical, electric high summer. An act drowned in tidal waves of screams that, while subsiding to mere cheers for Twinkle, Dusty and Cilla, hurled rampaging girls towards crash barriers where they'd be hurled back again by flushed bouncers, shirt-sleeved in the heat, and aggravatingly nearer to Mick, Georgie, Tom, Wayne, Ray, Donovan, Paul and Denny than those who'd give their souls to be. In the boiling mêlée further back, unluckier ticket-holders burst into tears, rocked foetally, flapped programmes and scarves, hoisted inexpertly daubed placards, tore at their hair, wet themselves and fainted with the thrill of it all.

# 8  "*Nobody I Know*"

"Paul McCartney came across at the time as being a bit
superficial. I think that he held his cards close to his chest."
— *Dave Davies of The Kinks*[1]

Bing Crosby, that most influential of pre-war singers of popular
song, hadn't realised that The Beatles composed their own material.
Until he did, he shared the view of evangelist Billy Graham – and
every other right-thinkin' North American adult – that they were
just "a passing trend".

A younger elder stateman of pop, Johnnie Ray, was of like
opinion, according to Bill Franklin, his manager: "When The
Beatles first came out, Johnnie said, 'Oh, I give 'em six months,'
and all the things everybody else did, but he got over it. Then we
had a very interesting encounter in London. Johnnie and I were
in a little club called the White Elephant, and Paul McCartney
came over and introduced himself. Paul was very nervous. He was
pawing the ground with his foot, and said some very nice,
complimentary things. Johnnie liked that. It made him feel great."

"I was amazed because he wouldn't talk to me," said Ray
himself. "I said, 'I'm glad to meet you Paul,' and he sort of shuffled
his feet and ran out the door."[2]

Johnnie was sufficiently impressed by McCartney and The
Beatles to record an idiosyncratic 'Yesterday' as Crosby was to
record 'Hey Jude' in 1969, but neither were so anxious to return
to the charts that they were driven to sift through Beatles albums
and, if lucky, demo tapes for a potential smash.

Others of their showbiz proper stamp did, among them, Crosby's favourite vocalist, Matt Monro. While keeping a weathered eye on Britain with scrupulous television plugs of his latest single, it had become convenient for Matt to relocate to the USA in order to commute to an ever-expanding workload there – and also record a body of work that would compare favourably with that of indigenous entertainers like his adolescent hero Perry Como as well as Tony Bennett, Dean Martin and even Sinatra, jackpot of all songwriters.

Among the most conspicuous chart climbers for Monro in the mid-1960s was the first ever cover of 'Yesterday', subject of over a thousand subsequent versions. As early as March 1967, it was approaching 500 – as announced by Dick James, director of Lennon and McCartney's publishing company Northern Songs.

"I just fell out of bed and it was there," divulged Paul. "I have a piano by the side of my bed, and I just got up and played the chords. I thought it can't just have come to me in a dream. It's like handing things in to the police; if no one's claimed it after six weeks, I'll have it."[3] 'Yesterday' was then launched into life with the provisional title of 'Scrambled Eggs' until the tailoring of lyrics that McCartney sang on disc accompanied by his own acoustic guitar strumming – and a string quartet, an early example of The Beatles' augmentation of conventional beat group instruments. Sitars, horn sections, orchestras, tape collage and other resources were yet to come.

Matt Monro's big band rendering of 'Yesterday' made the UK Top Ten in the teeth of a belated rival 'Yesterday' on Decca by Marianne Faithfull – with an accompanying choir – that was advantaged by apparent endorsement by sole composer McCartney ('and I never wished I'd written it,"[4] muttered John Lennon).

First refusal, however, had been given to Billy J Kramer ("it was too nicey-nicey for me") before 'Yesterday' was offered to Chris Farlowe, a white Londoner who was being bruited as "the greatest Blues Singer in the world today"[5]. Marianne Faithfull had dithered over it too. Then Matt Monro's headlining spot on *Sunday Night At The London Palladium* settled the matter – though McCartney's blueprint on the soundtrack album of *Help!*, The Beatles' second movie, scored in the States.

It was George Harrison's task to introduce 'Yesterday' onstage, viz, "For Paul McCartney of Liverpool, opportunity knocks!". George and the others had nicknamed Paul (not always affectionately) "The Star", partly because he seemed to have the most highly developed instinct – and desire – for riding the waves of showbusiness protocol whilst gilding the image of loveable and slightly naive lads from back-of-beyond taken aback by their celebrity – which probably accounts for his behaviour during the chat with Johnnie Ray. Paul's skill for combining necessary ruthlessness with keeping his popularity intact was freeze-framed in an episode centred on him at the window of a chartered aircraft that had just landed somewhere in the American Midwest...

A reception committee of town burghers and their hoity-toity children are waiting on the tarmac. Behind the glass, Paul is waving and smiling. From the side of his mouth, however, he is issuing instructions to Mal Evans, a principal of the road crew, to tell the assembly outside that he – Mal – had decided that, though The Beatles were delirious with joy at the thought of meeting them, they were in need of rest for that evening's show. I'm sorry you're disappointed, but, for their own good, I've had to disappoint the boys too. Thus Evans rather than Paul, John, George and Ringo was the *bête noire* via a strategy worthy of the most battle-hardened public relations officer.

Of all The Beatles too, Paul was the one most abreast with contemporary trends such as the injection of Oriental sounds into pop as originated by either The Yardbirds – or The Kinks on 1965's 'See My Friends' with its plaintive, whining vocal and droning guitars. Their lead guitarist Dave Davies would recall an encounter in a London club, the Scotch of St James, when "McCartney said, 'You bastards! How dare you! I should have made that record.'"[1]

After outlines dissolved, around late 1964, between what outsiders had understood to be the demarcation line of John (rhythm guitar)-George (lead guitar)-Paul (bass)-Ringo (drums), The Yardbirds left their mark on McCartney's lead guitar solo in 'Taxman' (from *Revolver*) on which you can detect shades of the abrasive passagework with which Jeff Beck lacquered 'Shapes Of Things', The Yardbirds then-current hit 45.

Above all, however, Paul listened hard to black music. "Paul loves Motown," Michael Jackson would observe when he and McCartney were friends. "He also loves gut music: early, early American black music like Elmore James – but if you want to see him smile, just start talking to him about 1960s Motown. He says he was a fan like everybody else – and since those years were really important to his career, his memories are very sharp, very sensitive about that time."[6]

Tamla-Motown, a black label based in Detroit, had manoeuvred its first fistful of releases into the US Hot 100 in 1960, beginning with Barrett Strong's 'Money (That's What I Want)'. By the mid-1960s, however, Motown – along with "soul" discs on other labels, notably Stax, its Deep South rival – was being saturation-plugged into the UK Top 50 by pirate radio. Nevertheless, as well as hits by the likes of James Brown, The Supremes, The Righteous Brothers, The Miracles, Nina Simone and Wilson Pickett, McCartney and others in the know were also *au fait* with both the back catalogue and the latest by even old timers such as The Drifters, Ray Charles, Fats Domino, Chris Kenner and Bobby Bland. Newer entries in what had once been called the "sepia" charts in the USA included The Soul Sisters' 'I Can't Stand It', Brenda Holloway's 'Every Little Bit Hurts' and further erudite gems that were infiltrating the portfolios of R&B units in Britain, now looking and sounding dangerously like straight pop groups.

While it was hip to say you preferred the black blueprints (or white in the exception of the "blue-eyed soul" of The Righteous Brothers), all kinds of British recording acts, famous and obscure, were trying on soul for size. 'I Can't Stand It' and 'Every Little Bit Hurts' had been thrust out as consecutive Spencer Davis Group A-sides as James Brown's 'I'll Go Crazy' was for the Untamed, and 'You've Lost That Lovin' Feelin'' for Cilla Black – while The First Gear had a go at Dobie Gray's 'The In Crowd', and The Fourmost heisted The Four Tops's 'Baby I Need Your Loving'. The Hollies were planning to cover the Tops's 'Reach Out I'll Be There' purely for the European market if the original missed – as Cliff Bennett And The Rebel Rousers were to do with Sam and Dave's 'Hold On I'm Coming'.

On the bill of the German leg of The Beatles' final world tour in 1966, Bennett and his band's set contained 'Got To Get You Into My Life', presented to Cliff in a dressing room one night by Paul McCartney on guitar and vocal, and John Lennon dah-dahing a horn section. Whereas The Beatles had attempted soul on disc with such as 'Money', 'Please Mr Postman' and The Miracles' 'You Really Got A Hold On Me' (all on *With The Beatles*) this new offering was a Lennon–McCartney original – "one of Paul's best songs,"[3] said John – in the more ebullient of Motown or Stax's house styles. Produced by McCartney and coupled with Bennett's self-penned 'Baby Each Day', this "best song I ever recorded" was to be Cliff's biggest smash, coming within an ace of Number One in Britain.

"When John and I first started writing songs," conceded Paul, "everything was a nick. Now that's a tip for budding songwriters. We pinched ideas from records all the time. There's nothing immoral or dishonest about it because the imitation's only a way of getting started. Like, you might hear 'Please Mr Postman' by The Marvelettes, and be knocked out by it, and want to do something in that style – so you could start with a line like, 'Sorry, Mr Milkman...' By the time the song's finished, you've probably got rid of the first line anyway. Maybe it doesn't sound even remotely like The Marvelettes either, but it's got you going, acted as the spark. For example, in my mind, 'Hey Jude' is a nick from The Drifters. It doesn't sound like them or anything, but I know that the verse, with these two chords repeating over and over, came when I was fooling around playing 'Save The Last Dance For Me' on guitar."[7]

The circle remained unbroken with Beatles numbers on a Supremes album, 1965's *With Love From Us To You*, and respective revivals of 'Eleanor Rigby' and 'Lady Madonna' by Ray Charles and Fats Domino. In 1967, Charles also did 'Yesterday', which, lasting a month low in the UK Top 50, couldn't have hoped to match Matt Monro's feat two years earlier.

The rainy winter that welded 1965 to 1966 had been party time too for The Overlanders with their Paul Friswell's contention that they "did Lennon and McCartney a favour"[3] via a faithful if unsolicited reproduction of 'Michelle', McCartney's bilingual ballad from The Beatles' *Rubber Soul* album. Friswell's cheek was mitigated when it became the first xerox of a Beatles LP track to top the UK singles chart.

'Michelle' suited the charitable Overlanders, a UK beat group long due a re-assessment as pioneers of folk-rock – and it was attitudes towards this genre that illustrated a major artistic difference between John and Paul. Lennon was fond of Bob Dylan, but McCartney had preferred Paul Simon, a New Yorker then doing the rounds of British folk clubs. 1965's *The Paul Simon Songbook* LP by this singing guitarist caught on with those who'd found Dylan too harsh or were shaking baffled heads now that he was taking the stage with a solid-body Stratocaster and a combo who used to back Canadian rock 'n' roller Ronnie Hawkins. Dylan's records reflected this as Simon's did the "poetic" gentleness that the writer of 'Blowin' In The Wind' had buried in alienating surreality and amplification.

Simon had still been in Britain when 'The Sound Of Silence', an opus with Art Garfunkel, was suddenly at Number One in the States. It almost did the same for The Bachelors in the UK chart, better placed as they were to plug their version on the domestic media. However, Simon and Garfunkel's original 'Homeward Bound' won the day against a cover by The Quiet Five. As this Bournemouth quintet had still spent a fortnight in the Top 50 with it, surely a revitalisation of this trendy songwriter's 'Richard Cory' could restore Them's broken fortunes. Decca even cancelled a single of 'Richard Cory' by The Animals to give their ailing Irish blood-brothers an unobstructed passage, but, with no airplay or actively functioning group to nourish it, Them's 'Richard Cory' flopped.

Them had made hay during what had come to be known as the "British Invasion" of North America, which may be dated from The Beatles' landing in Kennedy airport on 8 February 1964 with 'I Wanna Hold Your Hand' at Number One in the Hot 100. To the chagrin of The Four Seasons, The Beach Boys and other US acts on the same labels John, Paul, George and Ringo had been propelled by one of the most far-reaching publicity blitzes hitherto known in the record industry. While the intruders swamped the Hot 100, The Beach Boys' resident genius, Brian Wilson, had felt, both threatened and inspired artistically.

"I knew immediately that everything had changed, and that if The Beach Boys were going to survive, we would really have to stay on our toes," Wilson wrote in 2001. "After seeing The Beatles perform, I felt there wasn't much we could do to compete onstage. What we could try to do was make better records than them. My father had always instilled a competitive spirit in me, and I guess The Beatles aroused it."[8]

In reciprocation, *Pet Sounds*, The Beach Boys' most critically acclaimed LP, caused The Beatles' nervous backwards glances – with Paul McCartney citing Wilson as "the real contender"[9] rather than The Rolling Stones. Yet, during one Abbey Road session in 1966, Mal Evans was sent out to purchase *Aftermath*, the new Stones album – because, formidable though Lennon and McCartney's head start was, a year after their first original Stones A-side – 1965's 'The Last Time' – Keith Richards and Mick Jagger had penned all 14 tracks of *Aftermath*, which would net as rich a shoal of cover singles as *Rubber Soul* had done, among them one by The Searchers, who, if surviving Merseybeat's collapse, were finding it hard to crack the Top 50, let alone the Top Ten, nowadays.

If nothing else, The Searchers, Gerry, The Beatles *et al* had put Liverpool on the map. In doing so, the city's art scene garnered more attention than it might have done in the course of a less fantastic decade. In return, Liverpool artists remembered The Beatles at least in paintings like Sam Walsh's *Mike's Brother* (ie Paul McCartney) and *Lennon*[10] – as well as John Edkins's *We Love The Beatles* – shown in a posthumous exhibition at the Bluecoat in 1966. Less specific homage was paid in the ritual spinning of Beatles tracks during intermissions after the Cavern was refurbished that same year to host mainly poetry readings and like *soirées*.

Among recurrent acts now was the mixed-media aggregation known as "The Liverpool Scene"[11], founded by Adrian Henri and – epitomising the passing of the old order – ex-members of beat groups, The Roadrunners and The Clayton Squares. Bringing satirical humour as well as pop music to an audience biased against one or the other, The Liverpool Scene drank from the same pool as fellow latter-day Cavern regulars, The Scaffold who, still containing Paul's Brother, were to harry the UK Top Ten via the vexing catchiness of 'Thank U Very Much' – a response, apparently, to Paul giving Mike a Nikon camera – 'Lily The Pink' and 1974's 'Liverpool Lou'.

Over in Hamburg, there was more of a *fin de siècle* tang in the air, whether Kingsize Taylor on the verge of making despondent tracks back to England to become a Southport butcher or the bunkroom above the Top Ten being vacated for a reunion party after a show at the city's Ernst Merke Halle on 26 June 1966 by The Beatles. They and their entourage had completed dates in Munich and Essen before Hamburg where, just as the populace awoke, they arrived at the main station in a train generally reserved for royalty. Then they were whisked away in a fleet of Mercedes, flanked by a cavalcade of police motor-cyclists, to out-of-town seclusion in Tremsbuttel's Schloss Hotel.

A knees-up at the Top Ten had become impractical but a disguised McCartney and Lennon dared a nostalgic amble along twilit streets, and a few old faces such as Astrid Kirchherr and Bert Kaempfert were allowed past backstage security before showtime for selective reminiscences about the group's past that, through its amazing outcome, had attained flashback grandeur.

Along the Grosse Freiheit, the bands played on. As the age of Aquarius dawned, British beat groups still lingered there: doughty anachronisms still giving 'em 'Some Other Guy' and 'Besame Mucho', even as The Remo Four at the Star-Club and on *Smile!*, their 1967 Germany-only LP, crossed the frontiers between R&B and jazz. Not so adaptable, fellow Scousers Ian And The Zodiacs had followed Kingsize Taylor back to England to expire quietly after turning down 'Even The Bad Times Are Good', which, picked up by Essex's Tremeloes, made the Top Five.

During the global aftermath of domestic Beatlemania, John, Paul, George and Ringo had slumped too – at least as concert performers. Much of it was down to the insufficiently amplified music being drowned by screams, but the malaise was also psychological. It was a typical journeyman musician's memory, but Paul, depressed by the monotony of it all, had glowered from the window of a hotel in Minneapolis and wondered if this was all there was, just like he had in Allerton before opportunities beyond a conventional job like his Dad's had knocked. Imprisoned luxury in Minneapolis was just like imprisoned luxury in Milan. The Coca-Cola tasted exactly the same. If it's Wednesday, it must be Genoa. Box-office receipts could be astronomical, even when shows weren't always the complete sell-outs that they had been in 1964, but, essentially, you were in danger of getting stuck on the same endless highway as that travelled by the olde tyme rock 'n' rollers or black bluesmen of a pre-Beatles epoch.

Now you are on a chartered aeroplane to another stadium that could be anywhere in America. Eyes glazed, brain numb, you could fly forever. The highlight of the day isn't the half-hour lethargies of songs on the boards, but whatever restricted larks presented themselves in between. Contrary to what you read in the papers, you're more likely to drink in a what's-the-best-pint-you've-ever-had? ennui that anything resembling either *Satyricon* or a BBC mock-up of an imagined pop group drugs-and-sex orgy with pushers, groupies and loud-mouthed periphery almost smothering the noise of an interminable four-chord turnaround on an improvised stage.

In tomorrow's dressing room, you'll wait in wearied despair as shiftless equipment changeovers keep the second house in Detroit waiting. The stagehands loaf about, eating sandwiches and smoking. Isolated in the midst of it, what was there left to enjoy about such a debasing job in which, like them, you couldn't wait until knocking-off time?

The Beatles were in a protective bubble away from the shabbier aspects of life on the road. Yet enough concern about the delivery of the show lingered to deject Paul McCartney. It wasn't just fear of seizing up as an entertainer either as, when he finally got to bed, stress-related tension in his bones and muscles might have him lying as rigid as a crusader on a tomb. There was also the disturbing subliminal undertow that, according to the laws of averages and superstition, there was bound to be a major calamity whilst getting from A to B sooner or later – as there'd been for Johnny Kidd, killed in a smash-up near Preston, high-flying Buddy Holly and, in 1964, Jim Reeves, whose career also took a turn for the better with a posthumous UK chart-topper.

That royalties were still rolling in for compositions from 'Love Me Do' onwards was comforting in a way for Paul whenever he contemplated the crueller fate of other artistes – or found the creative process sluggish as it often was during endless centuries of self-loathing in interchangeable hotel suites when boredom had him investigating sound without substance on some new gadget or other.

During the 1966 world tour, the main diversions had been of the worst kind – an international incident in the Philippines when The Beatles had been all but savaged by a howling mob or death threats taken more seriously than any received previously when a comment about Christ by John was construed as "blasphemy" by right-wing sloganisers across the USA.

Yet, how could Paul be displeased with his lot? Even before embarking on this latest public journey, he could have dug his heels in and refused to go in the knowledge that he had enough put away for him and his immediate family to never need to work again. As a recent feature in the *TV Times* had stated: "You're a lucky man, Paul McCartney"[12]. This had been a reference not just to his swelling fortune but his proud courtship of a dashing, flame-headed actress named Jane Asher. She was the first daughter of the quasi-dynastic marriage of eminent Harley Street doctor Sir Richard Asher – and the Honourable Margaret Eliot, a professor at the Guildhall School of Music and Drama. Among her students had been Andrew King, future manager of The Pink Floyd, and a young George Martin.

Six years after he was taken on by EMI, George produced 1956's 'Nellie The Elephant', a giggly Parlophone novelty and *Children's Favourites* perennial by Mandy Miller, star of *Mandy*, an Ealing melodrama about a deaf girl. It was significant too as six-year-old Jane Asher's debut on celluloid. Her mother's connections also assisted a maiden appearance in professional theatre in the title role of *Alice In Wonderland* at the Oxford Playhouse while Jane was still completing her education at Queen's College, just round the corner from the Ashers' five-storey home in Wimpole Street.

When she first caught Paul's eye – backstage at Swinging '63, an all-styles-served-here pop spectacular at the Royal Albert Hall – 17-year-old Jane was in transition between minor child star of stage and screen, and more mature parts, having just spent her first week before the cameras in the horror movie, *The Masque Of The Red Death*. Had she wished, Jane could have urged her agent to negotiate a recording contract. A combination of personal vanity and a desire to maximise public exposure had already motivated the similarly placed Mandy Miller, Hayley Mills and Lynn Redgrave to preserve their warblings on disc; Mills racking up a US Top 20 entry with 1961's querulous 'Let's Get Together'.

Jane went no further than commenting on new singles as a panellist on BBC television's *Juke Box Jury*, though she'd been aware of The Beatles since seeing them on *Thank Your Lucky Stars*, plugging 'Please Please Me'. By his own account[13], she was more attracted initially to Mike McCartney, but before the Swinging '63 evening was over, Paul had seen her home and asked for a date.

For the first time in ages, he'd done the running. Compared to the skirt that had solicited him since he'd been famous, nicely spoken Jane was as a chained cathedral Bible to a cheap paperback novelette. She had "class", a maturity beyond her years reflected in a wasp-waisted confidence that had charmed every other male she'd ever known since reaching puberty. Suddenly, Paul was escorting her to the ballet, the opera, the classical theatre and other worlds of culture that were once outside a son of a Liverpool cotton salesman's index of possibilities.

Yet he was a hit with urbanely elegant Margaret Asher, who, affirms Andrew King, "was the one who told McCartney that he ought to go and get his clothes in Savile Row rather than Carnaby Street"[14]. She also invited him to move into the top floor at Wimpole Street for as long as it took for him to find a place of his own, now that The Beatles were in the process of uprooting from Liverpool. This, however, turned out to be as much of a social coup – and more – for Jane's brother Peter as it was for Paul.

As a day pupil at fee-paying Westminster School, Peter had formed an Everly Brothers-esque duo with a chap called Gordon Waller. Unlike others of their kind, this was more than a mere flirtation with pop prior to beavering away in the family business for a decent interval before being voted onto the board of directors, and becoming chairman by the time you were 40.

Peter and Gordon were sound enough to be signed to Columbia, another EMI label in 1964. Through knowing Paul, they were tossed 'World Without Love', a number that had been around since he was a Quarry Man. Any song with "Lennon–McCartney" as the composing credits was almost like a licence to print money then, so after 'World Without Love' had been ousted from Number One in Britain by Roy Orbison's 'It's Over', they were back with smaller chart entries – but chart entries all the same – in two more 1964 A-sides, 'Nobody I Know' and 'I Don't Want To See You Again', penned specially for them by Peter's sister's boyfriend.

Two years later, Paul handed them another opus, 'Woman', with the proviso that it be attributed to the fictitious "Bernard Webb" rather than "Lennon–McCartney", just to see if it would succeed on its more intrinsic merits. With his works now on the supermarket muzak bulletin as well as in the hit parade, Paul had leeway for playful financial experiments.

While 'Woman' tickled the Top 30 at home, it scrambled higher in the States where, if another upper-class duo, Chad and Jeremy from Eton, took the edge off their headway there, Peter and Gordon released five albums to every one in Britain. As a measure of their US eminence, Epic Records put out *Dave Clark Five Versus Peter And Gordon*, an LP on which both acts had one side.

The two were, nevertheless, on the wane by 1966 when the Ashers' lodger moved out to take up residence in a large but unostentatious Regency house along Cavendish Avenue, a convenient five minute stroll from Abbey Road. That same year, Paul also purchased – on Jane's recommendation – a rural bolt-hole where fans and media would have some search to find him.

A 50km (30 mile) stretch of cold, grey sea separated the northeast coast of Ireland from High Park Farm near Campbeltown, the principal settlement on Strathclyde's Mull of Kintyre, a desolate peninsula that, through McCartney, was to become known to a wider public than it might have warranted.

Campbeltown was just large enough for an airport to be a worthwhile commercial venture. Certainly, it was handy for Paul's commuting to and from London, even if this involved changing at Glasgow and was not as fulsome a forum for continuous thought as those long-haul flights across the planet's two largest oceans during The Beatles' final tour.

Jetting back to Britain two days after the last hurrah at San Francisco's Candlestick Park on 29 August 1966, Paul wrestled with occupational as well as personal stock-taking. Composition for The Beatles and others seemed the most potentially rewarding direction for him then, and it had been a false economy not to buy himself an expensive reel-to-reel tape recorder, once "too big and clumsy to lug around"[7], so that he could construct serviceable demos of the ideas – not just songs – that were streaming from him. Blessed with an over-developed capacity to try-try again, he grappled with his muse, drawing from virtually every musical idiom he had ever absorbed; some of them further removed from The Beatles' Hamburg core than any Star-Club bopper could have imagined.

For hours on end at Cavendish Avenue, he'd attack melody, rhyme and less specific fragments of lyrics and music from all angles, and some would start becoming more and more cohesive with each take. This escalating engrossment in recording caused him to splash out on a home studio. Soon, it was feasible – theoretically anyway – for every note of an entire album by Paul McCartney alone to be hand-tooled in this electronic den.

# 9 "I'm The Urban Spaceman"

"I'm alive and well, but if I were dead, I'd be the last
to know."

– *Paul McCartney*[1]

As Peter Asher had derived benefit from his affinity, so Barry Miles,
editor of *International Times* (*IT*), did when the cash-strapped
underground journal was bailed out with cheques from Barry's
pal, Paul McCartney, who also suggested that an interview with
him in an early edition would attract advertising from EMI and
other record labels. Moreover, when *IT* had been sped on its way
with a "happening" on a cold October night in 1966 at London's
barn-like Roundhouse auditorium, Paul – dressed as a sheik –
milled about with both proto-hippies and celebrities like
Michelangelo "Blow Up" Antonioni – the artiest mainstream film
director of the mid-1960s – and Marianne Faithfull in a cross
between a nun's habit and buttock-revealing mini-skirt.

Thousands more than can have actually have been there were
to reminisce about the free sugar-cubes that may or may not have
contained LSD; the huge bathtub of jelly; the ectoplasmic light-shows
that were part of the feedback-ridden act for The Pink Floyd and
The Soft Machine (in days before the definite article was removed
from their names) – and the latter's recital being interrupted by what
amounted to a simple audience participation number by Yoko Ono,
a Japanese-American "concept artist", who'd lately left the New
York wing of something called Fluxus. Quarter-page notices of her
forthcoming exhibitions surfaced like rocks in the stream in *IT*, but,

grimaced *IT* associate John Hopkins, "Yoko Ono's happenings were boring. She was the most boring artist I'd ever met."[2]

Thanks in part to sponsorship from Ono and more powerful allies like McCartney, *IT* was to muddle on into the 1970s, joining forces with *Oz* – regarded spuriously as its "colour supplement" – and the sub-*Rolling Stone Frenz* to produce *FREEk*, a daily newssheet for the 1970 Isle of Wight pop festival. There then followed a few one-off broadsheets pirated under the *IT* banner, and wanting in terms of constructive journalism and artwork.

In its 1967 to 1968 prime, however, *IT* leaked to back-street newsagents in Dullsville as the provincial sixth-former's vista to what Swinging London was thinking and doing. This was disturbing enough for Frankie Vaughan – who, incidentally, had covered 'Wait' from *Rubber Soul* – to launch a campaign to curtail the spread of the hippy sub-culture. "Hippies are leeches on society"[3], he declared at a public meeting, spurning a flower proffered by one such leech in the audience.

Fellow Scouser McCartney begged to differ: "The straights should welcome the underground because it stands for freedom. It's not strange. It's just new. It's not weird. It's just what's going around."[4] Sometimes, however, it was weird, unless, of course, you'd read the books, seen the films – and sampled the stimulants – necessary for understanding. Paul's *IT* interview, for example, was bloated with gaga truisms such as, "It's difficult when you've learned that everything is just the act and everything is beautiful or ugly, or you like it or you don't. Things are backward or they're forward – and dogs are less intelligent than humans, and suddenly you realise that whilst all of this is right, it's all wrong as well. Dogs aren't less intelligent to dogs, and the ashtray's happy to be an ashtray, and the hang-up still occurs."[5] To a readership uncomprehending, disbelieving or shocked into laughter, he also made the commendably honest admission that "starvation in India doesn't worry me one bit – and it doesn't worry you, if you're honest. You just pose. You don't even know it exists.

You've just seen the charity ads. You can't pretend to me that an ad reaches down into the depths of your soul and actually makes you feel more for these people than, for instance, you feel about getting a new car."[5]

After a field visit to Bangladesh in 1968, born-again Cliff Richard, regarded by then as almost as "straight" as Frankie Vaughan, was to concur with an uncomfortable "I don't pretend I felt any heartache for the people in the Third World or anywhere else for that matter."[6]

Via his management, Richard had been requested to articulate the Christian perspective in *The Process*, mouthpiece of the Church Of The Final Judgement, another publication that went the rounds of sixth-form common rooms. Cliff deigned not to reply, but, in issue number five, dedicated to "Fear", Paul McCartney "was not really afraid of people nor of the world ending or anything like that. It's just fear really, a fear of fear". In parenthesis, Jane Asher confided to the same questioner that she "used to be afraid of the world ending and all that five years ago," but has since "learned not to think about it"[7].

Yet, of all underground periodicals, McCartney's first loyalty was to *IT*. With deceptive casualness, he'd entered the life of Barry Miles, bespectacled, taper-thin and of similar bohemian vintage to Royston Ellis and Johnny Byrne, through Peter Asher. Jane's pop star brother had provided finance for Miles – who encouraged people to address him by his surname then – and John Dunbar, Marianne Faithfull's first husband, to open in January 1966 the Indica Gallery and Bookstore, dealing in merchandise of an avant-garde and fashionably mystical bent. A few months later, *IT* was born in its basement office.

Barry's recollections of his first acquaintance with the Beatle whose biography he was to write 30 years later[8], is worth quoting at length: "Paul helped the bookshop out with some loot occasionally. He made us some wrapping paper, a nice pattern. He just produced a big pile of it one day.

"I knew nothing about rock 'n' roll. When I first met McCartney, I didn't even know which one [of The Beatles] he was. The first time I really had a long talk with him was after Indica had just moved to Southampton Row in March 1966. When we were there, we saw a lot of Paul. He was almost mobbed one day, walking down Duke Street. He came beating on the door and we had to let him in, and there was this great horde of people following him. He'd been out looking for some kind of thread for Jane, who wanted it for a dress she was making.

"I thought it would be very good for The Beatles to know about avant-garde music – so I persuaded Paul to come along to a lecture by Luciano Berio at the Italian Institute. We got there and sat down, and almost immediately the press came bursting in with flashlights and so on. That was the kind of thing that happened all the time."[9]

Miles and McCartney became close friends to the degree of an insistence by the millionaire Beatle that he stand every round whenever they, John Dunbar, Peter Asher, John Hopkins *et al* spent an evening in one of few watering holes these days where Paul wouldn't have to listen with heavy patience to any stranger's starstruck twaddle.

As one who'd mixed with fustian intellectuals in Liverpool and Hamburg, McCartney wasn't ignorant of many of the well-read Barry's points of reference, and could hold his own amid the beer-fuelled polemics. Yet, his understanding of what literature was worth reading and what was not became more acute through knowing Miles and the Indica crowd. "Miles was a great catalyst," he agreed. "He had the books. We [The Beatles] had a great interest, but we didn't have the books. Once he saw that we were interested, particularly me because I used to hang out with him, he showed us new things – and I'd had a great period of being avant-garde, going off to France in disguise, taking in a lot of movies, which I later showed to Antonioni: very bizarre, but it seemed exciting at the time."[9]

Whenever he was under no immediate obligation to return to Cynthia and their infant son in the Surrey stockbroker belt, John Lennon would tag along too. Nevertheless, he digested many of the avant-gardenings second-hand. "John was so constricted living out in Weybridge," lamented Paul. "He'd come to London and say, 'What've you been doing?', and I'd say, I went out last night and saw Luciano Berio. That was quite cool. I've got this new Stockhausen record. Check this out. I think John actually said, 'I'm jealous of you'. He just needed to get out of Weybridge, watching telly. It wasn't his wife's fault. She just didn't understand how free he needed to be."[9]

Unhobbled by marriage and fatherhood, Paul's own evenings in at Cavendish Avenue might have found him flipping the three channels on his television before choosing to give the Stockhausen LP a spin. It got him as "gone" as a fakir in a trance. Reports of further self-improvements would raise puffy smiles of condescension from those for whom "culture" was second nature (and "pop music" and its practitioners beneath contempt). Such snobs may have assumed that Paul was exhibiting an observed reverence for what he felt he ought to appreciate, but didn't quite know why. Magnifying the gap between themselves and the common herd, they would not believe that one such as him could glimpse infinity during *Mikrophonie I* and *II*. Yet McCartney's devouring of such new experiences went further than just shallow dropping of names. Indeed, some of it was to infiltrate The Beatles' post-Candlestick Park output.

However, that the group was off the road didn't mean that McCartney was metamorphosing into an emaciated ascetic. His recreational pursuits were both far from sedentary and not always to do with intellectual curiosity. He and the other Beatles were as prone to untoward nonsense involving drugs and girls as any other in an elite of pop *conquistadores* whose disconnection with life out in Dullsville was so complete that their only contact with it most of the time was through personal managers, gofers – and narcotics dealers.

McCartney had been the last Beatle to sample LSD. "Paul is a bit more stable than George and I," explained John, "It was a long time before he took it, and then there was the big announcement."[10] If a latecomer, Paul was the loudest of all the group in the defence of LSD – "acid" – as a chemical handmaiden to creativity: "We only use one tenth of our brains. Just think what we could accomplish if we could tap that hidden part."[11]

You only had to tune in to the music wafting from California where LSD's paranormal sensations were being translated on the boards and on record by Jefferson Airplane, Clear Light, The Grateful Dead and further front-runners of the flower-power sound of the Haight-Ashbury – "Hashbury" – district of San Francisco. Once the musical wellspring of little beyond a few jazz clubs, the city was about to become as vital a pop capital as Liverpool had been.

During its 15-month Summer of Love, the proferring of sex and marijuana "joints" became a gesture of free-spirited friendliness, while the mind-warping effects of the soon-to-be outlawed LSD possessed its "Cavern", the Fillmore West's cavorting berserkers, shrouded by flickering strobes, tinted incense fumes and further audio-visual aids that were part-and-parcel of simulated psychedelic experience.

London sometimes surpassed this with events like the inauguration of *IT* at the Roundhouse, and, another *IT* benefit, the Fourteen Hour Technicolor Dream at Alexandra Palace on 29 April 1967 where The Move, The Pink Floyd, Tomorrow, John Children, The Flies (who urinated over the front row), the omnipresent Yoko Ono, you name 'em, appeared one after the other before tranced hippies and other updated beatniks, either cross-legged or "idiot dancing".

During the merest prelude to becoming a serious chart contender, the most exotic darling of the London underground around this time was Jimi Hendrix, a singing guitarist who'd been "discovered" walking an artistic tightrope without a safety net in New York's half-empty Cafe Wha?, and had been brought over to England to become almost the last major icon to come in from the outside of the British beat boom.

"The very first time I saw Jimi at the Bag O' Nails," recalled McCartney, "it wasn't who, but what is this? And it was Jimi. There weren't many people in the club, but at the next gig, me, Eric Clapton and Pete Townshend were standing in this very packed audience, all come to pay homage to the new god in town."[12]

On Paul's recommendation, Hendrix was booked for a watershed performance at the International Pop Music Festival in Monterey – an overground "coming out" of what was occurring a few miles up the coast in San Francisco and further afield. It was here that the fated Jimi's showmanship as much as his innovative fretboard fireworks – and his English accompanists' quick-witted responses to them – spurred a gallop to international stardom.

A contrasting surprise hit at Monterey was Ravi Shankar, the Indian sitar virtuoso, whose *West Meets East* album with the equally acclaimed violinist Yehudi Menuhin was issued just before 'Norwegian Wood' and 'Paint It Black' brought the sitar to a pop audience – though Shankar had been accused already by longtime devotees of "selling out" and of emasculating his art with Grammy-winning collaborations such as this.

Just as George Harrison had been the principal advocate of the application of Indian musical theories and instrumentation – and spiritual beliefs – to The Beatles' oeuvre, so McCartney was chiefly responsible for at least superficial use of the pioneering tonalities of Berio, Stockhausen *et al* in such as 'Carnival Of Light', a 14-minute tape collage that was the group's contribution to another Roundhouse "happening" early in 1967. The influence of the post serialist composers was evidenced too in 'Tomorrow Never Knows' in which only a repeated tom-tom rataplan and Lennon's battered lead vocal endowment on its trace of melody put it into the realms of pop at all.

On the same album, 1966's *Revolver*, McCartney shone brightest on 'Eleanor Rigby' – "Paul's baby, and I helped with the education of the child,"[13] quipped Lennon. She was, however, destined to die alone – with, seemingly, no one to welcome her through the pearly gates. That was how Eleanor had always lived until she expired in the church that was her only comfort, and was buried "along with her name" with just Father McKenzie, another lonely person, who darns his own socks, in attendance. Old maids would make further appearances in the corporate and solo canon of The Beatles – almost all through the offices of McCartney, who penned the bulk of 'Lady Madonna' and all of 1971's 'Another Day'.

Among acts that covered 'Eleanor Rigby' were The Vanilla Fudge – described in *IT* as "molten lead on vinyl"[14] – and supper-club crooner Johnny Mathis, thus demonstrating how it – and 'Here There And Everywhere', 'Penny Lane', 'When I'm Sixty Four' and further instantly familiar paeons mainly from McCartney – walked a safe and accessible line between the opposing styles of the day. Mellow sunshine rather than mind-zapping thunderstorm, they fitted perfectly into a period in which schmaltz was represented in the charts as much as psychedelia.

Now a vocalist of sub-Engelbert Humperdinck stamp, Malcolm Roberts was to rack up enough readers' votes in the *New Musical Express*'s popularity poll for 1969 to rank just below John Lennon in the "male vocalist" section. Likewise, for all its brush-strokes of surreal imagery, 'Penny Lane' nestled comfortably among easy-listening standards like Stevie Wonder's 'I Was Made To Love Her', Jose Feliciano-via-The Doors's 'Light My Fire', 'Brown-Eyed Girl' by former Them vocalist Van Morrison, Fifth Dimension's 'Up Up And Away', gently reproachful 'Pleasant Valley Sunday' by The Monkees and flower-power anthems like 'San Francisco' from Scott McKenzie.

'When I'm Sixty-Four', a recreation of a Jim Mac Jazz Band-type refrain, was the item that most fitted this brief on *Sgt Pepper's Lonely Hearts Club Band*. The most celebrated of all Beatles' long-players had sprung from late Abbey Road hours of cross-fades, stereo panning, intricately wrought funny noises and similarly fiddly console minutiae when the team were at the forefront of a trend for "concept albums" (which included "rock operas" and like *magnum opi*) – though others weren't far behind.

Mere weeks after *Sgt Pepper* reached the shops, 'Grocer Jack', a kiddie-chorused excerpt from *A Teenage Opera*, composed by Mark Wirtz, once a would-be German Elvis, was in the UK singles list. Nevertheless, while this built up anticipation for an associated album and stage show, the 'Sam' follow-up barely rippled the Top 40, and another 45rpm clip didn't even "bubble under". As a result, investors lost heart and the opera was abandoned.

Joe Average has heard even less of a concept LP that was realised by Paul McCartney late in 1965. As reported in the *Disc And Music Echo* gossip column[15], a few copies were pressed as Christmas presents for just the other Beatles and Jane Asher. It was said to be an in-joking send-up of a radio variety show with the irrepressible Paul as a one-man compère, singer, instrumentalist, comedian and all-purpose entertainer. If it ever existed, the roots of *Sgt Pepper* may lie in this *ultima thule*, this unobtainable prize for collectors of Beatles artefacts.

If one ever turned up in a memorabilia auction, it might bolster McCartney's assertion that it was he who came up with the basic notion of *Sgt Pepper*, "giving The Beatles alter-egos simply to get a different approach"[8], on a return flight from a holiday in Kenya in November 1966 – though he was to aver that "only later in the recording did Neil Aspinall [The Beatles' personal assistant] have the idea of repeating the 'Sgt Pepper' song, and The Beatles and George Martin began to use linking tracks and segues to pull it together."[8]

The *Sgt Pepper* era remains the principal source of countless hours of enjoyable time-wasting for those who collate "hidden messages" in the grooves and packagings of Beatles discs. While this is a subject worthy of 1,000 university theses, we can only scratch the surface here by attending to the most enduring so-called communiqué that supported a rumour that Paul McCartney had been beheaded in a road accident on 9 November 1966 and replaced by a *Doppelgänger*. All that actually happened was that he cut his lip that day in a mishap whilst riding a moped, but surely you can hear John say "I buried Paul" in a daft voice in the last seconds of 'Strawberry Fields Forever' – and at the end of 'I'm So Tired' on 1968's "White Album" (*The Beatles*), doesn't he mumble "Paul is dead. Bless him, bless him, bless him..."?

None of them were hits, but there was soon an impressive array of "Paul Is Dead" singles behind counters. Penetrating the crowded airwaves then were the likes of 'Brother Paul' by Billy Shears and the All-Americans, 'Saint Paul' from Terry Knight – future manager of Grand Funk Railroad – and Zacharias and his Tree People's 'We're All Paul Bearers (Parts One And Two)'. In a vocational slow moment after 'Light My Fire' in 1968, Jose Feliciano issued a 'Paul' 45 too. As an ex-Beatle, Lennon's snigger was almost audible when, not content with airing grievances against McCartney in the press, he sniped at him on disc in 1971 with 'How Do You Sleep?' from *Imagine*, confirming that Billy, Terry, Zacharias *et al* were "right when they said that you were dead".

Long before The Beatles' bitter freedom from each other, The Moody Blues had been falling apart too. During a commercially dangerous vinyl silence of not quite a year, Tony Secunda had been replaced as their manager by Brian Epstein, now nowhere as painstaking or energetic as he'd been when he'd taken on The Beatles in 1961. Therefore, with Epstein increasingly less available, and Decca only interested in consistent chartbusters, the group had been obliged to drastically reduce booking fees and soon inevitable cracks had appeared. First out was bass player Clint Warwick "because he was the only one married with a kid," elucidated Denny Laine. "For me, that was the beginning of the end. It changed the whole concept of the band. Because it levelled out with the Moodies – yet another tour of Germany, that sort of thing – it all got a bit insecure."

The vacancy was filled by a former member John Lodge who, according to Denny, "had had the job originally, but his girlfriend didn't want him to move out of Birmingham". Yet so anxious was Lodge for the Big Time that he sold some of his equipment to finance a pending tour of Europe where it was still feasible for the outfit to break even.

The tour took place without Laine who, anticipating Brian Wilson's role in The Beach Boys, was concentrating on writing and studio work before concluding that he couldn't be worse off solo. The ailing Moody Blues, nonetheless, were to be revitalised with 1967's 'Nights In White Satin', the hit 45 from *Days Of Future Passed*, an ambitious concept album with orchestra. From then on, it was plain sailing as album after platinum album refined a magniloquent style so nebulous in scope that such diverse units as Yes, King Crimson, ELO and Roxy Music were all to be cited irregularly as variants of The Moody Blues blueprint.

As for Denny Laine, "I was adrift for a bit. I went to Spain for two years in a village in the house of an American guy who was also studying flamenco. I came back with the idea of doing a folky, acoustic-style thing, but with strings. For a few months, he was backed by The Electric String Band, an amplified string quartet from the Royal Academy of Music – "technicians", Denny called them – plus a drummer and electric bass guitarist. "It was a bit of a nightmare actually," Denny admits now, "because the technicians were all so busy doing other things. It was fun for them, but they didn't find it easy. They were all soloists, really good players. A lot of good ideas came from them."

The advanced nature of Laine's singles with this ensemble, 'Say You Don't Mind' and 'Too Much In Love', was demonstrated when Colin Blunstone's exact copy of the former crept into the Top 20 in 1972. However, getting a satisfactory concert sound for The Electric String Band was problematic. Yet a final engagement, supporting Jimi Hendrix at London's Saville Theatre – in which Brian Epstein had a controlling interest – "went really well," in its leader's estimation, "and a lot of people from the business were there. Then the string players had to go to Russia to tour and things drifted off again."

In need of careers advice, Denny arrived on the off-chance at his distant manager's Belgravia doorstep during 1967's August bank holiday. He received no answer to his knock. Inside, Brian Epstein was expiring in a drug-induced slumber.

He was found on the Sunday afternoon. At around 4pm, eight-year-old Ruth McCartney, daughter of Jim McCartney's second wife, Angela Williams, had been visiting her step-brother and his Beatles in Bangor, a university town where the Welsh mainland nears the island of Anglesey. She and Angela had been bidding him farewell when he'd been requested to take an urgent telephone call. She was to learn its content on arrival back home in Hoylake, over the river from Liverpool, two hours later. The telephone there was ringing too. George Harrison's mum was on the line with an example of how the story had become confused. Brian, she told Angela, had shot himself.

By then, the truth The Beatles had refused to avow had inflicted itself. They could no longer not believe it. An attempt to soothe their anguish had been made by the Maharishi Mahesh Yogi, the Indian guru who'd been running the weekend course in transcendental meditation that, at George Harrison's urging, they'd all been attending at the University of Bangor.

The appeal of a community more enclosed than the innermost pop clique was attractive enough for The Beatles to study meditation further at the Maharishi's yoga-ashram – theological college – in the Himalayas the following spring. Though politicians might covet the pop deity's unlooked-for manipulation of widespread opinion, a charismatic head of a supposed spiritual movement is often on a par with the most adored guitar god – but with a stronger self-certainty about everything he says and does. How else are orthodox religions able to maintain mass subscription to tenets that coming from a street-corner crank would draw only jeers from the few who stop to listen? What else explained the ascendancy of the likes of Sun Myung Moon and, before his disgrace, the US evangelist Jimmy Lee Swaggart over their followers? In a Hindu city, would the notion that communion wafers and wine turn into the body and blood of Christ forestall mockery? Conversely, what is the Christian party-line on the Hindu ascetic's ingenious modes of self-torture? What about tarot cards, not walking under ladders and black cat bones? Spirituality – or, if you prefer, superstition – has less to do with logic than what St Denis held as "perfect unreasonability".

Even prior to his association with Indica, Paul McCartney had explored Buddhism and Hinduism as well as mystical and esoteric Christianity, but had not been completely convinced by any of them. Furthermore, while he continued to practice meditation, even designating a room in his house for that specific purpose, his jet-legged return from India was a fortnight ahead of George and John, and his most piquant memory of the visit one of a solitary session on a flat roof when "I was like a feather over a hot-air pipe. I was just suspended by this hot air, which had something to do with the meditation – and it was a very blissful thing."[16]

Back to the day-to-day mundanities of being a Beatle, Paul was still living down *Magical Mystery Tour*, the made-for-television movie – and their first major post-Epstein project – of which he'd been both the instigator and main producer. To disaffected observers – and, indeed, to John, George and Ringo now and then, his methodology had appeared slap-dash – as if he was making it up as he went along, which he was much of the time. Concordant with the bare bones of the "plot" – summarised by the title – there was much spontaneity, improvisation and scenes that seemed a good idea at the time. Worse, though some clutter fluttered onto the cutting-room floor, its focus still remained vague – but maybe that was almost the point.

The finale was a big-production number, 'Your Mother Should Know', written by Paul, and recorded the week before Brian

Epstein's sudden passing. Like 'When I'm Sixty-Four', it was at one with a fad for olde tyme whimsy that had prevailed in the hit parade since 1966's chart-topping 'Winchester Cathedral' – all vicarage fête brass and posh megaphoned vocals – by The New Vaudeville Band. In its wake came such as Whistling Jack Smith's 'I Was Kaiser Bill's Batman', boutiques like 'I Was Lord Kitchener's Valet' and experiments – by The Beatles too – with dundreary side-whiskers, raffish moustaches and similar depilatory caprices that prompted a Mancunian costumier to manufacture fake ones so those without the wherewithal to sprout their own could still "Make The Scene With These Fantastic New Raves".

On the strength of their debut 45, 'My Brother Makes The Noises For The Talkies', The Bonzo Dog Doo-Dah Band ran in the same pack, but, as it turned out, they defied entirely adequate categorisation – except that, though the outfit's *raison d'être* was centred on getting laughs, they were more Scaffold than Freddie And The Dreamers in that they conveyed in pop terms that strain of fringe-derived comedy that was to culminate with *Monty Python's Flying Circus*.

"In 1966, we decided to expand our style," explained Neil Innes, who was, with Vivian Stanshall, the group's principal composer. "We did 1950s rock 'n' roll, flower-power, anything went – and started writing our own stuff. It only took a year to develop. If it got a laugh, it stayed in the act. On the cabaret circuit and then the colleges, and we were earning as much as any group with a record in the charts. We were liked by people like Eric Clapton as a band most of them would liked to have been in – even though we were never mega recording artists."

Their eventual modicom of Top Ten success – with an Innes opus, 'I'm The Urban Spaceman' – was testament to courage in remaining true to their strange star, but it was, however, secondary to an eye-stretching stage act, which earned them both a cameo in *Magical Mystery Tour*, and a weekly turn on the anarchic ITV children's series, *Do Not Adjust Your Set*.

"I wrote 'Urban Spaceman' in one afternoon," said Innes with quiet pride, "Our producer, Gerry Bron, was fairly strict about studio time, and Viv Stanshall complained about this to Paul McCartney, who he'd met down the Speakeasy. Paul came along to the 'Urban Spaceman' session, and his presence obliged Gerry to give us more time. Paul also had great recording ideas – like double-tracking the drums, and putting a microphone in each corner of the playing area to catch Viv's garden hose with trumpet mouthpiece as he whirled it round his head.

"I was quite keen to do a follow-up that was sort of humorous but still catchy. We selected 'Mr Apollo', which was once like that. Most of it was mine, but Viv got hold of it, and it ended up well over acceptable single length – because it wasn't until 'Hey Jude' that you could get away with it."

# 10 *"Goodbye"*

"She wore impeccably applied make-up, including long, fluttering false eye-lashes. It wasn't long before she zeroed in on Paul."

– *Peter Brown*[1]

In Brian Epstein's final months, the same questions had come up over and over again. Plain fact was that the contract was up for renewal anyway, and, according to hearsay, his stake in Beatles' affairs would have been reduced, though they wouldn't have carried on totally without him.

Therefore, though Brian might not have approved of Apple Corps, had he lived, he probably wouldn't have been able to do much to prevent it. On paper, nevertheless, it made sound sense, combining a potential means of nipping a huge tax demand in the bud and a diverting enterprise that could equal profit as well as fun. This was a common ploy of wealthy pop stars down the ages, whether Frank Sinatra's Reprise record company, Who singer Roger Daltry's trout farm, Dolly Parton's "Dollywood" amusement park or Reg Presley of The Troggs's Four Corners Vision film company.

Apple Corps was intended to house all manner of artistic, scientific and merchandising ventures under The Beatles' self-managed aegis. By 1970, however, it had been whittled down to Apple Records, a label whose releases were monitored by EMI with all kinds of middlemen taking a cut.

Yet, once upon a time, Apple had been visualised as the most public expression of the underground's "alternative economy", but as much its embodiment as the free open-air rock concerts that pocked post-flower power Britain's recreational calendar. So common and large-scale were these altruistic happenings in London – as instanced by the Blind Faith "supergroup" and then The Rolling Stones in Hyde Park's natural amphitheatre and Procol Harum near the tumulus in Parliament Hill Fields – that reaction when scanning billings in *IT* or *Time Out* had shifted from a sardonic "Yeah, but how much is it to get in?" to a jaded "Hmmm, is that all that's on this time?"

Motives, as always, were suspect. The Stones' amassing of an audience of over half-a-million – the largest assembly for any cultural event ever contained by the capital – was, sneered cynics, great publicity, helped sell records and provided raw footage for a TV film. Apple, nevertheless, seemed at first to be genuinely if romantically anxious to give a leg up to deserving causes from the pottering weekend inventor whose converted garage is a grotto of bubbling test-tubes, electrical circuits and Heath Robinson-like devices, to smocked and bereted sculptors chipping at lumps of concrete in upstairs bedrooms, to night porters composing symphonies that would otherwise never be performed.

The Beatles were on such a person's side. They alone understood the difficulties of gaining recognition and finance, having had to struggle for so long themselves before George Martin lent an ear to their efforts. In addition, with Barry Miles the Aaron to his Moses in *IT*, "Paul McCartney asked me to point out that Apple exists to help, collaborate with and extend all existing organisations as well as start new ones. It is not in competition with any of the underground organisations. The concept, as outlined by Paul, is to establish an underground company above ground as big as Shell, BP or ICI, but, as there is no profit motive, The Beatles' profits go first to the combined staff and then are given away to the needy."[2]

If nothing else, Apple was wonderful foolishness. Governed by overweening expressive ambition, it flung indiscriminate cash at the talented, the hopeful and the hopeless until alarming bank statements dictated otherwise. The record company, even with The Beatles as its flagship act, cut back too. Recording manager Peter Asher dispensed straightaway with its Zapple subsidiary for indulgences like George Harrison's knob-twiddling *Electronic Sounds*, and spoken-word items such as a jettisoned 24 album series of in-concert monologues by the late Lenny Bruce who, for those outside his native USA who've ever heard of him, is remembered vaguely for a brand of blue *humor* (not humour) that may appeal to anyone who prefers *This Is Spinal Tap* to *The Glam Metal Detectives*.

Apple's chief non-Beatle triumph was Mary Hopkin, whose records were produced – and, in the case of 1969's 'Goodbye', composed – by McCartney. An 18-year-old soprano, Hopkin was known already in the parallel dimension that is the Welsh pop scene. Until a winning appearance on ITV's *Opportunity Knocks*, her abilities had been directed at the Welsh-speaking market mostly via slots on BBC Wales's weekly pop showcase, *Disc A Dawn*. She began making headway east of Offa's Dyke after fashion model Twiggy brought her to McCartney's attention.

At her father's insistence, some of her B-sides were in Welsh, but her debut Apple A-side, 'Those Were The Days', was in pop's international tongue, and thus began Hopkin's three-year chart run in fine style by spending most of 1968's autumn at Number One after ending the two week reign of seven-minute 'Hey Jude' (which, nevertheless, lasted over two months at the top in the States). Mary's attainment was all the more remarkable in the light of a shorter rival version by the better-known Sandie Shaw, who was still wished "the best of luck" in an Apple press release.

John Lennon had been put in charge of another female vocalist in which Apple had been "interested". Unlike John Hopkins, he hadn't found Yoko Ono boring at all, very much the opposite. As well as taking the place of Cynthia in his bed, Yoko also superseded Paul as a lovestruck John's artistic confrère and filler of the void left by Stuart Sutcliffe as a adjunct personality. She was a mate in every sense; John nutshelling their bond with: "It's just handy to fuck your best friend."[3]

As it had been with Astrid and Stuart, Yoko and John began styling their hair and dressing the same. Paralleling Astrid too, Yoko was the older and, on the face of it, more emotionally independent partner. Through her catalytic influence, the world and his wife were confronted with a John Lennon they'd never known before, one for whom The Beatles would soon no longer count any more than they had for Stuart after he'd made up his mind to return to painting.

Apart from Cynthia, how could anyone begrudge Yoko and John their joy? Many did after *The News Of The World* front-paged the rear cover of *Unfinished Music No 1: Two Virgins*, the couple's first album together. It was a back view of themselves hand-in-hand – and stark naked. The front photograph was too indecent for a self-called family newspaper.

This, like the rest of John and Yoko's many funny-peculiar pranks in the name of art, didn't "give me any pleasure"[4] wrote Paul later, but he showed at least cursory solidarity by accompanying John and his inseparable Yoko to an appointment with EMI chairman Sir Joseph Lockwood to discuss the distribution of *Two Virgins*. He also allowed the inclusion of a shot that almost-but-not-quite revealed all of himself too in the pull-out poster that was part of the "White Album" packaging.

It had been snapped by Paul's new girlfriend from New York, Linda Eastman. Ultimately, he'd been unlucky with Jane Asher – to whom he'd been engaged since January 1968. She'd made an unexpected entry into the Cavendish Avenue master bedroom where another young lady – a New Yorker too – clutched a hasty counterpane to herself. Paul had always been incorrigibly unfaithful; it was one of the perks of his job, but this was the first time he'd been uncovered. Nevertheless, he and Jane weren't over immediately. Indeed, they'd seemingly patched things up when they attended Mike McCartney's wedding in July, but the damage had been done, and was permanent.

A free agent again, Paul chased a few women until they caught him – albeit only fleetingly, but there was no one for the press to take seriously for several months – though it would have been quite a scoop had a tabloid editor got wind of an incident at the Bag O' Nails when McCartney attempted to chat up Rolling Stone Bill Wyman's Swedish sweetheart, Astrid.[5]

It was in the same London night club that Linda Eastman had introduced herself to Paul in 1967, shivering with pleasure at the smile he flashed from the other side of the room. He in turn was to be impressed by a disarming self-sufficiency that would not permit him to be bothered by the fact that she was a divorcée – and the mother of a six-year-old, Heather. In any case, it would have been hypocritical of him not to have been morally generous.

From a family of prominent showbusiness attorneys, Linda was quite accustomed to the company of professional entertainers. This was compounded by her skills as a freelance photographer, and her social intercourse with pop musicians visiting or resident in New York.

Not all such encounters were cordial. Late one 1967 evening in Louie's Bar, a Greenwich Village hang-out with sawdust on the floor and a juke-box, she was one of a clique that included singer-songwriter Tim Buckley, whose introspective melancholy was jazzier than most. He was also something of a boor, bragging later of seducing Linda – who'd taken publicity shots of him in a local zoo earlier in the week – after he'd been boozing heavily that night at Louie's, and had been spectacularly sick as a result. How could she resist?

Apparently, she did – which may be why an ill-natured Buckley also told his guitarist, Lee Underwood, that, following a Rolling Stones press conference in New York, "Mick [Jagger] spent a night with her, and she wrote about it in an American teen magazine."[6] If it ever existed, the article in question has not come to light – nor proof that any liaison between Jagger and Eastman went further than a wistful embrace beneath the stars at the conclusion of a night out.

Linda was on good terms too with The Animals. It was on an assignment at the Harlem Apollo for *Ebony* magazine that she made a lifelong friend of their singer, Eric Burdon. "Linda showed me how to move through that city of cities," enthused Eric. "It was there that we got our first tabs of LSD on the floor of Ondine's night club. Never a participant, Linda was always there to make sure we got home safely after tripping the light fantastic in our favourite place, Central Park. One morning as Barry Jenkins [drummer] and I marvelled at the skyscraper walls that loomed over the city's green sanctuary, Linda snapped away, capturing some of my favourite images of that time."[7]

Another Animal, Chas Chandler had been Linda's escort at the Bag O' Nails for the concert by Georgie Fame And The Blue Flames that was also the occasion she met Paul. Two years later, she was gripping the Beatle arm with a bright, proprietorial grin, and there was less anger than amusement from Heather's father, a geophysicist named Melvin See, when his daughter and ex-wife moved into Cavendish Avenue less than six months after the split with Jane Asher.

Beatles traditionalists did not regard this upheaval as profound an erosion of Fab Four magic as John's estrangement from Cynthia, and the entrenchment of that dreadful Yoko – with whom he was now recording chartbusting singles with an ad-hoc Beatles splinter group, The Plastic Ono Band. Her baleful presence at Abbey Road had exuded too from the needle-time on the "White Album", most notably in 'Revolution 9', dismissed by most as interminable musical scribble. In tacit concurrence, it had been faded out after Paul had been duty bound to mention it without critical comment during his track-by-track discussion of the album – all four sides of it – on Radio Luxembourg on the Friday in November when it was released.

As fans may have expected, Paul had been responsible for the track that mirrored *Rubber Soul*'s 'Michelle' as the biggest-selling cover from the "White Album", namely 'Ob-la-di Ob-la-da', inspired, so one story goes, by the Jamaican patois of Georgie Fame's percussionist, Speedy Acquaye. In March 1969, a Benny Hill television sketch centred on a disc jockey obliged to host an early morning radio show after a night on the tiles. Exacerbating his hungover queasiness was a listener's request for "any platter by Grapefruit, Cream – or Marmalade!" This gag was an illustration of the latter outfit's chart-topping success with a shrewd Yuletide copy of 'Ob-la-di Ob-la-da'. As four of this quintet were Glaswegian, they celebrated by miming it on *Top Of The Pops* in national costume: the Clydeside boys resplendent in sporrans, gorgets, clan tartans *et al* with their English drummer in redcoat gear as a reminder of Culloden.

Each new edition of the weekly programme hammered home to Denny Laine the extent to which his fortunes had declined since 'Go Now'. After Brian Epstein's death, he'd returned to Tony Secunda – "who understood me. Any thing I wanted to do he backed me." So began the great Balls debacle.

This so-called "supergroup" emerged from the ashes of the Ugly's (*sic*), an undervalued Midlands act led by vocalist Steve Gibbons. On its last legs by 1968, it also contained guitarist Trevor Burton whose assets included his standing as an ex-member of the hit-making Move and an effusion of "image" – constant scowl, protuberant eyes and Brooding Intensity. The change of name to Balls was Burton's suggestion. Next came Secunda's directive to migrate to a bungalow in the Hampshire village of Fordingbridge – and, later, to a farmhouse near Reading – as trendy Traffic had to their isolated cottage on the Berkshire Downs.

Though employing the same producer, Jimmy Miller, "getting it together in the country" wasn't without problems for Balls. "A lot of madness went down," growled Trevor, "a lot of drugs too." However, an exploratory bash at a local hall was encouraging, and a lucrative record company advance was promised. By then, Denny had been roped in – so Burton was led to believe – as a bass player, but, according to Laine, "the idea was that we were going to swap instruments around, and bring different people in for different things."

A Burton composition, 'Fight For My Country' – attributed variously to "Balls", "Trevor Burton", "Trevor Burton and Balls" and "Burton, Laine and Gibbons" – surfaced as the only record release after an age of trying out different players; among them Alan White from The Plastic Ono Band. "Some of what became The Electric Light Orchestra were involved," said Denny, "but they weren't worldly enough for me, and I got bored with their lethargic conversation. I wanted guys with energy, who'd been around a bit more."

After an erratic string of college bookings as an acoustic trio – Denny, Trevor and Steve – "Tony Secunda and Jimmy Miller fell out over money," snapped Laine, "and that was the end of that. Then Ginger Baker [former drummer with Blind Faith] came to my house one night and asked me to join Airforce. It was a shambles – too many players all trying to outdo one another, not enough discipline."

As well as percussion, Baker's post-Blind Faith big band was heavy with under-employed Brummies – Burton and Traffic's Steve Winwood and Chris Wood as well as Denny – and Birmingham Town Hall was a fitting debut performance. Most stuck it out for just one more engagement – at the Royal Albert Hall – where a rambling and unrepentantly loud set was captured on tape. From this was salvaged a single, Bob Dylan's 'Man Of Constant Sorrow', sung in Laine's fully developed "hurt" style.

Airforce was one example, but about twice a month from around the middle of 1966, the music press would report a schism in – or complete disbandment of – one group or other; either that or a key member setting himself apart from those with whom he'd been in earshot for every working day since God knows when.

Manfred Mann took formal leave of Paul Jones at the Marquee; Yardbirds vocalist Keith Relf edged into the Top 50 with a solo 45, and the firing of Jeff Beck from the group wasn't far away. Another lead guitarist, Dave Davies, enjoyed two 1967 hits without his fellow Kinks, and Wayne Fontana had cast aside his backing Mindbenders. It was Eric Burdon And The Animals now – just as it soon would be Don Craine's New Downliners Sect.

Georgie Fame had abandoned his Blue Flames, and had plunged boldly into 1966's self-financed *Sound Venture* LP with jazz veterans like Stan Tracey, Tubby Hayes and The Harry South Big Band. The Walker Brothers were to part after a final tour, and Brian Poole and The Tremeloes were recording separately. Alan Price had had several Top 20 entries as an ex-Animal, while Van Morrison had made a less sweeping exit from Them.

All four Beatles were uncomfortably aware that some sort of crunch was coming for them too. John's activities with Yoko and The Plastic Ono Band were bringing it closer by the day. Who could blame Paul, George or Ringo for pondering whether a relaunch as either a solo attraction or in a new group was tenable? Was it so unreasonable for Paul especially to hold in his heart that either way, The Beatles would be recalled as just the outfit in which he'd cut his teeth before going on to bigger and better things?

# 11 "Wedding Bells"

"It was a fabulous band to play with, The Beatles, and we played together long enough to get very comfortable with each other on the music side."

*– Paul McCartney*[1]

Weeping female fans mobbed London's Marylebone Registry Office on that dark day – 12 March 1969 – when Paul and his bride tied the knot. Next, the marriage was blessed at a Church local to Cavendish Avenue. To limit the chances of an outbreak of Beatlemania, neither George, Ringo nor John – who was to get hitched to Yoko a week later – showed up at either building, and a police raid on Harrison's Surrey home and the subsequent discovery of controlled drugs upset his plans to attend the Ritz Hotel reception.

On the BBC's *Six O'Clock News*, girls who'd witnessed the newlyweds exit from the registry office were not undismayed by the last bachelor Beatle's choice, even if most had expected it to be Jane Asher. Though their views weren't broadcast, some had speculated whether or not Linda was pregnant.

She gave birth to Mary on 28th August 1969 (yes, I can count too) in London, though, as it would be with half-sister Heather and two younger siblings, Mary was to look upon East Gate Farm near Rye, Sussex, as home. During what amounted to eventual years of house-hunting, Paul and Linda would restrict themselves to the southeastern shires. The more wooded trackways of Surrey,

Hertfordshire and Essex may have been considered – though, for the renowned who preferred the bright lights of the metropolis, sufficiently secluded havens were hidden too in Little Venice, Hampstead and Holland Park.

Cavendish Avenue, however, was to remain McCartney's principal address for at least as long as The Beatles endured – though they weren't much of a group anymore by the second half of 1969. Increasingly rare moments of congeniality occurred most frequently when not all of them were present at Abbey Road. The old brusque tenderness between Paul and John, for instance, was caught in a photograph taken during a session when, with the former on bass, piano and drums, they were the only Beatles heard on 'The Ballad Of John And Yoko', the worst A-side since 1964's 'Can't Buy Me Love'. It had been composed by Lennon as he continued painting himself into a corner with Yoko, going so far as to change his middle name by deed poll from "Winston" to "Ono" in a ceremony on the flat roof of Apple's central London office.

This was also the location of that famous traffic-stopping afternoon performance – The Beatles' last ever – with organist Billy Preston, their old pal from the Star-Club. "That idea came from the bottom of a glass,"[2] said Paul of this most captivating sequence from *Let It Be*, the *cinéma vérité* follow-up to *Help!*. Elsewhere on celluloid and in private, you could slice the atmosphere with a spade now that Paul's boisterous control of the quartet's artistic destiny had gathered barely tolerable momentum since John's unofficial abdication as *de facto* leader of the four. A Beatles obsessive could date this from as far back as Lennon's murmured "you say it" before Paul's count-in to the reprise of the title song of *Sgt Pepper*.

It wasn't all smiles at business meetings either. The crux of most disagreements was that McCartney advocated his own father-in-law, Lee Eastman, to disentangle Apple and The Beatles' disordered threads, while Lennon, Harrison and Starr favoured

Allen Klein, a New York accountant who Eastman – and, by implication, Paul – disliked and distrusted.

It was scarcely surprising, therefore, that each Beatle was readying himself for the end after his individual fashion; Ringo, for instance, consolidating his then promising film career, and George attempting, purportedly, to compose a stage musical and the soundtrack to a western, neither of which came to fruition – though it was he who was to emerge in the first instance as the most engaging and commercially operable ex-Beatle after the grand *finale* of Abbey Road.

Because everyone involved understood that there weren't to be any more Beatles after that, a spirit of almost *Sgt Pepper*-ish co-operation pervaded. As healthy too in their way were the flare-ups that replaced the irresolute nods of the "White Album" and *Let It Be*. Of all of them, none was so bitter as the one over Paul's 'Maxwell's Silver Hammer'. This was overruled as a spin-off single in favour of a double A-side of George's 'Something' – and 'Come Together' by John, the most vehement opponent of 'Maxwell's Silver Hammer'. It was, he thought, a glaring example of what he and George derided as "granny music". Yet, while it was suspended over a jaunty, see-saw rhythm, the wordy libretto reveals that homicidal medical undergraduate Maxwell Edison bumps off his date, a reproving lecturer and the judge about to sentence him for murder.

Regardless of content, *Abbey Road* as a whole had a clearer sound than *Let It Be*'s associated album, which had been doctored by US producer Phil Spector, whose muddy bombast and heavy handed orchestration was frowned upon by McCartney, and his poor opinion was echoed by studio engineer Glyn Johns. Yet, issued out of sequence, ie after *Abbey Road, Let It Be* earned another gold disc for The Beatles, albeit a Beatles who couldn't care less anymore.

# 12 *"Love Is Strange"*

"A curious mixture of the quiet, retiring man and the natural stage performer."

*– David Gelly*[1]

By 1970, *Beatles Monthly* had ceased publication.[2] From the same publisher, two more glossy monthlies dedicated to Gerry And The Pacemakers and The Rolling Stones had fallen by the wayside long before through falling subscriptions. This, however, wasn't the case with the Beatles periodical, far from it, but "because they are not The Beatles," explained the editorial, "but four separate personalities now."

It seemed silly for those who still styled themselves "Beatle people" to be anything but pessimistic about a predictable future that held the group's total disintegration. Yet, if The Beatles themselves weren't functional as a recording entity, it was a strange week if a version of a Lennon–McCartney number wasn't among the supplicatory flotsam-and-jetsam that washed up round a record reviewer's typewriter.

'It's For You' – one that Paul and John wrote for Cilla Black in 1964 – had just been exhumed by US vocal group Three Dog Night, and was a frequent spin on John Peel's *Top Gear* on BBC Radio One. A highlight of Blonde On Blonde's act at that same year's Isle of Wight festival was 'Eleanor Rigby', whose sad-sack verses and baroque arrangement suited the style of this Welsh "nice little band" admirably. It was also revived by Dozy, Beaky, Mick and Tich, once Dave Dee's Bostons – while both Wilson Pickett and a certain Gerry Lockran had had the unmitigated audacity to issue respective cracks at 'Hey Jude' in January 1969 when the original had barely left the charts; Pickett even cracked the Top 30 on both sides of the Atlantic with his.

That same month, Badfinger peaked at Number Four in Britain with Paul's 'Come And Get It' – which did almost as well in the States, despite competition from a xerox by The Magic Christians, named after the movie in which it was heard no less than five times.

*The Magic Christian*'s second male lead was Ringo Starr – for whom McCartney arranged Hoagy Carmichael's 'Stardust' on *Sentimental Journey*, a forthcoming album of showbiz chestnuts. As calculatedly "square" had been Paul's 'Thingummybob', an A-side penned for Yorkshire's Black Dyke Mills Band. He put in an appearance at the recording session in Bradford, having taken on the commission because, firstly, "I still have a soft spot in my heart for brass bands, it's a roots thing for me."[3] It was also as challengingly distant from 'I Saw Her Standing There' as it was from 'Tomorrow Never Knows'.

*Eeeeee*, my grandad loved bands when he were a lad. Called John Foster and Son Limited Black Dike Mills Band when it took shape from denizens of the Old Dolphin pub in the village of Queenshead, the Black Dyke began with a repertoire that "contained regimental music that inspired England's heroes in the several wars of the French Revolution."[4] In case you're wondering where you'd heard the name, at the Grand Brass Band Competition at Manchester's Belle Vue in 1864, the Black Dyke carried off the cup with The London Victoria Amateurs, The 4th Lancashire Rifle Volunteers and The Holmfirth Temperance amongst runners-up. The greatest day anyone could ever remember concluded – as was proper – with the massed participants blasting up the National Anthem.

By the late 1960s, the Black Dyke were, perhaps, the kingdom's most renowned brass band – though, of similar antiquity, The Brighouse And Rastrick Brass Band had better luck with a treatment of 'The Floral Dance', which all but topped the charts at the apogee of punk, almost a decade after 'Thingummybob' bit the dust. So did the nondescript one-series-only ITV situation comedy, starring Stanley Holloway, for which it was the theme tune.

Yet The Black Dyke Mills Band weathered Apple's subsequent ditching of them as easily as it had all the changes of personnel over the previous century or so. Just as it predated them, so the ensemble outlasted The Beatles for whom the end became publicly nigh when McCartney announced his resignation on 11 April 1970.

"I suppose it ceased to be a working partnership months ago," admitted Paul to journalist Anne Nightingale, "but the Beatles' partnership goes on for seven more years, and this is why I want out now. The other three of them could sit down now and write me out of the group. I would be quite happy. I could pick up my cash and get out. I don't know how much is involved, but I don't want Allen Klein as my manager."[5]

Neither for now did he wish to endure the unpleasantnesses that occur when human beings congregate in a recording studio. During the mild winter that had seen in the new decade, how much more gratifying it had been to tape by multiple overdub enough for an eponymous solo album on four-track equipment in the privacy of Cavendish Avenue and his home-from-home in the Mull of Kintyre. Other than some backing vocals by Linda, Paul – now bearded to the cheekbones – had sung and played every note. With the help of a manual, he had now become sufficiently schooled in the equipment's aural possibilities to commence a day's work with nothing prepared. Without the emotional overheads of working with John, George and Ringo, he layered instrument upon instrument, sound upon sound, for hours on end, anchored by a metronome or retractable "click-track".

Following some fine-tuning in "technically good" Abbey Road and a "cosy" complex in Willesden, *McCartney* was finished to the last detail – or at least the last detail its creator had any desire to etch. "Light and loose" was how he described it in a press release – a "self-interview" – that also got off his chest a lot of feelings about Lennon, Klein ('I am not in contact with him, and he does not represent me in any way') and other issues including the "personal differences, business differences, musical differences" with The Beatles.

Some of its consumers were to find a copy within a package that, after much angered to-ing and fro-ing between Paul and the Klein conclave, reached the shops in April 1970, a fortnight before the valedictory *Let It Be*, and just after *Sentimental Journey*. Without spawning a spin-off 45, McCartney shifted an immediate two million in North America alone, and the general verdict at the time was that it was OK but nothing brilliant. Perhaps it wasn't supposed to be, even if The Faces, fronted by Rod Stewart, thought highly enough of 'Maybe I'm Amazed' to revive it a year later (as would McCartney himself in 1976).

Overall, the album captures a sketchy freshness, even a stark beauty at times. Certainly, it was much at odds with more intense offerings of the day, whether Led Zeppelin, Deep Purple, Man, Black Sabbath, Humble Pie and other headbangingly "heavy" outfits or the "pomp-rock" of ELP, Yes and borderline cases like Pink Floyd and The Moody Blues, castigated for preferring technique to instinct – and *McCartney* couldn't be accused of that.

While the likes of Man and ELP appealed to laddish consumers lately grown to man's estate, self-doubting bedsit diarists sailed the primarily acoustic waters of the early 1970s denomination of singer-songwriters ruled by James Taylor as surely as Acker Bilk had ruled British trad jazz. While there were elements of the same self-fixated preciousness of Taylor, Melanie, Neil Young and their sort, *McCartney* wasn't anywhere as mannered in its embrace of, say, a paeon to its maker's wife ('The Lovely Linda') – and *Let It Be* leftovers ('Teddy Boy') and, the first track ever aired in Britain (on *Pick Of The Pops* one Sunday afternoon), 'That Would Be Something', still being performed by McCartney in the 1990s.

Most of his first true solo effort had resulted from a kind of purposeful mucking about that didn't suggest that Paul McCartney was ready to soundtrack the 1970s as he had the Swinging Sixties with John Lennon, especially after the two's artistic separation was to be confirmed when The Beatles dissolved formally in the Chancery Division of the London High Court on 12 March 1971.

Inevitably, too much would be expected of Paul, John, George and, if you like, Ringo – but whether the much-anticipated *McCartney*, *John Lennon: Plastic Ono Band* and Harrison's *All Things Must Pass* had been tremendous, lousy or, worse, ordinary wasn't the issue for the sort of fan for whom just the opportunity to study each one's sleeve was worth the whole price of what amounted to a new ersatz-Beatle album. It was adequate that it just existed. Nevertheless, like The Rolling Stones, Bob Dylan and Frank Zappa, though McCartney, Lennon and Harrison would rack up heftier sales and honours as individuals, the repercussions of the records they'd made in the 1960s would resound louder. Having gouged so deep a cultural wound collectively, whatever any of them got up to in the years left to him was barely relevant by comparison, no matter how hard he tried.

Paul, in particular, acquitted himself well as a chart contender, made nice music, but none of it made the difference that The Beatles had. His first post-Beatles single, 'Another Day' – as melancholy as 'Eleanor Rigby' – zoomed to a domestic Number Four on 4 March 1971, and began a journey to one position short of this in the US Hot 100 a week later. All that stood in his way to the very top in Britain before the month was out was 'Hot Love' from T Rex, glam-rock giants, whose "T Rexstasy" was as rampant among schoolgirls as Beatlemania once was, and "Rollermania" was to be when Edinburgh's Bay City Rollers – in their gimmick bow-ties and half-mast tartan trousers – were hyped as "the new Beatles". *Plus ça change*.

Lennon's extreme strategies had taken him beyond the pale as an orthodox pop star, while Harrison insisted that he "wouldn't really care if nobody ever heard of me again"[6] after his finest hour at the forefront of the *Concerts for Bangla Desh* in August 1971. McCartney, however, wasn't so happy about someone else having a turn as the teenagers' – or any other record buyers' – fave rave. At the same age – 28 – Roy Orbison had been revered as something of a Grand Old Man of pop during the 1963 tour, but he'd had a receding chin, jug-handle ears and pouchy jowls like a ruminating hamster.

The allure of Paul's yet unwrinkled good looks, his hair remaining on his head and his relative boyishness were belied only by the sorry-girls-he's-married tag that had so irritated the adulterous John before the coming of the second Mrs Lennon when "I really knew love for the first time"[7].

Paul was happily married too, and, like John, intended his missus to get in on the act. Linda had endured piano lessons as a child, but had come to loathe the carping discipline of her teacher. Yet she was sufficiently self-contained to disassociate the music from the drudgery. Indeed, when the dark cloud of the lessons dissolved, she and her school friends had often harmonised *a cappella* for their own amusement in imitation of 1950s vocal group hits such as 'Earth Angel' (The Penguins), 'Chimes' (The Pelicans) and 'I Only Have Eyes For You' (The Flamingos).

Many other outfits of this vintage gave themselves ornithological appellations too – The Crows, The Orioles, The Feathers, The Robins and so forth. It's been said that, with this in mind, Linda, heavily pregnant with a third daughter, modified Paul's original suggestion of "Wings Of Angels" to just plain "Wings" as a name for the group he planned to form for both stage and studio.[8] As with Procol Harum and, since 1969, Pink Floyd, lack of a preceding article was *à la mode*. That there was already a US entity called Wings with a recording contract too was of no apparent consequence.

After recovering from the premature birth of Stella – named after both her maternal great-grandmothers – in London on 13

September 1971, Linda began her diffident tenure in Wings, vamping keyboards as well as ministering to overall effect as a singer. Unlike Yoko Lennon, she was a timid songbird, and wasn't willing initially to walk a taut artistic tightrope with her vulnerability as an instrumentalist. "I really tried to persuade Paul that I didn't want to do it," she protested. "If he hadn't said anything, I wouldn't have done it."[9]

The other more experienced members recruited shared her doubts: "Linda was all right at picking things up, but she didn't have the ability to play freely. If we'd had her and another keyboard player as well, we would have been fine, but Linda was given too much to do. She was a professional though. She got paid like the rest of us."

Thus spake Denny Laine, who had been engaged on an album of his own when summoned to the Mull of Kintyre in August 1971. He'd also been party to a half-serious attempt to put together a "supergroup" drawn from other supergroups with George Harrison, Rick Grech and Eric Clapton from Blind Faith, and Plastic Ono Bandsman Alan White. This was during the interregnum between Balls and the Airforce fiasco. When 'Man Of Constant Sorrow' was issued in autumn 1970, Ginger Baker's post-Blind Faith big band had crash-dived for the last time, thanks mostly to its drummer-leader's heroin dependency – so grave that his "works" had been an established if discreet part of dressing room paraphernalia.

"Ginger had to go away and get better," sighed Denny, "and I was swept under the carpet after Tony Secunda took on T Rex and got them a deal in America. Robert Stigwood wanted me to hang in there, and gave me a retainer. A couple of months later, I got a call from Paul."

McCartney had first met his future lieutenant when Denny Laine And The Diplomats had supported The Beatles at a poorly attended booking at Old Hill Plaza near Dudley back on 11 January 1962. Each had since stayed in the picture about the other's activities, and so it was that "Paul knew I could sing, write and play, and so he called me. It knocked me sideways a little because I wasn't used to being a sidekick, but I admired Paul. That was the first time I'd been with a band with someone more famous than me."

It was also the first time Laine had been in a band with someone of the same Christian name. At the drum stool for several months before Laine's coming was Denny Seiwell, who McCartney had discovered in New York during a thin time in a career that had lifted off when Seiwell completed a spell in a US army band, playing music in an area bordered by John Philip Sousa and The Black Dyke Mills Band. Demobilisation found him in Chicago and then New York, beating the skins in jazz clubs and landing occasional record dates where the versatile Seiwell proved equally at ease attending to "godfather of soul" James Brown's anguished raps as the easy-listening country-rock of John Denver. By 1970, however, he was living a hand-to-mouth existence in the Big Apple where the McCartneys, purportedly, stumbled upon him cluttering a sidewalk along the Bronx. "We thought we'd better not pass him by," recalled Paul-as-Good Samaritan, "so we picked him up, put him on a drum kit, and he was all right."[9] There was another more pragmatic reason for taking him on. "The other New York session guys Paul had approached wanted a lot of dough," elucidated Denny Laine, "and only Denny Seiwell agreed with the amount offered".

As he – and wife Monique – were also amenable to uprooting to Britain, Seiwell seemed to be just what McCartney needed. As well as being an adaptable and proficient time-keeper, his blithe dedication to his craft was refreshing to Paul after the malcontented shiftlessness of certain Beatles in the months before the end. "The important thing is understanding, willingness," judged Paul, "a personality that fits in."[1]

With US guitarists Dave Spinozza and Hugh McCracken – as well as sections of the New York Philharmonic Orchestra – earning their coffee breaks with infallibly polished nonchalance, Seiwell's period in the former Beatle's employ had started with *Ram*, an album that was to be attributed to "Paul and Linda McCartney". Neither presumed to dictate notes and nuances to sidemen with close knowledge of each other's considerable capabilities through working together on countless daily studio sessions, but ran through the basic essentials of every number.

The outcome was a no-frills precision that lent the majority of *Ram*'s 12 selections a dispiriting squeaky-cleanliness as if the hand-picked and highly waged players couldn't accomplish what Paul alone – for all his wispiness and casually strewn mistakes – had committed to tape instinctively on home-made *McCartney*.

This opinion was echoed by contemporary critics – with the *NME*'s "a mixed bag of psychedelic liquorice all-sorts"[10] a prototypical reaction to the compositions *per se*. In what amounted to a personal attack, the now-radical *NME* also denigrated the McCartneys as a smug, bourgeois couple too long and maybe guiltily detached from the everyday ennui of the lengthening dole queues in 1970s Britain.

Yet a public that didn't read the music press were willing to assume that *Ram* and its spin-off singles would grow on them like most of *Sgt Pepper* had after repeated listening. Raw fact is that *Ram* topped the UK album list, though 'Back Seat Of My Car' struggled wretchedly to the edge of the Top 40. That *Ram* stalled at second place in *Billboard*'s Hot 100 was mitigated by its US-only 45, 'Uncle Albert/Admiral Halsey' – freighted with sound effects and stiff-upper-lip vocal – going all the way, despite *Rolling Stone* dismissing the album as "the nadir of rock"[11].

*Rolling Stone*'s perspective was shared with those who imagined themselves sensitive and unopposed to the polarisation of pop in particular styles since the late 1960s as jazz had been for years. "Traditional" could be represented by both Engelbert Humperdinck and Rolf 'Two Little Boys' Harris. "Mainstream" was capacious enough to contain Marmalade, The Faces, James Taylor and, chart newcomers from Indiana, The Jackson Five – while The Jeff Beck

Group and The Moody Blues squeezed in amongst modernists like Traffic and Renaissance. No more providers of teenage entertainment in their way than Engelbert, Soft Machine and Yoko Ono were among brand leaders of the avant-garde.

Formerly "the Tommy Steele of Scotland", Alex Harvey, one of the support acts to Johnny Gentle and the Silver Beatles, was to belong in more than one of these categories as the leader of The Sensational Alex Harvey Band via a discography that embraced both the vile transit camp scenario of Jacques Brel's 'Next' and a revival of Tom Jones's singalong 'Delilah'. Though Paul McCartney planted feet in more than one camp too, Alex hadn't much time for *Ram*: "Do you think McCartney makes records just to annoy me personally, or does he want to get up everybody's nose with his antics?"[12]

Comparisons of Paul's output with that of his former creative confrère were inevitable, and the conclusion of the record industry *illuminati* was that Lennon was cool and McCartney wasn't. Because of a cathartic projection of himself as 'Working Class Hero' on raw and intense *John Lennon: Plastic Ono Band*, Lennon was an executant of "rock" – which only the finest minds could appreciate – while McCartney peddled ephemeral "pop".

In retrospect, the chasm between Paul and John's first efforts as ex-Beatles was not unbreachable, not least because both extolled the virtues of harmony and equality in emotional partnerships – married love, if you prefer – to the level of ickiness. Nevertheless, 'Working Class Hero' contained rude words, and that mighty Cerberus *Rolling Stone* (to whom Lennon had just granted a frank, unashamed and circulation-enhancing two-part interview) had surmised that his singing on 'God' – fifth track, side two – "may be the finest in all rock", and the whole LP was "a full, blistering statement of fury". Thus McCartney and *Ram* were made to seem even more shallow and bland.

As far as John was concerned, Wings was just the latest vehicle for what he still ridiculed as Paul's "granny music". Lennon said as much in his natter to *Rolling Stone*, and was about to exact vengeance on vinyl – in a composition entitled 'How Do You Sleep?' – against what he'd perceived as a lyrical attack on him in 'Three Legs', a *Ram* selection that could have been ditched without any hardship. A McCartney interview in *Melody Maker* headlined "Why Lennon Is Uncool" prompted a bitter riposte from John on the readers' letters page the following week. Adding injury to insult, Ringo – who damned *Ram* with faint praise in print – had drummed on *John Lennon: Plastic Ono Band*, while George had endorsed Lennon's venom by gladly picking guitar and dobro on nasty 'How Do You Sleep?'.

Matters didn't improve with the issue of *Wild Life*, Wings's maiden album, in time for 1971's Christmas sell-in. Four months earlier, engineer Tony Clarke had been summoned to the Mull of Kintyre farmhouse to assist on tracks that were recorded as soon as they'd been routined. What struck him was how much was accomplished in one day compared to the months of remakes, jettisoned tracks and trifling mechanical intricacies that had to be endured from others. Understanding that it was the margin of error that had put teeth into *McCartney*, if not *Ram*, Paul was as jaded with endless multi-track mixing, and made transparent his desire for *Wild Life* to be as belligerently "live" as possible – no arguments, no needless messing about with dials – and on to the next track.

However, for all its brisk finesse, *Wild Life* stalled on the edge of the Top Ten in both Britain and the USA – a tangible comedown by previous commercial standards. It was even less of a critical success than *Ram*, asking for trouble as it did with a capricious revival of The Everly Brothers' 'Love Is Strange' from 1965, and so-so originals that were also pounced upon as symptoms of creative bankruptcy. After a decade on the run – of snatched meals, irregular sleep and pressure to come up with the next Number One – who could blame McCartney for resenting anyone who begrudged a back-street lad who'd climbed to the top of the heap, letting go, stopping trying to prove himself?

"I think I've got some idea of the way he feels about things," reckoned Denny Laine, "because I've been through the same stuff myself. The longer you go on, the tougher it is in lots of ways. People expect more and more of you. For Paul, having been part of the best rock 'n' roll band in history, it must be very heavy. I admire him so much, the way he handles it and doesn't let it interfere with his music."[1]

Just as commendable was that too much convalescent sloth wasn't McCartney's way. "After a few days, I get the feeling I want to be doing something musical," he'd tell you, "so I go and play the piano or guitar for pleasure. It's generally at moments like this that an idea will occur to me – almost as if it's been waiting to come out. The best way to write a song is for it to write itself. Some of the best things I've done have happened like that. They turn up like magic."[1]

"I just don't know how he does it," gasped Linda, but, to paraphrase Mandy Rice-Davies, she would say that wouldn't she? A disaffected listener's angle might be that *McCartney*, *Ram* and *Wild Life* weren't magic, just music – though Paul seemed to have fun on them. Yet you could understand his attitude. Above the tour-album-tour sandwiches incumbent upon poorer stars, McCartney could wait until he felt like going on the road again whilst making music for the benefit of himself rather than a public that would assure a former Beatle at least a moderate hit then, even with something like *Wild Life*.

Paul himself was to say of *Wild Life*, "OK, I didn't make the biggest blockbuster of all time, but I don't think you need that all the time. *Wild Life* was inspired by Dylan, because we'd heard that he just took one week to do an album. So we thought, 'Great, we'll do it a bit like that, and we'll try to get just the spontaneous stuff down and not be too careful with this one.' So it came out like that, and a few people thought we could have tried a bit harder."[8]

Bob Dylan had sunk into an artistic quagmire too by the early 1970s, though his stumblings on disc were shrugged off by sympathetic pundits as writer's block. He was also, they reckoned, a possessor of genius rather than anything as common as the mere talent that was Paul McCartney's. In retrospect, nevertheless, *Wild Life*, if skimpy rather than grippingly slipshod, was enjoyable enough after the manner you'd expect from an album that, like Kingsize Taylor's Hamburg long-player, had next to no time to record – and even 'Bip Bop', *Wild Life* at its most inconsequential was to make more rock 'n' roll sense when Wings oozed rather than exploded onto the stage after a launch party at the Empire Ballroom, Leicester Square, London on 8 November 1971.

A small army of Paul's famous friends – Elton John, Keith Moon, Ronnie Wood of The Faces, all the usual shower – rallied round for the celebration. As the champagne flowed and the paper plates piled up at the buffet, the founder of the feast reserved a little of that well-known charm for every guest that entered his orbit, doling out a few minutes of chat each to witnesses and participants in some of the stirring musical exploits of the past and present, whether John Entwistle – whose Who could no longer take hits for granted – or Jimmy Page with his Led Zeppelin's fourth album yet to be dislodged from Number One in both Britain and the States.

Paul's new hand-made suit hadn't been quite ready that afternoon, but he wore it anyway with the tracking stitches for all to see. Perhaps it was an Art Statement, like. Maybe the entire evening was. Most conspicuously, the entertainment laid on was nowhere to be found on the map of contemporary rock. Seated on the Empire podium was tuxedoed Ray McVay and his Dance Band, lifted by time machine from the pre-Presley 1950s. Their Victor Sylvester-esque duties included accompanying a formation dance team; inserting rumbles of timpani at moments of climax during a grand prize raffle, and providing a framework for those who wished to hokey-cokey the night away or pursue romance to lush stardust-and-roses ballads that wouldn't have been out of place on Ringo's *Sentimental Journey*.

Seizing the opportunity to rewind his life in another respect too, Paul had decided that, while he wasn't intending to hump equipment or coil even his own amplifier leads, Wings were to re-enter the concert arena with small, unpublicised, even impromptu engagements. During the drive back from The Black Dyke Mills Band session, he'd stopped in a Bedfordshire village pub where, in a fit of exuberance, he'd sat down at the saloon bar piano and, without preamble, hammered out some Beatles numbers plus an instrumental that none of the astonished clientele recognised as father Jim's 'Walking In The Park With Eloise'. This wasn't the first or last such episode from one who needed to perform as a drug addict needed his fix.

Nearly all the essential elements were intact to enable Wings to tread the boards. Largely through Denny Laine's urging, another guitarist was roped in. Born and raised in Londonderry, Henry McCullough had cut his teeth in The Skyrockets and then Gene and the Gents, two of around 600 horn-laden showbands operational in Ireland in the early 1960s.

An entertainment institution peculiar to the Ireland, the showband ruled the country's dance halls with a polished mixture of across-the-board favourites, *salvo pudore* in-song comedy and the onstage glamour of braided costumery and neat coiffure. Dressed as if they'd come direct from the set of *Oklahoma!*, colleens sat on strategically placed stools, looking patiently pretty whilst waiting their turns to display synchronised dance steps, add vocal counterpoint or even sing lead as a breath of fresh air in a sphere dominated by Guinness-swilling male bonding.

Changeless and changed after rock 'n' roll, the showbands diverged into ones that stuck to the tried-and-tested guidelines, and ones that aspired to be highly proficient non-stop copyists of whatever North American pop commotions were stirring up the nation. However, such an inordinate amount of the old corn remained that Henry McCullough on the bandstand would wonder if he'd remembered to collect the eiderdowns from the dry-cleaners as he strummed rote-learnt 'Que Sera Sera', 'Sparrow In The Treetop' and 'Noreen Bawn'.

Musicians whose tastes lay in the same rebellious direction marked time too in the payroll of old stagers who thought that you couldn't go wrong with Jim Reeves, and couldn't grasp what had come over these young shavers who were biting the hands that fed them with their constant machinations to include this crazy, far-out music in the show.

There remains bitter division about the showband's influence on both Irish and world pop. It is often too easy to forget that this tight-trousered lead vocalist or that clenched-teeth guitarist may have got his first break by falling meekly into line in a professional showband. Mind-stultifying as it was to them, it was a toehold on showbusiness and, more importantly, a guaranteed income. Yet those veterans predestined to be mainstays of Them, Taste, Thin Lizzy – and Wings – were not so generous in recounting how they'd mastered their assorted crafts in the ranks of The Skyrockets, The Fontana, The Clubmen, The Dixies, The Swingtime Aces *et al*.

Late in 1966, Henry chose to outlaw himself from the stuffy if lucrative showband functions on which he depended for a living to throw in his lot with The People, a combo of psychedelic kidney from Portadown. Being enormous in Armagh wasn't, however, enormous enough, and the group migrated to London where they were renamed Eire Apparent after being taken on by Chas Chandler, now gone from The Animals to behind-the-scenes branches of the music business. As he also had The Jimi Hendrix Experience on his books, Chandler was in a strong position to obtain both a contract for Eire Apparent on Track, the Experience's label, and support spots to Hendrix both in Britain and the USA. Moreover, McCullough was rated as a guitarist by the discerning Jimi, who produced an Eire Apparent album.

Obliged by visa problems to return to Ireland during an Eire Apparent trek round North America in 1968, Henry passed through the ranks of Sweeney's Men, a renowned folk-rock outfit who were about to thrust tentacles into the folk circuit on the other side of the Irish Sea, notably as the surprise hit of that summer's Cambridge Folk Festival. Founder member Johnny Moynihan acknowledged that "Henry put funk into it. He'd just pick up on traditional tunes and they would come out in his playing. One night, we were playing in Dublin, and after the gig, Henry jumped in a car and drove like mad to catch the end of a John Mayall concert elsewhere. This told us what direction he was heading in, and when he was offered a job with Joe Cocker, he took it. He naturally gravitated towards it."[13]

McCullough's arrival in Cocker's Grease Band coincided with Denny Cordell's production of the group's 'With A Little Help From My Friends' wrenching Mary Hopkin from Number One in November 1968. He was backing Joe still when that grizzled Yorkshireman was acclaimed by the half-million drenched Americans who'd braved Woodstock, viewed from a distance of decades as the climax of hippy culture and, via its spin-off movie and albums, the yardstick by which future Cocker performances would always be measured.

For Henry, any Woodstock euphoria was blunted when Cocker ditched the Grease Band to tour the States as *de jure* leader of retinue known as Mad Dogs And Englishmen, but drawn principally from Los Angeles "supersidemen" – including a "Space Choir" and no less than three drummers from that smug élite whose unsparingly snappy jitter was described as "tight", "economic" and by that faintly nauseating adjective "funky".

Back in London, McCullough was one of a Grease Band that were hired to assist on the tie-in double-album to the West End musical, *Jesus Christ Superstar*. This proved to be useful as a bartering tool for a deal with EMI's "progressive" subsidiary, Harvest. Nevertheless, despite a *Top Of The Pops* slot and relentless touring to plug an eponymous LP, the group was no more by the close of 1971.

Henry fell on his feet with Wings for all Denny Cordell's reservations: "When he played well, Henry was a genius, but he could only play in one certain bag, and you had to get him just right. Otherwise, he was very mercurial. He'd just fall out of it."[14]

Paul McCartney was prepared to take a chance on Henry McCullough just as he was on Linda's hit-or-miss keyboard-playing – because, so he reasoned, "Linda is the innocence of the group. All the rest of us are seasoned musicians – and probably too seasoned. Linda has an innocent approach which I like. It's like when you hear an artist say, 'I wish I could paint like a child again'. That's what she's got. If you talk to an artist like Peter Blake, he'll tell you how much great artists love the naivety of aboriginal paintings. Linda's inclusion was something to do with that."[9]

As well as pre-empting punk's more studied guilelessness, Linda McCartney was, according to Eric Burdon, an unwitting pioneer of female visibility in mainstream rock: "I think Linda played a part in paving the way for more female performers to join the boys' club called rock 'n' roll."[15]

For those who prized technical expertise, she served as a bad example of this, beginning with her professional concert debut on Wednesday, 9 February 1972 at the University of Nottingham. The date and venue had been chosen arbitrarily as Wings cruised by car and caravan up the spine of England the previous morning. Turning off the M1 somewhere in the Midlands, they wound up at the university campus and volunteered their services. Room was made for them to do a turn during lunch hour the next day in the student's union auditorium.

Seven hundred paid 50p (81 cents) admission to stand around as Wings strutted their stuff – principally olde tyme rock 'n' roll and excerpts from *Wild Life*. Permitting himself the luxury of apparent self-indulgence, Paul didn't give 'em 'Yesterday', 'Let It Be' or, indeed, any of the good old good ones from The Beatles' portfolio as he took lead vocals on everything apart from reggaefied 'Seaside Woman', penned solely by Linda. Elsewhere, 'Henry's

Blues' was a rambling instrumental showcase for McCullough, while 'Say You Don't Mind' had been rehearsed but left out at the insistence of its composer, who feared disobliging comparisons to Colin Blunstone's elegant resuscitation, then poised to slip into the spring Top 20. A few blown riffs, flurries of bum notes, vaguely apocalyptic cadences and yelled directives were reported, but pockets of the audience felt a compulsion to dánce to as nice a little band as Blonde On Blonde – and Paul McCartney's first performance on a *bona fide* stage since Candlestick Park.

The 90 minutes Linda spent to the left of Denny Seiwell's kit passed quickly – surprisingly so – in a blur of *son-et-lumière* heat and audience reaction as remotely unreal as conch murmurs, but for all her panicked vamping in Z minor or whatever key a given number was in, the general feeling as cigarettes were lit and beer-can rings pulled later was that she'd done OK.

Similar casual and unannounced bashes – mostly at other colleges – filled the calendar for the next fortnight. By the final date in Oxford, Linda was solidly at the music's heart, and, for the most part, it had been an agreeable jaunt for a Paul McCartney unbothered by keening feedback bleeps, one of the sound crew blundering on to sort out a dead amplifier, a mistimed falling curtain, audience interruptions or anything else that wasn't in a slap-dash script. While the gear was being loaded afterwards, he'd chatted freely with fans, autographing both copies of *Wild Life* fresh from the pressing plant and a dog-eared *Beatles For Sale*.

Either on piano or at the central microphone too, he'd been joking and swapping banter during proceedings that were epitomised by an amused cheer on the second night – in York – when Linda, crippled with nerves, forgot her cliff-hanging organ introit to *Wild Life*'s title track. Response generally was as heartening as might be expected from crowds enjoying both an unexpected diversion from customary mid-term activities and a surge into the bar afterwards, having participated, however passively in the proverbial "something to tell your grandchildren about".

# 13  "Mary Had A Little Lamb"

"They smelled of the farm. They brought their kitchen smells
with them – parsley, garlic and the country freshness."
– *Eric Burdon*[1]

While advised by payroll courtiers, McCartney had never been a
corporation marionette. Almost from the beginning – when he'd
been late for the very first business discussion with Brian Epstein
– Paul, for all his apparent conviviality, had been a disquieting and
tenacious presence around Brian, maintaining an acute and
sometimes unwelcome interest in every link of the chain from
studio to pressing plant to market place.

Since their manager's death, the sundering of The Beatles and
the formation in 1969 of what was to become McCartney
Productions and then MPL Communications, whether he made
wise or foolish executive decisions, Paul alone would accept
responsibility for them.

Nevertheless, certain wolves were kept from the door on his
behalf by appointed accountants and lawyers who waded through
mazy balance sheets, computer run-offs and musty ledgers to ensure
that assorted incoming monies would be divided as agreed and
sent via complicated but fixed channels to a frequently disenchanted
client. Taking care of much McCartney business were Eastman
and Eastman Inc, a relationship based not so much on profit as
family affinity – and friendship, particularly with brother-in-law
John Eastman, who had been present at the Mull of Kintyre when
Paul reached his decision to leave The Beatles.

Both on paper and in practice, it was an ideal arrangement. Dignified and quietly besuited – albeit with an occasional penchant for brightly coloured socks – John had acquired the cautious confidence to strike a bellicose stance when necessary in negotiation, and a brain that could, at a moment's notice, spew out dizzying facts and figures. Some eyelids would grow heavy, but at least he had clients' best interests in mind, and Paul would think highly enough of him to ask him to be best man at his second wedding 30 years later.

In 1972, the most immediate concern of McCartney's investors was the mercantile possibilities of Wings's follow-up to *Wild Life*. With this in mind, stadium managers from every major territory were on the line to McCartney Productions, yelling "Klondike!" at the prospect of a round-the-world carnival of Beatles-sized magnitude.

The only snag was that the heavyweight wouldn't fight – well, not for the world championship – yet. As he had with that first low-key sweep round England with Wings, Paul not so much plunged headfirst as dipped a toe *sur le continent* with mainly 3,000 rather than 20,000 seaters over seven summer weeks that covered France to Germany, Switzerland to Finland. The group travelled in a customised double-decker bus, just like Cliff Richard and his retinue of wonderful young people had in 1962's *Summer Holiday*, a film musical of cheery unreality. In keeping with this, McCartney was *éminence grise* behind a film of the tour – for a purpose that was then non-specific – that split-screened in-concert footage with a twee cartoon about a rodent family with human characteristics and a paterfamilias called Bruce McMouse, who dwelt beneath the floorboards of each stage where Wings performed.

Owing largely to publicity that was "non-aggressive" to the point of being nearly as secretive as that for the show in Nottingham, ticket sales were erratic, even forcing a cancellation at a venue in Lyons. It had been quite a while – Barcelona in 1966 with John, George and Ringo – since the peacock had shown his feathers in Europe. In the wings at the Arles Theatre Antique, Zurich's Congress Halle or the Messuhalli in Helsinki, Paul steeled himself to face facts, but he needn't have worried. Barrages of whistling, cheering and stamping greeted him before he sang a bar of the opening 'Bip Bop'.

Attendance figures notwithstanding, Wings were received with affection for what onlookers now understood they ought to expect. The set was longer and, as instanced by a projected array of rural, coastal and lunar scenes on a backcloth during the second half, more elaborate than before. Nevertheless, with the 'Long Tall Sally' encore the only nod towards The Beatles, the audiences heard much the same as their British counterparts plus Leadbelly's "Cottonfields" – subject of a 1970 revival by The Beach Boys – and sides of two recent singles and two yet to come.

First up had been 'Give Ireland Back To The Irish'. Perhaps not really by coincidence, John Lennon had just recorded 'Sunday Bloody Sunday', an album track that was also inspired by the bomb-blasting, bullet-firing malevolence in Northern Ireland rearing up again with the incident in Londonderry that January when 13 were shot dead by British soldiers during a civil rights demonstration.

With increasingly more attention-seeking and deadly tactics from both loyalist and republican cells of fanaticism, both inside and outside jails that were regarded as prisoner-of-war camps, the tension pervaded the whole province, whether it was "Bloody Sunday"; the "dirty" protests in the Maze prison where hunger strikers' eyes burned like coals; frightened customs officials armed with every fibre of red-tape bureaucracy could gather or the jack-in-office malice of the young polytechnic janitor who stuck an "out of order" sign on a working lift to compel a visiting English pop group to lug its equipment up five punishing staircases to the auditorium, and down again when the show finished by the early hour ordained in the curfew regulations.

Allusions to current affairs had been hitherto as rare as winter roses in both Paul McCartney's songs and interviews. In any case, the difficulty with topical ditties is what becomes of them when they are no longer topical or the topic gets tedious? Yet Paul's doctrinal statement about the Troubles, rather than a sidestepping support of general pacifism, topped the hot-blooded Irish lists, while struggling elsewhere in the teeth of radio bans and restrictions, even with an alternative instrumental version on the flip-side.

To redress the balance, Wings followed through with 'Mary Had A Little Lamb' – yes, the nursery rhyme – which, like the National Anthem, turned out to have verses other than the one everyone knew. "It wasn't a great record," confessed McCartney – and in this, he was at one with nearly all reviewers, even if, aided by four contrasting promotional shorts, it rose higher in the domestic chart than its predecessor.

"I like to keep in with the five-year-olds," he beamed, but, six months later, what did this corner of the market make of 'Hi Hi Hi' – which went the scandalous way of 'I Can't Control Myself' by The Troggs, The Rolling Stones' 'Let's Spend The Night Together', 'Wet Dream' from Max Romeo and, climactically, Jane Birkin and Serge Gainsbourg's 'Je T'Aime...Moi Non Plus?'

Excluded from prudish airwaves for sexual insinuation too, offence had been taken when the word "polygon" was misheard as "body gun", interpreted (like "sex pistol') as a euphemism for "prick", "cock", "willy", need I go on? Whether it was or wasn't the wrong end of the stick, the stick still existed – and with none of the clever word-playing double-entendre of, say Cy Coleman's 'The Ball's In Your Court' ('where the competition is stiff'), direct from Broadway. Yet, partly because disc jockeys began spinning the perky, reggaefied B-side, 'C Moon', 'Hi Hi Hi' was Wings's biggest British hit thus far, going flaccid at Number Three as 1972 mutated into 1973.

The new year got underway with Paul tying at 15 – with David Bowie, Van Morrison and Randy Newman – in the "world vocalist" section of the *NME* readers' popularity poll, and the UK issue in March of syrupy 'My Love', a taster for a forthcoming album. If sent on its way with the expected critical rubbishings, the single would be a US Number One whilst just scraping into the domestic Top Ten. Paul's status as a non-Beatle as much as that as a former Beatle was further confirmed by a *Melody Maker* journalist's random survey among schoolgirls shuffling into the Bristol Hippodrome, the first stop on Wings's first official tour of Britain that May. "What's your favourite Paul McCartney song?" "Dunno," replied one moon-faced female before pausing and adding, "Oh yeah – 'My Love'."

No longer the dream lover of old, he had emerged as a cross between admired elder brother, favourite uncle – and, for some, a character from *The Archers*, BBC Radio Four's long-running rustic soap opera. If he wasn't living the so-called "simple life" after he'd moved to East Sussex, he was living it hundreds of miles away on his farm in Scotland. At either, the landscape melted into another endless summer day with not a leaf stirring, a touch of mist on the sunset horizon and a bird chirruping somewhere. Then the seasons changed from gold to marble, and, as they did, the log fire would subside to glowing embers, and the harvest moon in its starry canopy would shine as bright as day over the vastness of the story-book countryside. He, Linda and the girls seemed the very epitome of domestic bliss while they trod the backwards path towards the morning of the Earth.

Even in the bluster of the city, who could fail to adore Britain where female traffic wardens called you "love', cigarettes could be bought in ten-packs, pubs were more than buildings where men got drunk and the humour – as opposed to *humor* – of *Monty Python's Flying Circus* repeats clearing the ground for such as *Fawlty Towers* and *Ripping Yarns* to heave UK television comedy out of the mire of "more tea, Vicar?" sit-coms or half-hours fraught with innuendo about wogs, poofs and tits?

Remaining thus on his native soil, Paul McCartney was flying in the face of the cold and rain, no ice in your Coca-Cola except in the poshest lounge bars, only three television channels and the snarled-up motorways to and from his two principal residencies. Crucially, there were also the burdensome Inland Revenue demands on the rich that had already driven The Rolling Stones to temporary exile in France, Bad Company to Guernsey, Dave Clark to a fiscal year in California and Maurice Gibb of The Bee Gees to the Isle of Man.

While Rye's most renowned addressee was commuter-close to McCartney Productions, only the odd flight overhead from Gatwick airport miles away need remind him of what was over the hills in London, New York and Hollywood. It had left its mark on Paul's songwriting already – in, for example, 'Heart Of The Country' on *Ram*, and would continue to do so in the likes of the imminent 1973 B-side 'Country Dreamer' – actually taped in one of his backyards – and, most memorably of all, 1977's 'Mull Of Kintyre'.

Shrouded by meadows, greenery, exposed oak rafters, stone-flagged floors and Peace in the Valley, Paul had been all for the quietude and fresh air, even penning a feature about the most northerly of his arcadian shangri-las for the newspaper in Campbeltown (for which he was paid the standard National Union of Journalists fee). Whereas they might have pressed ivory or fret, the 31-year-old musician's fingers became hardened from fencing, logging and moving bales.

Yet, while he did not join Ringo Starr on so voracious a social whirl that he'd hide rings under his eyes with the mirror sunglasses that became a standard party accoutrement from that time, what Paul could barely enunciate was that there were times when he missed the limelight as he forwent opportunities to reactivate his old magnetism at dazzling showbiz soirées where a murmur would reach a crescendo as he entered as a signal for all the younger pop stars and their acolytes to drone round him like a halo of flies.

He was to encounter that in macrocosm when mingling with other locals at coffee mornings, jumble sales and parents evenings at the nearby state schools where, unlike the fee-paying Harrisons and Starkeys, he and Linda were to send their offspring. In and about Rye or Campbeltown where nothing much was calculated to happen, year in, year out, the most exciting daily excursion was the uncomplicated ritual of shopping for groceries as Paul and Linda became an everyday sight, hand in hand around the parish. At first, Paul's hesitant smile had not rested on individuals, but had been diffused to the general multitude. He couldn't help but be aware that his arrival once at a barber's in Rye for a self-conscious short-back-and-sides was as profoundly disturbing an experience for others in the queue as noticing the Queen having her hair tortured into a Hendrix Afro in its sister establishment.

Yet soon he was chatting about field drainage, nativity plays, winter farrowing and muck-spreading with the best of them – as demonstrated by him kicking up a fuss when Hibernian stag hunters presumed it was OK to cross his land, and a less justifiable one when staff at the junior school joined a national teachers' strike in November 1986; his disapproval immortalised by one lucky amateur photographer whose back view of a McCartney stamping off in a pique across the playground, front-paged *The Times Educational Supplement*.[2]

At dinner parties with other parents, a relaxed Paul would bring his hosts up to date with Stella's reading, while insisting on one chronicled occasion that they eat in the ambience of the kitchen rather than the less free-and-easy dining room.

In contrast to Mal Evans dashing across busy Abbey Road to the fish-and-chip shop, and as tasty as the repasts of his Rye and Campbeltown circles, was the roast dinner washed down with home-brewed ale at record entrepreneur Richard Branson's new Manor Studios. Half-hidden by woodland some 30km (20 miles) northwest of Oxford, these were used by Wings for two exploratory days that were marked less by the aural results – mostly mixing – than a pointed complaint from a neighbour to police about noise caused when, during a humid night, members of Wings kept opening a studio door otherwise almost permanently shut. During boring mechanical processes at the console, the group also enjoyed facilities that were more agreeable than the clinic-doss house paradox of certain urban complexes they could name – where you got to know by sight individual biscuit crumbs, and followed their day-to-day journeyings up and down a ledge, where an empty can of orangeade might also linger for weeks next to a discarded swab-stick dirtied from cleaning tape heads.

How more civilised it was to be served deferential meals at the huge oak table in the cloistered Manor's ancient hall with its stained glass, crossed swords, exposed beams and half a tree blazing in the fireplace. Alien to a mediaeval baron, however, were the swimming pool and the snooker den – not to mention a studio that had attracted Fairport Convention, Vivian Stanshall and, as American as Stanshall was English, Frank Zappa.

Of British studios, Zappa preferred those few in London that, for all their environmental shortcomings, were several technological steps ahead of the Manor – and so did McCartney, who had fashioned most of the second Wings album, *Red Rose Speedway*, in no less than five different metropolitan locations including Abbey Road. No spectator sport, the recordings themselves were only the most expensive part of a process that, before session time was even pencilled in, had started with Paul rehearsing the material with un-*Wild Life*-like exactitude, balancing ruthless efficiency with the old sweetness-and-light.

With his producer's hat on, McCartney also decreed theoretical apportionment of trackage; the short-listing of devices and effects, and the overall operational definition. Never had he been out on a longer limb, but he kept whatever trepidations he had about his presently maligned skills as a console *savant* in check. Nevertheless, much as at least six engineers employed might have respected the ex-Beatle's learned if sometimes irritating procrastinations over, say, degree of reverberation overspill allowable on the keyboards, Glyn Johns for one had had his apparent fill of being head-to-head with Paul inside the control room.

Partly because he'd been one of McCartney's chief supporters during the *Let It Be* unpleasantness, Glyn had been put in charge of the technological donkey work for the latest effort. Yet Paul's comprehensive logging of production methods since 'My Bonnie' with Bert Kaempfert had ripened in him the self-assertion to issue jargon-ridden instructions, and make recommendations about equalisation, vari-speeding, bounce-downs, spatial separation and so forth that, if not guaranteed to achieve the effect he desired, he considered worth investigating. Tiring of the majestic slowness of conjuring up sounds that may or may not have met McCartney's headache-inducing requirements, Johns, allegedly, washed his hands of *Red Rose Speedway*.

As to the finished product, titles like 'Big Barn Red' and 'Little Lamb Butterfly' were reflective of the maturing McCartney family's rural contentment, and a confirmation that Paul's capacity for "granny music" was bottomless. *Rolling Stone* judged *Red Rose Speedway* to be "rife with weak and sentimental drivel"[3]. The way other detractors laid into it too, you'd think that it made Gareth Gates sound like Zappa jamming with Hendrix. Certainly, Gareth, Will Young, Peter André or some weedy present-day boy band could do as well with a revival of 'My Love' as its originators did in 1973.

Anyway, how could *Rolling Stone*, the *NME* or the newer *Zig-Zag* turn their noses up at a disc that in the USA spent a month lording it over the likes of Dawn, Elton John, Barry White, The Osmonds, The Carpenters, Stevie Wonder plus The Stylistics, Harold Melvin and his Blue Notes and any number of other velvet-smooth acts from trend-setting Philadelphia that kept North American FM radio in tasteful focus with vocal burbling of lovey-dovey mush over limpid sweetening of strings, vibraphone and woodwind plastered over a muted rhythm?

It may have afforded McCartney a wry grin when 'My Love' was brought down at the end of June by George Harrison's 'Give Me Love (Give Me Peace On Earth)', but that lasted only a week before the latest by Billy Preston took over. Ringo's turn would come during the autumn when 'Photograph' – co-written with George – climbed to the top of that same Hot 100. Starr did it again – just – in January when, on knocking off Eddie Kendricks's 'Keep On Trucking', he ruled pop for seven glorious days. Before the year was out, John Lennon would stick it out for a week up there too with 'Whatever Gets You Through The Night' – and so would Wings with 'Band On The Run'.

# 14 *"Crossroads"*

"It took us ages to become a good band – partly because
we kept changing the other personnel."

*– Denny Laine*

The Wings show that crossed Britain in summer 1972 passed
without incident other than a road manager bringing on a birthday
cake for Denny Seiwell at Newcastle City Hall where the bill-
toppers were joined for the encore by support act Brinsley Schwartz,
harbingers of the pub-rock movement.

In the first instance, Wings too had been a reaction against
the distancing of the humble pop group from its audience, and
the isolation of stardom from the everyday. Empathy with
ordinary people going about their business did not extend,
however, to police who had appeared backstage with the
promptness of vultures after a performance in Gothenberg the
previous August. It had come to their ears that controlled
substances, to wit 200g (7oz) of marijuana, had been discovered
in a package from Britain addressed to McCartney. The tedious
wheels of the Swedish legal process had been set in motion, and
fines had to be paid before Wings could continue with dates in
Denmark, the next country on the itinerary.

Paul passed this off as a farthing of life's small change, even
hurling a metaphorical stone after his prosecutors by confiding to
a journalist's cassette recorder straightaway that he intended to
smoke some more of the stuff as soon as the opportunity arose.
Such insolence may have provoked the unwelcome interest of the

constabulary local to Campbeltown, who, so a PC Norman McPhee testified at the Sheriff's Court on 8 March 1973, visited High Park for a routine check on the absent owner's security arrangements. Glancing in one of the greenhouses, McPhee, fresh from a course in drugs identification, recognised cannabis plants, cultivation of which was counter to the provision of the 1966 Dangerous Drugs Act, section 42.

Interrupting work on a forthcoming ITV special entitled *James Paul McCartney* to answer the summons, the McCartneys were free to go after coughing up £100 ($160), a mere bagatelle for an ex-Beatle, as there was no question of the narcotic being used for any purpose other than personal consumption. As it had been in Sweden, James Paul McCartney seemed unremorseful, even facetious, as he brushed past the *woompf* of flashbulbs afterwards.

A few hours later, he was back in London, focussing his attention once again on *James Paul McCartney*, under the direction of Dwight Hewison, whose curriculum vitae included Elvis Presley's televised comeback over Christmas 1968. Paul's prime-time spectacular for Britain and the States was among the first such undertakings in which the "rushes" – uncut footage – were filmed on videotape, thereby bypassing the false economy of holding up proceedings for the laborious development of cheaper cine-film.

Sequences included a "voxpop" street scene and some cheery community singing of 'Pack Up Your Troubles', 'April Showers', 'You Are My Sunshine' and further tin-helmeted whimseys and *Sentimental Journey*-type warhorses from the Chelsea Reach, a Liverpool pub, by Paul, Mike McGear and other McCartney relations plus Gerry Marsden and the boozer's regulars. Nevertheless, the greater part of *James Paul McCartney* was excerpts from a late afternoon concert before a studio audience, and staged scenarios, among them an outdoors 'Mary Had A Little Lamb', and a choreographed and moustachio-ed Paul in a white tail suit and pink tuxedo with a high-stepping Busby Berkeley-esque dance troupe. More significant than this blatant concession to showbiz proper was the inclusion of several Beatles numbers such as an acoustic 'Michelle', a passer-by's unique 'When I'm Sixty-Four' and back to Paul for 'Yesterday' just before the closing credits.

While *Melody Maker* sneered at the "overblown and silly extravaganza"[1], it was to run a two-part feature, obsequiously headlined "Wings – Anatomy Of A Hot Band"[2], after according the ensemble's third album, *Band On The Run*, and the single that preceded it, 'Live And Let Die', grudging praise.

*Melody Maker* noted too the involvement of George Martin in 'Live And Let Die', the first time he'd worked with McCartney – or any Beatle – since Abbey Road. The song had been commissioned as the theme for the James Bond flick of the same name with the lightweight Roger Moore, rather than Sean Connery, in the title role. Martin also served as McCartney's champion when the movie's co-producer, Harry Salzman took it for granted that the Wings version was a useful demo for the use of Welsh *chanteuse* Shirley Bassey or someone like her. "I was completely nonplussed," recalled Martin, "and in my best tactful way, I had to suggest that if he didn't take the thing more or less as it stood, I didn't think Paul would like him to have the song. Eventually, it did sink through and I got the job of doing the film score, but it was a nasty moment."[3]

Martin's soundtrack earned him a Grammy, and *Live And Let Die* was nominated for an Oscar after almost-but-not-quite reaching Number One in the US. While 'My Love' had demonstrated that chart supremacy could give false impression of Wings's standing with the critics, 'Live And Let Die' cut the mustard, and, for the time being, most of them let McCartney in from the cold. They also listened sympathetically to *Band On The Run*, a combination of force and melody that yielded a cathartic send-up of Lennon and his Plastic Ono aggregations in 'Let Me Roll It' as well as hit singles in 'Helen Wheels' (a track remaindered from the UK pressing), 'Jet' and its complex and million-selling title track. Vignettes of around five different melodies to strung-together lyrics, the latter seemed to be a medley, albeit a more marketable proposition than such disparate precedents as 1957's 'One For The Road' – drinking songs by pugilist Freddie Mills – and The Pretty Things' 'Defecting Grey', a dry-run for *SF Sorrow*, the first "rock opera".

Because Paul's favourite Studio Two at Abbey Road had been block-booked already, Wings had chosen to record the album at the only other EMI complex then available – in Lagos, Nigeria – and, even then, they were obliged to transfer to the same city's ARC Studios (owned by Ginger Baker) and endure the scowling disapproval of hired local musicians who resented what they'd perceived as non-African pop stars "plundering" the continent's musical heritage – though, as Michael Jackson was to confirm, this never went deeper in McCartney's case than the sonic possibilities of its instruments: "He goes to hotels in Africa and Jamaica, bringing back different sounds, sticks and some drums."[4]

As well as being accused unfairly of cultural burglary, the McCartneys were mugged in broad daylight by the occupants of a kerb-crawling car not long after Paul had been poleaxed by a respiratory complaint.

It never rains but it pours, and there'd been something rotten in the state of Wings before they'd so much as booked the flight from London. It had set in when Henry McCullough slumped into a glowing huff over what McCartney remembered as "something he really didn't fancy playing"[5]. This was symptomatic of a general antipathy felt by both McCullough and Denny Seiwell towards the group's music, Linda's keyboard abilities and some of the antics in *James Paul McCartney*. Since *Wild Life*, the poisoning of Wings's reputation by pens dipped in vitriol didn't help either.

Five days after the guitarist had resigned by telephone, Seiwell threw in the towel too, mere hours before the rest left for Africa. He'd decided he'd be better off as a freelance sessionman – while McCullough landed a recording contract with Dark Horse, a label founded by George Harrison – who could guess what Paul had been like as a bandleader. By 1977, however, Henry was back on small UK stages in the employ of such as Carol Grimes and Frankie Miller.

Without him and Seiwell, the troubled making of *Band On The Run* had continued with Denny Laine and Paul often finding themselves with headphones on, playing an unfamiliar instrument. Yet from the internal ructions, the tense 'atmospheres', the drifting from pillar to post, from studio to unsatisfactory studio, surfaced the first Wings album that was both a commercial and critical triumph, back and forth at Number One at home and the Hot 100, and the first Wings LP to be issued in the Soviet Union.

The release of the album and its singles hadn't been accompanied by a tour of any description, simply because Wings didn't have the personnel then. Therefore, before they could hit the road again, a search began for a replacement guitarist and drummer. Among those considered for the latter post were, purportedly, Rob Townsend of a now-disbanded Family; Davy Lutton from Eire Apparent, heard already on a 1972 session for Linda McCartney's 'Seaside Woman'; Mitch Mitchell who'd worked for Johnny Kidd, Georgie Fame and Jimi Hendrix and Aynsley Dunbar, whose musical resume was as impressive, having served time with The Mojos, John Mayall's Bluesbreakers, his own Aynsley Dunbar Retaliation and The Mothers of Invention.

Next, Wings were driven to advertise in the music press, thus bursting a dam on a deluge of hopefuls from cruise ships, night clubs, nice-little-bands, pit orchestras, ceilidh outfits, hotel lounge combos, you name it. To accommodate those on a short-list, Paul rented London's Albury Theatre, and hired an existing group to play four numbers with every contender while he, Denny and Linda listened in the dusty half-light beyond the footlights.

It was a long and sometimes mind-stultifying chore that led McCartney, 50 drummers later, to conclude that "I don't think auditions are much use. We won't do it again. We'll just look around quietly, go and see people playing with different bands – but it was quite an experience: 50 different drummers playing 'Caravan' [a mainstream jazz standard]."[8] Yet Paul saw it through to the bitter end, pruning the list down to five, who were to sit in with Wings. Then there were two to be each subjected to a full day – that included an interrogatory dinner – with their prospective colleagues.

There was nothing to suggest that 31-year-old Geoff Britton wasn't the *beau ideal*. He was versatile enough to have coped with stints in both rock 'n' roll revivalists The Wild Angels and East Of Eden, one of Britain's most respected executants of jazz-rock – though best remembered for a novelty hit with 'Jig-A-Jig', a barn-dance reel. Geoff's black belt in karate had been a reassuring asset at the more unrefined engagements that either of these groups played.

Yet, the pop equivalent of the chorus girl thrust into a sudden starring role, Geoff turned out to be living evidence of McCartney's "I don't think auditions are much use". For a start, he was too loose-tongued for Paul's liking when talking to the press, implying, for example, that he was the fittest and most clean-minded member of Wings because, unlike the others, he was a non-partaker of either junk-food or drugs.

He was also unhappy about the financial arrangements, and was at loggerheads almost immediately with both Denny Laine – "a bastard"[5], snarled Geoff – and the new guitarist, Jimmy McCulloch – "a nasty little cunt"[5].

Jimmy's short stature had been seized upon for publicity purposes when he was a mainstay of Thunderclap Newman, the entity responsible for anthemic 'Something In The Air', a post-flower power call-to-arms commensurate with a period when, with Vietnam the common denominator, kaftans had been mothballed as their former wearers followed the crowd to genuinely violent anti-war demonstrations and student sit-ins.

The line-up was completed by singing drummer Speedy Keen and middle-aged multi-instrumentalist Andy Newman, an ex-Post Office engineer, whose heart was in jazz. Though the most conspicuous features of 'Something In The Air' were Keen's nasal tenor and Newman's interlude on piano and saxophone, a particularly enduring visual image was captured in an inspired photograph of Andy dressed as a 'ello-'ello-'ello policeman towering over Jimmy as a short-trousered urchin with a football under his arm.

'Something In The Air' topped the domestic chart for three weeks in summer 1969, and reached the US Top 40 by autumn, a climb aided in part by its inclusion – with Badfinger's 'Come And Get It' – in the soundtrack to *The Magic Christian*. This coincided with the release of the hit's belated follow-up, 'Accidents', which lingered for one solitary week in the British Top 50. Sales were as modest for the associated album, *Hollywood Dream*, even after *Rolling Stone* suggested that Keen was the group's producer, Pete Townshend of The Who, in disguise.

By 1971, Thunderclap Newman was no more, and Jimmy, a working musician since his Glaswegian schooldays, landed a prestigious stint with John Mayall, whose previous lead guitarists had included Eric Clapton, Peter Green and, Brian Jones's successor in The Rolling Stones, Mick Taylor. He then stepped into the shoes of the late Les Harvey in Stone The Crows, fronted by Maggie Bell, a sort of Scottish Janis Joplin but minus the onstage histrionics. The group was, however, on its last legs, and Jimmy had been one of Blue, a nice-little-band connected genealogically with Marmalade, when, on the recommendation of Denny Laine, a friend of several years standing, he was invited to play on 'Seaside Woman'.[6] After he gave as creditable a performance on a Mike McGear solo album at Strawberry Studios in Stockport, Jimmy became a member of Wings in June 1974, two months after Geoff Britton.

Thus reconstituted, Wings continued with sessions half a world away in Nashville, where Paul had already finished a nepotic

'Walking In The Park With Eloise' with assistance from Chet "Mr Guitar" Atkins – co-producer of many early Elvis Presley smashes – Floyd "Mr Piano" Kramer and others of that self-contained caste that could improvise the orthodox "Nashville sound" peculiar to the Hollywood of country-and-western music. By the 1970s, however, Nashville had embraced more generalised pop, though of a kind not uninfluenced by C&W's lyrical preoccupations and melodic appeal. As such, 'Walking In The Park With Eloise' – the one written by Jim McCartney – was issued as a single by The Country Hams and was to remain one of Paul's (and his father's) eternal favourites of all the material he ever recorded.

While the McCartney brood were observed during their six weeks in Nashville, eating regularly at the fashionable Loveless Motel restaurant – famous for its smoked ham, biscuits and peach jam – they slept on a farm outside the city. It was owned by songwriter Curly "Junior" Putnam, who was still reaping a rich fiscal harvest from 'Green Green Grass Of Home', a 1966 global chartbuster for Tom Jones. Otherwise, he'd meant nothing to the world at large, except to those who derive deep and lasting pleasure from studying raw data on record labels – until immortalised by Wings in 'Junior's Farm', issued as a hit single late in 1974 with a strong B-side, 'Sally G', penned by Paul after sightseeing Nashville's red-light district.

In its own right, 'Sally G' crept into the US Top 40, while Paul's production of Scaffold's treatment of 'Liverpool Lou', a sea shanty that had flowered from the same stem as 'Maggie May', fared better in Britain than a crafty 1963 rendering by Dominic Behan, brother of playwright Brendan. Among further items in which the McCartneys were involved during the exploratory period that followed *Band On The Run* were *I Survive*, an intriguing *faux pas* of an album that gained Adam Faith his first *Top Of The Pops* slot in a donkey's age; 'July 4' by Australian vocalist – and protégé of the leader of a now-disbanded Dave Clark Five – John Christie and 'Let's Love', a song by Paul that had more intrinsic value than a bottle of wine when presented to Peggy Lee after the couple joined her for dinner in her suite at London's plush Dorchester Hotel. If not amounting to much in sales terms, that Lee – an international entertainer since 1938 – was "thrilled" by this gift from one she'd perceived to have "loads of class"[5], was as luxuriant a feather in McCartney's cap as her 1965 version of Ray Davies's haunting 'I Go To Sleep' had been for the Kink composer.

During the gaps between records and tours, it was quite in order for lower-ranking Wings musicians to undertake individual projects too – as Denny Laine did with a 1973 solo LP, *Ahh...Laine*, which he'd started when in Airforce, backed by personnel from Stone The Crows. Whatever McCulloch and Britton's plans of like persuasion were – or whether they even had any – are not known, because, at a press conference in New York on 22 October 1974, the McCartneys mentioned that dates were being pencilled in for a tour of ten countries. This, they said, was intended to last over a year, albeit with breaks lengthy enough for the making of an album to follow another one that would be out prior to the first date.

Fans from Bootle to Brisbane were on stand-by to purchase tickets, but, as it was with "the Phoney War" – the lull between Neville Chamberlain's radioed declaration and the first blitzkriegs – the interval between Paul and Linda's announcement and the opening night (at the Southampton Gaumont not quite a year later) was long enough for many to wonder if the tour was ever going to happen.

The most pressing hindrance was centred on the apparently irresolvable antagonism between Britton on the one hand and McCulloch and his less expendable pal Laine on the other. So far, Geoff had kept his fists, if not his emotions, in check, but breaking point wasn't far away. Perhaps a punch-up might have cleared the air. Nevertheless, during sessions in New Orleans's Sea Saint Studios for Wings's fourth album, *Venus And Mars*, McCartney cut the Gordian knot by finding a drummer who'd get on better with Denny and Jimmy.

The job went to Joe English, a New Yorker who had been summoned to assist on *Venus And Mars*, following Geoff Britton's crestfallen return to England. Joe was esteemed by trombonist Tony Dorsey, hired to lead the four-piece horn section being assembled for the tour, mainly on the strength of his experience in the same capacity for soul shouter Joe Tex. Dorsey was also among those with first refusal on numerous studio dates in Los Angeles – which was where he'd entered the orbit of Joe English.

Like Denny Seiwell before him, Joe was, by his own admission, "on the bottom"[7]. This had followed six years of vocational contentment as one of Jam Factory, a unit that had criss-crossed North America, second-billed to the likes of Jimi Hendrix, The Grateful Dead and Janis Joplin. The group's disbandment allied to a messy divorce triggered poverty and general psychological upset, but he'd been thrown a lifeline with a chance to back Bonnie Bramlett, once of Delaney and Bonnie and Friends, drawn from that Los Angeles studio crowd who were the very epitome of that cocksure sexism that informed the stock rock-band-on-the-road in the pre-punk 1970s.

English was spared the monotony of listening to any detailing of the previous night's carnal shenanigans on the Bramlett tour bus when he took up the post with the less aggressively friendly Wings in time for the unleashing of *Venus And Mars* and its first single, 'Listen To What The Man Said', in May 1975.

Because *Band On The Run* had been deemed a commendable effort, both were guaranteed a fair hearing by reviewers – and sufficient advance orders to slam the album straight in at Number One in every chart that mattered. 'Listen To What The Man Said' also went to the top in the States, but, true to what was becoming a precedent, fell slightly short of that in Britain. The 'Letting Go' follow-up traced a similar scent in macrocosm, nudging the US Top 40 while stopping just outside it at home. By a law of diminishing returns, however, a third A-side, 'Venus And Mars' itself, actually climbed higher than 'Letting Go' in the States while missing completely at home, becoming McCartney's first serious flop since The Beatles.

This was but a petty dampener on the overall success of an album that the majority of listeners judged to be pleasant enough, but something of a holding operation, for all its vague star-sign "concept", complete with a *Sgt Pepper*-esque reprise of the opening track, and the penultimate 'Lonely People' – them again – linked to a jaw-dropping version of the contrapuntal theme to *Crossroads*, the long-running ITV soap opera, set in a Midlands hotel and then broadcast during forlorn afternoon hours between the *News In Welsh* and the children's programmes – and, surmised McCartney, "just the kind of thing lonely old people watch"[5].

It was flattery of a sort that the Wings version of 'Crossroads' was churned out over the closing credits before the series – in its original format – finally went off the air over a decade later, following the dismissal of Noele Gordon as central character "Meg Mortimer". Denny Laine may have been the originator and principal advocate of the Wings's cover, having been acquainted with Gordon when she was host of *Lunch Box*, that lightest of ITV's light entertainment shows, on which he and his Diplomats had been resident.

Denny was also lead vocalist on 'Spirits Of Ancient Egypt' as Jimmy McCulloch was on 'Medicine Jar', a number he'd penned with Stone The Crows' drummer, Colin Allen. This corresponded with a spirit of willing concession by McCartney that emanated not only from the grooves of the album, but also during the preliminaries to the long-anticipated tour – for which Laine had also been earmarked to sing 'Go Now' – with Paul tackling Mike Pinder's descending piano ostinati and solo – and a revival of Paul Simon's 'Richard Cory'. Moreover, Jimmy and Denny (playing a twin-necked Gibson) were to break sweat with duelling guitars during controlled "blowing" sections in a couple of numbers elongated for that very purpose.

It had been decided too that the two colours and two orbs that dominated the album sleeve were to be a recurring image in both the tour merchandise and the costumes worn on a carpeted stage in the midst of scenery sufficiently minimal and plain to accommodate back-projections such as the one for 'C Moon' – a reproduction of one of the Magritte paintings Paul had been collecting since 1966. This one depicted a candle with the moon where a flame ought to be.

The props were being constructed while Wings rehearsed five days a week just north of London in EMI's hangar-like film studios, which were surrounded by a wilderness of weeds and coarse grass that was engulfing gear that had outlived its celluloid usefulness – like two flights of ornamental stairs, half a Spitfire and an equally rusty German U-boat.

Inside, as well as the classic two guitars-bass-drums set-up, a grand piano stood on a rostrum for Paul's use, while Linda was now banked by a clavinet, mellotron and mini-moog, new-fangled keyboards that made her Hammond organ seem like a Saxon church in Manhattan. Sight-reading at stage-right behind English's drum kit, the horn players were all-American apart from Howie Casey blowing tenor saxophone just like he had with Derry And The Seniors.

Howie was a comfortable familiar – and so were Linda and Denny, but if Paul was expecting a smooth ride, he was to be disappointed. "No! It's too fuzzy," he shouted, having halted the group mid-song, "The harmonies aren't sharp enough. We've really got to concentrate all the time here, otherwise it'll go limp – and don't scoop up to that last note. Let it fall away naturally."[8] The next half-hour was spent attacking five offending notes from different angles until they matched the boss's "head arrangement".

Gradually, direction and outcome shone through with sharper clarity, specifically when "We got to a point at one time where we were very gloomy, moaning that it wasn't gelling – and that made it worse, of course. So in the end, we had a discussion-cum-argument about the whole thing, and everybody got it out of their system. Each of us would play his own bit instead of looking over his shoulder at the next man – and it seemed to work. That's when we started believing in it. It became real for us that day, and everybody felt much happier."[8]

The litmus-test was an *in situ* bash before an invited audience that included Ringo Starr, Harry Nilsson and others who didn't necessarily want to like it: "record company people and so forth," noticed Paul. "It showed up a lot of holes in the show, bits that needed to be tightened up."[8]

Encouragingly, only those in the know picked up on these in Southampton on 9 September 1975 – though, belying the atrocious sound quality of the trek's first bootleg – a cassette entitled *McCartney In Hammersmith* – a general improvement became perceptible to eight North Americans and a Japanese lady with the resources to attend every stop of the once and, wishfully, future Beatle's passage round the globe.

When his Wings weren't either on an aeroplane or waiting in the departure lounge for the next one, they hurtled along the motorways, freeways and *autobahns* in a state-of-the-art coach as luxurious as a first class railway carriage with attached diner and toilet – so much so that it excited the idle upward stares from traffic-jammed car drivers whose exhaust pipes belched out their envious impatience.

Between the Australian and European legs of the tour, the dramatis personnae convened at Abbey Road to get to grips with *Wings At The Speed Of Sound*, another good rather than great album, on which Paul's delegation of artistic responsibility extended as far as featuring Joe English as lead singer on 'Must Do Something About That' – while Linda's soprano was to the fore on 'Cook Of The House'. Denny and Jimmy were permitted one each too – on, respectively, 'Time To Hide' and, another McCulloch–Allen opus, 'Wino Junkie'. Paul, nevertheless, was loud and clear on the attendant hits, 'Let 'Em In' – and the rather self-justifying 'Silly Love Songs', which, like the album, shot to the top in the USA, Number Two in Britain.

During this and other lay-offs during the tour, the man that *Melody Maker* had front-paged lately as "Just An Ordinary Superstar"[9] made time to attend to MPL, now the largest independent music publisher in the world with 'Happy Birthday To You', 'Chopsticks' – the most recognised (and irritating) piano solo ever composed – and key Broadway musicals (including *Hello Dolly, Chorus Line* and *Annie*) amongst its litter of lucrative copyrights.

Of more personal import, however, were the US rights to Buddy Holly's best-known songs at a knock-down price, owing to comparative indifference to him on his home territory. In Britain, it was a different story. A London Teddy Boy called Sunglasses Ron – so it is fabled – wore his trademark shades day and night from Holly's death until his own in the mid-1990s. The first tribute on vinyl, however, was that of Marty Wilde with 'You've Got Love', a medium-paced jollity whose title said it all, on the 1959 LP, *Wilde About Marty*.

The Searchers, Dave Berry and Peter and Gordon were among those whose pragmatic admiration during the 1960s beat boom had brought forth workmanlike versions of 'Listen To Me', 'Maybe Baby' and the chartbusting 'True Love Ways' respectively, while The Hollies were responsible for a 1980 album that was devoted to Holly.

In the age of the "supergroups", Humble Pie gave us 'Heartbeat', but before that Blind Faith's revamp of 'Well...All Right' was conspicuous for a snake-charmer riff, altered lyrics and a typical instrumental work-out over the fade.

Already, the 1970s had produced Steeleye Span's *a cappella* experiment with 'Rave On' and Mud's Number One in the same style with 'Oh Boy!' – while on the horizon was Wreckless Eric's 'Crying Waiting Hoping'.

Capitalising on this latest evidence of the four-eyed Texan's lasting popularity in the land he visited just once, the 40th anniversary of his birth was marked by the first of McCartney's yearly Buddy Holly Weeks in London. Beginning on 7 September 1976 – midway between two months in the USA and the tour ending as it had begun in Britain – it climaxed with a showbiz luncheon at which guest of honour Norman Petty, Holly's studio mentor, presented a startled Paul with the cuff-links that, so he told the watching throng, had been fastening Buddy's shirt when his corpse was carried from the wreckage of the crashed aircraft.

Later celebrations – in other cities too – would embrace concerts by what was left of The Crickets; rock 'n' roll dance exhibitions; Buddy Holly painting, poetry and songwriting competitions; the opening of a West End musical about him; a "rock 'n' roll Brain Of Britain" tournament – and song contests, although the 1996 winners (a trio with a jungle-techno crack at 'Not Fade Away') at the finals in London's Texas Embassy Cantina had some of their thunder stolen by an "impromptu" jam fronted by Gary Glitter, Dave Dee, Allan Clarke of The Hollies, Dave Berry and – you guessed it – Paul McCartney.

Paul was vocal too in his objection that a 1979 bio-pic, *The Buddy Holly Story*, "was hardly the true story". Putting action over complaint, he financed *The Real Buddy Holly Story*, a documentary screened on BBC2 in 1985 with interviewees that included Keith Richards, Holly's brothers and, using The Quarry Men's scratched 78rpm 'That'll Be The Day' as an audio aid, Paul himself – who also gave viewers 'Words Of Love' to his own acoustic six-string picking. In parenthesis, he was, purportedly, to be supplicated in vain four years later to sink cash in Clear Lake, Iowa's Surf Ballroom – the site of Holly's final performance, and now threatened with demolition – or at least use his celebrity to convince state authorities that the place might be a remunerative tourist attraction.

Back in 1976, however, McCartney's primary Holly-associated concern was supervising *Holly Days* on which Denny Laine, like The Hollies, paid his respects over an entire album. As exemplified by, say, 1960's *I Remember Hank Williams* by rockabilly balladeer

Jack Scott or Heinz's *Tribute To Eddie* [Cochran] three years later, this was not a new idea, but, spawned in Scotland in the same homespun way as *McCartney*, its heart was in the right place, even if it didn't beat hard enough to tempt many to buy either *Holly Days* or its two 45s, 'It's So Easy' and 'Moondreams'.

Nothing from *Holly Days* was trotted out when the tour resumed or on in-concert *Wings Over America*, said to have shut down George Harrison's *All Things Must Pass* and his *Concerts For Bangla Desh* as the biggest-selling triple-album of all time. Moreover, in among its reminders of Wings and the solo McCartney's chart strikes were ambles as far down memory lane as 'Yesterday' and 'I've Just Seen A Face' (also from the non-soundtrack side of *Help!*); 'Lady Madonna' and the "White Album"'s 'Blackbird', and, restored to its raw pre-Spector state, 'The Long And Winding Road' off *Let It Be*. Paul seemed, therefore, to be coming to terms with both his past and present situation as he conducted Wings with nods and eye contact while never sacrificing impassioned content for technical virtuosity. As codas died away or as someone wrapped up a particularly *bravura* solo, he'd direct the adulation of the hordes towards others under the spotlight, and beam as salvos of clapping recognition undercut, say, the opening chords of Denny's 'Go Now'.

Ultimately, Paul McCartney had ensured that his Wings gave the people what they seemed to want – and the consensus in North America was that he'd put up a better show than George Harrison, whose trek round the sub-continent late the previous autumn had also contained a quota of Beatles numbers among the solo favourites – though these had been marred by George's persistent laryngitis, his taking of unpardonable lyrical liberties and unappealing re-inventions such as a 'My Sweet Lord' at breakneck speed. Hardly the last word in mister showbusiness, he hadn't endeared himself to the crowds either with on-mike admonishments like "I don't know how it feels down there, but from up here, you seem pretty dead to me."[10]

John Lennon had sent Harrison a bouquet of first-night flowers, and had attended a couple of the troubled concerts, trooping backstage afterwards to say hello and join in heated inquests into the graveyard hours. He, George and Paul had also contributed songs and lent studio assistance to Ringo Starr's eponymous 1973 album. Though this was coloured as a bastardised Beatles collection, no track had involved all four in the same place at the same time – though 'I'm The Greatest' came close with Starr, Harrison and Lennon at the session in Los Angeles' Sunset Sound Studio. McCartney had wanted to pitch in too, but turgid bureaucracy and his recent run-ins with the law had delayed the granting of a US visa.

Embroiled as they were still in the fiscal turmoils of Apple, it wasn't exactly hail-fellow-well-met between Paul and the others – or, for that matter, between the others themselves – but there was talk of Paul, George, John and Ringo amalgamating again on maybe a casual basis when Allen Klein – now a villain of the darkest hue to Lennon, Starr and Harrison as well – was out of the way. Fanning dull embers for Beatlemaniacs too were reports of at least three out of four ex-Beatles caving in to overtures to do it all again for either a charity or some individual with more money than sense. "God, it's like asking Liz Taylor when she's going to get together with Eddie Fisher again,"[11] Linda cracked back at another broken-record enquiry on the subject – because neither wild horses nor net temptations that worked out at hundreds of thousands of dollars per minute each for just one little concert could drag the old comrades-in-arms together again.

John's public reviling of Paul, and Paul's more veiled digs at John had continued after the 'Three Legs'–'How Do You Sleep?' episode. "'Imagine' is what John's really like," McCartney had informed *Melody Maker*. "There was too much political stuff on the other album."[11]

"So you think 'Imagine' isn't political?," parried Lennon in the same publication the following week. "It's 'Working Class Hero' with sugar on for conservatives like yourself."[11]

Yet no printed or vinyl insult could erase a private mutual affection, cemented together as they were by an extra-sensory understanding of each other's creative appetite, by George and Ringo and by 17 years of joys and sorrows. From New Orleans, McCartney had telephoned Lennon and caught himself asking if John wanted to lend a hand on *Venus And Mars*. John didn't materialise, but Paul did for an evening of coded hilarity and nostalgic bonhomie at the open house that was a well-appointed beach villa in Santa Monica where John was living during a 15 month separation from Yoko.

Not so rose-tinted would be the 1974 night in New York when Paul and Linda fell in with John who was on his way to call on a new-found friend, David Bowie. According to the latter's girlfriend, Ava Cherry, the visit was rather confrontational: "David wasn't really friendly with Paul and Linda. There was this tense feeling. Every time Paul started to say something, Linda would jump in and not let Paul talk. I don't think she liked David very much, and the feeling was mutual."[12] The dialogue deteriorated further when, after listening to the host's new *Young Americans* twice through, Paul snapped, "Can we hear another album?"

His remark was all the more barbed because John had made a pronounced creative investment in *Young Americans*, going so far as to co-write its chief single, 'Fame'. Having absorbed "Philly Soul" deeply, *Young Americans* was as slick as John's other recent sojourns in the studio weren't. These included hacking chords as Mick Jagger emoted 'Too Many Cooks', a Chicago blues obscurity, during shambolic sessions ostensibly for a Harry Nilsson album, *Pussycats*, at Los Angeles' suburban Burbank Studios, whilst taping its demos back at Santa Monica.

Jack Bruce thrummed bass on 'Too Many Cooks', but Paul McCartney elected to man the drum kit when he looked in at Burbank, and ended up on an approximation of 'Midnight Special', once in The Quarry Men's repertoire. A few days later, he was rattling the traps again at a musical "at home" in Santa Monica.

Present too would be Nilsson, guitarist Jesse Ed Davis (Eric Clapton's understudy at the *Concerts For Bangla Desh*), "supersideman" saxophonist Bobby Keyes and blind singing multi-instrumentalist Stevie Wonder – Tamla-Motown's mollycoddled former child-star, who'd been recipient of an affectionate message in Braille on the sleeve of *Red Rose Speedway*.

As there were so many distinguished participants, the results were committed to tape for posterity – and the inevitable bootlegs – on equipment borrowed from Burbank. Paul was most conspicuous with a vocal extemporisation on a go at Santo and Johnny's 'Sleepwalk', an instrumental hit from 1959, but the clouds parting on the gods at play revealed nothing more remarkable than a session crew's meanderings during some tiresome mechanical process at the mixing desk.

Regardless of quality, however, it encapsulated a Lennon and McCartney reunion of sorts, though it wasn't the harbinger of any permanent liaison. "You can't reheat a soufflé,"[13] concluded Paul, who thought no more about sitting in with John and his cronies than he did of similar rambles with Bob Dylan at a party in Joni Mitchell's Californian home a few months later.

Nonetheless, there lingered enough fond shared memories from the days of The Quarry Men, Hamburg *et al* for further get-togethers with John, musical and otherwise, outside the context of the ledgers, computer run-offs, board meetings and the rest of the prevailing business that was taking place over division of the Apple empire.

Lennon and McCartney, however, finished on a sour note on Sunday 25 April 1976 when Paul returned unexpectedly, guitar in hand, to a harassed John's New York apartment after spending the previous evening there. "That was a period when Paul just kept turning up at our door. I would let him in, but finally I said to him, 'Please call before you come over. It's not 1956 [*sic*] anymore. You know, just give me a ring.' That upset him, but I didn't mean it badly."[14]

Without formal goodbyes, the two friends went their separate ways, and were never to speak face-to-face again. How could either have guessed that John had less than five years left?

Wings would be over too by then. Indeed, Jimmy McCulloch and Joe English hadn't stuck around long enough to be heard on the most memorable British hit by a group, that, by autumn 1977, had pared down to just the McCartneys and Denny Laine.

## 15 "Japanese Tears"

> "'Galveston' is about wanting to get back home and now the war is over, I can relate the song to 'Mull Of Kintyre', which I also do in concert. They have the same feeling about them."
>
> – *Glen Campbell*[1]

Perhaps he wasn't the most fitting bearer of sad tidings in this case, but John Lennon, the "bad influence" from Quarry Bank, heard about 73-year-old Jim McCartney's death of bronchial pneumonia in March 1976 before Paul did. From New York, John telephoned to break the news.

In transit between Copenhagen and Berlin with Wings, Paul was absent from the cremation, unlike brother Mike, who lived near his father's Cheshire home. While he'd cried his tears, Paul had decided that Jim would have understood that the show must go on. Besides, the tour would serve as occupational therapy, even if, when the music was over for the day, there'd be heartache.

One outcome of Paul's emotional convalescence was a gradual estrangement from step-mother Angela and 14-year-old Ruth. They'd continued living in the house that Paul had bought his father, but he made it clear that he didn't intend to maintain them financially anymore. Within a decade Angela had reverted to her previous surname, Williams, and had told her story to a daily newspaper. "We don't exist," she was to mope in another periodical in 1995, "Paul has written us out of his life. I write and send Christmas cards, but never receive a reply."[2]

Correlated with the beginning of life without her elder step-brother was Ruth's ascent as a professional entertainer. From childhood, she had attended singing and dancing lessons, and was already composing on guitar and piano. Her stylistic determination was what she called "the spectacle": that strata of mainstream pop that embraced the likes of Liza Minnelli, Barbra Streisand and, with a nod to the glam-rock that was still in vogue during her schooldays, Gary Glitter. Indeed, Glitter's tour manager, Mike Mingard, was intermediary in setting up an artists' management company in Birkenhead – with Angela and Ruth as co-directors.

Despite his reluctance to keep these two in the manner to which they'd become accustomed, Paul, like the fated socialite in 'Richard Cory', "spread his wealth around" in other matters. When Wings were in Texas that May, for example, he and Linda bought a horse that had escaped from its paddock and happened to be ambling along the roadside as the tour bus nosed by. Four months later, the US leg of the tour was marked by a no-expenses-spared party on a Beverly Hills estate where celebrity-spotters noted the arriving Mercedes, Bentleys, Porches and Roll-Royces, and speculated about who could not been seen behind their smoked windows.

By contrast, the punk-rock – or, if you prefer, New Wave – storm gathered in Britain, and pub-rock tumbled from its zenith of chart entries for the likes of Ace and Dr Feelgood, and its executants either fell by the wayside or adjusted themselves to changing times – as did Nick Garvey and Andy McMasters of Ducks De Luxe, who resurfaced as half of The Motors. Garvey was also destined for a walk-on part in the life of Paul McCartney, the millionaire superstar epitome of all The Sex Pistols, The Damned, The UK Subs and the rest of them detested.

McCartney was loathed further for a mid-1970s visibility – in Britain anyway – that was comparable to that of a recurring ITV advertisement. There he was with Linda in a comedy sketch on *The Mike Yarwood Show*; grinning and facing the lens in an after-hours cluster of small-talking luminaries at a Rod Stewart concert at London's Olympia, and sharing a joke with Mick Jagger when the Stones appeared at 1976's Knebworth Festival. The McCartneys' pre-recorded personal greetings punctuated the in-person funny stories from the past when Liverpool boxing champion John Conteh – pictured with Kenny Lynch, Christopher Lee and other worthies on the front cover of *Band On The Run* – was subject of an edition of *This Is Your Life*.

More pragmatically, Paul seemed to be omnipresent on *Top Of The Pops*. As well as miming this or that latest single in an official capacity, there were on-camera sightings of him and his wife jigging about amongst the studio audience, sometimes lending manifest if unsolicited support to younger contenders. "By far the nicest thing that's ever happened to me on the show," recollected David Essex, "was back in October 1975 when I reached Number One with 'Hold Me Close'. It so happened that during the number, Paul and Linda McCartney, who were in the audience at that time, actually jumped up and joined in the chorus with me. It was a great moment, very special, and I'll never forget it."[3]

Amused by the memory, presenter Simon Bates would reconjure "one occasion when I was on, and, of all people, Paul McCartney strolled on to the stage. Now this is totally live, and he said, 'Hi, Simon. I'm here to plug my new record.' It was the first time in a long time that a Beatle [*sic*] had appeared live on the show."[3]

Maybe Paul only seemed to put in an appearance every time you switched on prime-time television simply because there were so many sit-coms at the time with central characters that looked like him: John Alderton in *Please Sir*, acrylically garbed Richard O' Sullivan (in *Man About The House* and *Robin's Nest*), the late Richard "Godber" Beckinsale in *Porridge*... Muddling through a weekly half-hour in, perhaps, a classroom, shared flat or, in Beckinsale's case, prison, all sported the neat, dark-haired mop-top, clean-shaven face and aspects of the chirpy persona that was the public image of "Fab Macca", who was, he declared to a waiting press corps, "over the moon"[4] about the birth of his and

Linda's first son – James – on 12 September 1977. Eight days later, he authorised the publication for all the world to see of an official photograph of the little 'un and his enraptured parents.

Elsewhere, however, it was far from fond smiles and baby-talk. Jimmy McCulloch resigned from Wings in September 1977, just prior to their knuckling down to a new album, *London Town*. He preferred to take his chances with a reformed Small Faces, one of few 1960s acts tolerated by leading punk entertainers. Nevertheless, it became rapidly and painfully transparent that all the group's fans, old and new, wanted were the sounds of yesteryear, as poor sales of two "comeback" albums against healthy chart strikes for the reissued 'Itchycoo Park' and 1968's 'Lazy Sunday' testified. With no glad welcome back assured from McCartney, McCulloch was to try again with his own outfit, The Dukes, who bit the dust soon after a 1979 album for Warner Brothers failed to live up to market expectations, and Jimmy being found stone-dead on the floor of his Maida Vale flat with the quantity of morphine, cannabis and alcohol inside his body that led the necessary inquest to record an open verdict.

By then, Joe English was an evangelical Christian, a pop-star-who'd-seen-the-error-of-his-ways, expounding the Bible and preparing a 1981 gospel album, *Lights In The World in Nashville*. He'd lasted fractionally longer in Wings than Jimmy McCulloch before tiresome "months and months sitting in recording studios"[4], waiting his turn to drum, led English to weigh up his self-picture as a musician and the cash benefits of being the last among unequals – behind Paul, Denny and one he considered a poor vocalist and keyboard player – in a group infinite numbers of rungs higher than Jam Factory had ever been.

Joe's decision to slip his cable during sessions for *London Town* – taped in part on board a converted minesweeper bound for the Caribbean – seemed justified in the aftershock of *Rolling Stone*'s condemnation of the finished product as "fake rock, pallid pop and unbelievable homilies that's barely listenable next to Wings's best work."[5] That was the worst review – as disheartening as anything written about *Red Rose Speedway* – but only the most snowblinded McCartney devotees weren't disappointed by *London Town*, for all the meticulousness that hadn't stopped at just music. Hesitation and then annoyance had chased across Paul's face when inspecting a cover on which a tinge of blue marred an otherwise two-tone shot of him, Linda and Denny against a background of Tower Bridge. Upon further reflection, however, he came to quite like it, agreeing maybe with the Confucian adage, "Honour thine error as a hidden intention" as applied to the errant photographer – who, having disposed of the original, was obliged to keep redeveloping the negative until the mistake was repeated.

This subtlety was lost on fans. Their appetites for fresh Beatle-related merchandise unsated by *London Town*, a few fell back on something called *Thrillington* on discovering that, though carrying a logo other than Parlophone, Apple, MPL or Polydor in Britain, it was, nonetheless, a pseudononymous Paul McCartney LP, this track-by-track retread of *Ram* for an orchestra augmented by the cream of London's session players, a recorder ensemble and France's Swingle Singers, a choir best known for addressing itself to jazzy adaptations of Johann Sebastian Bach in a wordless style that has the effect of predetermined mass scat-singing.

The sleeve notes alluded to the fictional life of a Percy "Thrills" Thrillington, the musical jack-of-all-trades responsible for vinyl contents taped in 1971 to be stored away until dusted off to plug a gap for Beatles–McCartney curiosity-seekers between *Wings Over America* and *London Town*.

Paul catered for more mainstream tastes with a vengeance via 'Mull Of Kintyre', a 45 recorded in, well, the Mull of Kintyre during a lengthy respite from the rigours of *London Town*. When spun in the middle of a radio interview in Australia, it prompted the hushed sentence, "Well, I've never heard such a load of crap in my life," from Gerry Marsden. Taking to heart less reactions like this than someone's conjecture that most North Americans wouldn't know what this "mull of kintyre" – or was it "Ma looking tired'? – meant, let alone be able find it on a map, McCartney promoted its coupling, 'Girls School', as the A-side in the States, where it crawled to a modest Number 33.

Yet, as much co-writer Denny Laine's baby, this eulogy to Paul's Hebridean abode was a howling domestic success, replete as it was with the pentatonic skirling of a Scottish pipe band to stoke up a seasonal flavour in keeping with its release in time for 1977's December sell-in with its homecomings, mistletoe and Timex commercials. Ploughing a similar furrow to 'Sentimental Journey', World War II singalong 'Home Town' – the one about "those corny country cousins of mine" – 1969's 'Galveston' from Glen Campbell and the verses before the convict is marched to the gallows in Curly Putnam's 'Green Green Grass Of Home', 'Mull Of Kintyre' was Wings's first UK Number One, shutting down 'She Loves You' as the kingdom's biggest-selling 45. Milkmen from Dover to Donegal whistled it, and there was no finer rendition of 'Mull Of Kintyre' than by a nine-year-old schoolboy named Matthew who, at a fête I attended in a south Oxfordshire village the following spring, clambered onto the makeshift stage, lowered the microphone and delivered it *a cappella* in an impromptu but pitch-perfect treble.

A man's gotta do what a man's gotta do. For Wings themselves, such as they were, plugging 'Mull Of Kintyre' via both a promotional film on location in – you guessed it – and slots on Yuletide TV variety and chat shows, was all in a day's work until well into January. Yet while Paul was thus mutating into as much of a British showbiz evergreen as Max Bygraves, he was to be the only ex-Beatle to figure still in *Melody Maker*'s yearly poll.

*London Town* also fared better commercially than contemporaneous offerings by both George Harrison and Ringo Starr. As for John Lennon, he had, to all intents and purposes, thrown in the towel since the birth of his and Yoko's only surviving child in 1975, seemingly rounding off his post-Beatles career that October with a self-explanatory "best of" retrospective, *Shaved Fish (Collectable Lennon)*.

Paul succumbed too with 1978's *Wings Greatest*. Padded out with 'Another Day' and 'Uncle Albert/Admiral Halsey', this 12-track compilation embraced further major smashes for Paul as a non-Beatle up to and including 'Mull Of Kintyre'. By its very nature, *Wings Greatest* showed up *London Town*, still only a few months old, in an even poorer light, despite the second of its singles, 'With A Little Luck' tramping a well-trodden path to the top in the Hot 100 and slipping quietly in and out of the Top Ten at home.

It had been preceded by 'Goodnight Tonight', a hit 45 that, like 'Mull Of Kintyre', had nothing to do with either *London Town* or the work-in-progress on the next album, *Back To The Egg*. Less than a fortnight after its release came a remix, which met disco fever, then sashaying towards its John Travolta zenith, more than halfway.

If you sat that one out, you could groove to 'Daytime Nighttime Suffering', buried on the B-side, but rated by aficianados as one of McCartney's most evocative compositions since The Beatles. It was also among the first Wings tracks to feature two new full-time members.

Both were more steeped in all things Beatles than anyone who had gone before. Laurence Juber had started to learn the guitar seriously only after hearing 'I Want To Hold Your Hand', while the first LP that drummer Steve Holly bought was *Sgt Pepper's Lonely Hearts Club Band*. The enthusiasm of these tractable young men was matched by skills acquired mostly on the London studio circuit where they'd crossed paths with Denny Laine. Consequently, each had been procured in summer 1978 by Denny for executive approval by Paul. While Steve was blessed with a talismanic surname, neither posed any limelight-threatening challenge to the high command or were outwardly frustrated songwriters or lead vocalists.

Neither minded being indiscernibly audible on the *Back To The Egg* session for 'Rockestra Theme' and 'So Glad To See You Here', preserved on celluloid because of arrangements that Cecil B de Mille might have approved had he been a late 1970s record producer with the run of Abbey Road and with the biggest names in British rock only a telephone call away. Led Zeppelin's John Bonham alone sent the console's decibel metre into the red, but he was but one-sixth of a percussion battalion that also included Speedy Acquaye and, from The Small Faces, Kenney Jones.

"Keith Moon was going to turn up too, but unfortunately he died a week before,"[6] explained Paul. Nonetheless, fingering unison riffs on electric guitars were Denny, Laurence, Pete Townshend, Hank B Marvin and Pink Floyd's Dave Gilmour. "Jeff Beck was going to come and Eric Clapton," sighed McCartney, "but they didn't. Beck was worried about what would happen if he didn't like the track."[6]

Beck also suffered from tinnitus – which 'So Glad To See You Here' and 'Rockestra Theme' might have worsened when even Bonham's Led Zeppelin cohort, John Paul Jones, one of no less than three bass players, fought to be heard amid the massed guitars, drums, keyboards and horns.

While they made outmoded monophonic Dansette record-players shudder, the two items weren't the flat-out blasts you may have imagined on top-of-the-range stereo. They held their own, however, on *Back To The Egg*, but that isn't saying much as the album for all its diversity was subjected to a critical mauling as vicious as that for *London Town*. If none of them, in their heart-of-hearts, expected it to be astounding, the faithful bought enough copies of lacklustre *Back To The Egg* to push into Top 20s, home and abroad, but the singles, 'Old Siam Sir' and the double A-side, 'Getting Closer' and 'Baby's Request' snatched but the slightest chart honours.

Paul had offered the latter to the venerable Mills Brothers, whose humming polyphony in concert had impressed him during a recent holiday in France. It wasn't, however, a mutual admiration society as it had been with Peggy Lee after she'd gladly clasped

'Let's Love' to her bosom. Perhaps befuddled with jet-lag and not sure which ex-member of those upstart Beatles was actually chatting to them, the Brothers had had the nerve to demand payment for recording what they didn't hear as much of a song – nowhere near the fighting weight anyway of 'Paper Doll', 'Till Then', 'You Always Hurt The One You Love' or any given one of their own hits that had predated the charts.

McCartney's name on the record label would have guaranteed a degree of attention from radio station programmers, just as his achievements prior to any 'Old Siam Sir' folly had sold out Wings's winter tour of England with side-trips to Edinburgh and Glasgow. This coincided with the calculated issue of 'Wonderful Christmastime', which, like 'Mull Of Kintyre', was a hit parade contender during a time of year when the usual rules don't apply. How else had Dickie Valentine's 'Christmas Alphabet' eased 'Rock Around The Clock' from Number One in December 1955? Why did repromotions of Slade's 'Merry Christmas Everybody' keep registering somewhere in the lists years after the disc's optimum moment in 1973? After years of minor entries at most, Gary Glitter was to be back on his Top Ten perch in 1984 with 'Another Rock And Roll Christmas' before falling back on a nostalgia netherworld where current chart status had no meaning.

The Christmas single is, with the "death disc", one of pop's hardiest forms – and Paul's effort in 1979, spurred by a reggae version of 'Rudolf The Red-Nosed Reindeer' on the B-side, and publicity generated by the tour, was guided with almost mathematical precision into the UK Top Ten. Needless to say, music press organs that were still fawning to a person who was once called "Johnny Rotten" despised 'Wonderful Christmastime'.

Mean-minded critics, flop singles, the turnovers of personnel, the arguments, the ultimatums, the eternities in the studio, none of that mattered once Wings kicked off with 'Got To Get You Into My Life', hit their stride with 'Maybe I'm Amazed' and had everyone in this Odeon or that Gaumont involved; fretting when

Paul showed signs of flagging, glowing when he got second wind and giving vent to an ear-stinging bedlam of applause after a particularly fiery 'Band On The Run'. As if they'd all sat on tin-tacks, the volume would rise momentarily to its loudest when, after 'Goodnight Tonight', Paul entered a solitary spotlight with his acoustic six-string for 'Yesterday'. Up there was his reward for working so hard: the acclamation of the great British public. That was better than any filthy lucre or terrible review of his latest LP.

As the artificial show cascaded during 'Wonderful Christmastime', Paul was in his element. The here and now was too important – and magical – to worry about The Mills Brothers and 'Baby's Request' or what the *NME* had printed about 'Wonderful Christmastime'. He had the people eating out of his palm in the way he'd imagined when in a brown study during physics at the Institute.

By way of a dress rehearsal, the group put on a free concert at Paul's old school the day before three nights at Liverpool's Royal Court, his first "home game" since The Beatles played the Empire in December 1964. There's a scene in the 1955 film melodrama *Blackboard Jungle* where a teacher tries to establish rapport with unruly pupils by spinning a disc from his treasured collection. "It's just a guy singing," was the general response. "Guys singing are a dime a dozen."

To Liverpool at large, Paul McCartney at the Royal Court was more than just a guy singing. Veiled in flesh, the Local Boy Made Good was reappearing before his people like Moses from the clouded summit of Mount Sinai to the Israelites.

Yet even some of those who'd paid touts half a week's wages for a ticket were more level-headed – though when Paul piled into 'Twenty Flight Rock' towards the end of the set, the oldest among them might have indulged in knowing nods and inner binges of maudlin reminiscence about a callow bunch called The Quarry Men – or were they The Silver Beatles? – who, through the fantastic outcome of their metamorphosis into the showbusiness sensation of the century, had attained a sort of romantic nobility. While none expected the murky waters of the Mersey to part, the show was on the scale of, if not a Cup Final or Muhammed Ali's last fight in Las Vegas, then the original Animals reunion bash at Newcastle City Hall or The Troggs in the open air of Andover's Walled Meadow in 1977. Only a miracle could have rescued either of them from anti-climax too.

McCartney's whereabouts when not within the Royal Court was a red rag to a media that had decided that if the slightest thing could be sensationalised about his descent on the city, then sensationalised it would be. There wasn't a newspaper editor on Merseyside who wouldn't promise a king's ransom for an exclusive or a candid snapshot, but journalists needed to spin an impossibly likely tale to gain admittance to a suite as protected as Fort Knox after the hiding place was rumbled and its switchboard blockaded with enquiries.

A regional television crew was kept waiting for a rumoured walkabout by the lad from Allerton – though one afternoon, he and Linda (whose forced or otherwise Scouse accent was noted) boarded the Royal Iris, the "ferry across the Mersey" on which The Beatles had twice supported Acker Bilk in the old days.

By the time The Beatles headlined with Lee Castle and his Barons on the selfsame vessel for another 'Riverboat Shuffle', just before lift-off with 'Love Me Do', Bilk had been old hat. Yet via the continuing rotation of the seasons of pop, the Somerset clarinettist had enjoyed an unexpected British Top Ten windfall – with an opus entitled 'Aria' – in the late 1970s when the going was ostensibly hard for all manner of elder statesmen of the Swinging Sixties as The Sex Pistols raced towards Number One with their banned 'God Save The Queen', and countless outfits all over the realm were formed in their image: short hair, ripped clothes held together with safety pins and horrible onstage racket with guitars thrashed at speed to machine-gun drumming behind some ranting johnny-one-note who acted as if he couldn't care less whether you liked it or not.

Even in the teeth of the standing-room-only tour, Paul may have pondered where he fitted into an industry voracious as always for new faces to exploit and discard for a fickle public. Precisely where did he belong in a Britain in which such as the *NME* had been tacitly biased towards the grassroots developments of pub-rock, punk, the Mod revival and whatever was on the way next? Its staff's lampooning of "dinosaur" acts encompassed those it considered either over-the-hill such as The Grateful Dead or wholesomely Americanised like Fleetwood Mac, who were as far from the splendid blues band they once were as Steve Winwood would be from The Spencer Davis Group with 1980's *Arc Of A Diver*, on which more US sound laboratories would receive "special thanks" than humans. Articles about him and his sort would be slotted well towards the back, just before the box adverts for disco equipment.

If McCartney was deemed worthy of as little room too, maybe he wasn't bothered. Most of his following had been disenfranchised by punk, and being mentioned in the same pages as the Pistols, Damned, Stiff Little Fingers and so on was of meagre consequence to him now that he had reached a plateau of showbusiness so unassailable that another single in the British charts or even a US album going platinum would be a mere sideshow.

He didn't need Wings anymore either. No time was better for letting go of the group than after Paul's extradition from Japan on 25 January 1980, following nine days as Prisoner No 22 in a Tokyo gaol. This had put the tin-lid on a tour of the country. He only had himself to blame, though a story persists that Yoko Ono, overwhelmed with spite after a strained telephone conversation with him two days earlier, had prodded nerves to ensure that when Wings threaded their way through the customs area at Narita airport, Paul would be the one instructed to open his suitcase.

Sure enough, a polythene bag of marijuana leaped out from on top of the spare underwear, toilet bag *et al*. Parodoxically, the culprit was suppressing an almost uncontrollable urge to laugh out loud as, handcuffed, he was hustled by uniformed men into custody and hours of circular questioning, as if in a parody of *Midnight Express*. A drama of a US student arrested for possession of hashish, and sentenced to open-ended years in a squalid Turkish prison, it had been *the* hit movie of 1978.

"PAUL IN CHAINS!" screamed a headline on breakfast tables back home while the subject of the report beneath it sank into an uneasy slumber in the detention centre where the local prosecutor had demanded he be sent. Lying there, McCartney groped for reasons why the case – which carried a maximum sentence of seven years hard labour – would or would not be pursued. Bouncing his thoughts off both Linda, John Eastman and a representative of the British Consul during their visits, he built up an damning case against himself before concluding that, while Japanese drug laws were stringent, harsh and effective – in all probability because of the island's position as a vital confluence of southeast Asia's trafficking thoroughfares – the authorities were embarrassed at having such a celebrity *keto* behind their bars, and they didn't know what to do about it.

The tour's promoter – a Mr Udo – concurred with this: "Much loss of face for me," he seethed. "Much loss of face for Minister of Justice also."[7] Yet as the hours dragged by with no word either way about his fate, Paul could either carry on wringing his hands or just shut his mind to the horror of the situation, make at least a half-hearted attempt to be pleasant to the guards and the other prisoners and slide into a routine of sweeping his cell, folding up his bedding and mattress and further compulsory chores. He also began a diary of this extraordinary chapter of his life to occupy hours when he'd otherwise be drowning in despair.

He was responding well to prison life when his belongings were returned to him and he was escorted by a dozen police officers onto the next connecting flight to London. In essence, it wasn't much different to not quite two decades ago when he and Pete Best had been bundled out of Germany for arson.

As he had after the Maharishi's tutorials in 1967, Paul insisted that he was never going to touch narcotics again, whilst either continuing or resuming his habit – as demonstrated by two related if minor run-ins with the law in 1984 when he and Linda were reprimanded and made to pay fines as inappreciable as the amounts of dope with which they'd been caught.

Nevertheless, while the nasty experience in Tokyo was yet to fade, McCartney may have had every intention of staying out of trouble. "I'll never smoke pot again,"[8] he assured one British tabloid the afternoon after his inglorious farewell to the Land of the Rising Sun. Days later, Fleetwood Mac touched down at Narita for a performance at the Nippon Budokan Hall. This was was preceded by a press conference top-heavy with topical discussion about drugs. Next morning, "WE DON'T SMOKE MARIJUANA SWEAR FLEETWOOD MAC!" drew the reader's attention to the front-page of the English-language *Japan Times*.[9]

By then, the McCartneys, weak with relief, were home at last. That Denny Laine – and the two new boys – had left Japan nearly a week earlier may have struck Paul as disloyal. While his glorious leader's freedom was hanging in the balance, Laine had been preoccupied with another solo album. Preceded by a 45 of self-produced remakes of 'Go Now' and 'Say You Don't Mind', the resulting all-original endeavour contained items with Wings that Paul had allowed him to use – as well as another single, 'Japanese Tears', an attempt to come to terms with topical events close to his heart. Issued in May, its sentiments were worthy enough, and the old conviviality between Denny, Linda and Paul hadn't dissipated immediately. Nevertheless, the seeds of Denny's departure and the subsequent demise of Wings had been sown.

# 16 "(Just Like) Starting Over"

"If I'd have been Paul's manager, I'd have slapped a huge Band-Aid over his mouth for three weeks after John died before I allowed him to speak."

– *Ruth McCartney*

As far as I'm concerned, Paul McCartney's most important contribution to society has been his very pragmatic support of animal rights. Any argument that his celebrity and wealth created the opportunity to do so is irrelevant. Others of his kind were sufficiently hip to understand that, like, cruelty to animals is wrong, and were active after a detached, sweeping, pop-starrish fashion in verbally supporting vegetarianism, anti-vivisection *et al.* Sometimes – because it was trendy – they'd attempted not eating meat for maybe a few weeks before the smell of frying bacon triggered a backsliding. Then they'd be noticed once again in a motorway service station, autographing a table napkin whilst masticating a pork pie; ordering a paté de foie gras to go with a minor Beaujolais in a Montparnasse restaurant – or indulging in new and disgusting passions for huntin', fishin' and shootin' with monied neighbours for whom blood sports had been second nature from childhood.

Though as much a member of the rock squirearchy as anyone else, Paul stuck at vegetarianism, following a road-to-Damascus moment one Sunday lunchtime in the Mull of Kintyre. He was settling down to a main course of roast someone-or-other with the family whilst gazing out at an idyllic rural scene of lambs gambolling round their mothers in a meadow. After at least three decades since he pushed away his plate that afternoon, he's still tucking into non-meat dishes exclusively, preaching the gospel of animal welfare, sinking hard cash into all manner of associated organisations and generally keeping up the good work started by him and his first wife.

The eventual founder of a multi-national vegetarian food company, Linda's picture remains the emblem of the still-expanding, constantly improving and award-winning Linda McCartney range of products stocked in a supermarket near you. Her role model may have been Mary, former wife of Peter Frampton, singing guitarist with *Humble Pie*. Mary's non-meat *Rock 'N' Roll Recipes* was published in 1980, several years before *Linda McCartney's Home Cooking*, still the world's biggest-selling recipe book of its kind.

Both Linda and Paul had tried vegetarianism in the 1960s. He, for instance, had been obliged to do so anyway at the Maharishi's ashram. Yet, when filling in the *New Musical Express*'s "Lifelines" questionnaire early in 1963, McCartney had chosen Chicken Maryland as his "favourite food"[1]. This was a rare treat during that year's travelling life of wayside cafés and snatched and irregular chips-with-everything snacks that coarsened the palate. It had been the same in meat-happy Hamburg where Bratwurst sausage was the equivalent of fish-and-chips, and menus in establishments like Der Fludde, Harold's Schnellimbiss and Zum Pferdestalle – which translates as "the Horses' Stable" – favoured horsemeat steaks, Labskaus – a mélange of herrings, corned beef, chopped gherkins and mashed potato, topped with a fried egg – and *Deutsch bifsteak*. A search for a nut roast would be fruitless as all over Europe a vegetarian was regarded generally as a crank and an inconvenience for dinner party hosts.

None of The Beatles had, therefore, ever considered adopting vegetarianism seriously, even when they had the means to order more than beans-on-toast. On the run around the world, gourmet dishes with specious names – furst puckler, trepang soup, veal

Hawaii, – pampered stomachs yearning for the greasy comfort of cod and chips eaten with the fingers.

By the final months of Wings, however, the catering on the road was, at Paul's insistence, entirely meat-free – though, after the lamentable incident in Tokyo, he wasn't to tour again for years, no matter how hard his various investors pleaded. Among these was CBS, who had joined the queue of major US labels supplicating him for his services as soon as executive washroom whisperings filtered through that he, Ringo Starr and George Harrison were about to shower Capitol Records with writs, alleging breach of contract and money owed.

Looking for a new record company was as chancy as looking for a new girlfriend, and now that the legal professional had insinuated its complex mumbo-jumbo into pop, deals could not be mapped out over lunch as Brian Epstein's had been with Billy J Kramer in 1963. One of the hottest properties in the industry, Paul was in a position to call shots about marketing procedure. If there was the slightest deviation from the ascribed riders, wild horses wouldn't drag him out to utter one solitary syllable or sing a single note on an album's behalf.

It was a tall order but CBS was most prepared to obey, and had also proferred the unprecedented enticement of rights to *Guys And Dolls*, *The Most Happy Fella* and further musicals containing all manner of showbiz standards by the late Frank Loesser. "That was the only thing CBS could give him that the others couldn't," laughed company executive Harold Orenstein. "Lee Eastman was always copyright hungry."[2] Thus Paul McCartney melted into CBS's caress for the next five years.

His maiden single under the new regime, 'Coming Up', wasn't accepted without comment by a marketing division that preferred the greater depth of sound on an in-concert version by Wings. Nonetheless, for Orenstein and those whose concept of quality was based on columns of figures, the huge advance and the sacrifice of the Loesser catalogue was a sound investment. Indeed, there was an immediate upward turn of the CBS profit graph when Paul bounced back to Number One in the States with 'Coming Up', aided by a promotional video featuring him in various guises as every member of a band. This was an apt taster for the maiden CBS album, *McCartney II*, which returned to his solo debut's homespun and virtual one-man-band ethos.

Such contrivances were not uncommon from the late 1970s. Jon Anderson of Yes had scored in the UK album Top 40 with *Olias Of Sunhollow* in 1976 – while Eddy Grant, former linchpin of The Equals, was to do likewise with 1981's *Can't Get Enough*. Issued, like *McCartney II*, in 1980, the green sleeve of Steve Winwood's *Arc Of A Diver* was as much of a fixture in student halls of residence as Che Guevara's mug had been years earlier. However, it spread out of the campuses and into *Billboard*'s Top Five, and, less instantly, to Number 13 in Britain. As it was with Paul's latest, every note had been hand-woven by Winwood personally via multiple overdubbing in the privacy of the studio he'd had built on his country estate in the Cotswolds.

Winwood, Anderson, Grant and McCartney had each built up instrumental backing tracks using a lot of synthesizers and often adding drums last, when the rhythm had already been invested into a given number. Such methodology prompted antagonism from those who prized the exhilaration of the impromptu from flesh-and-blood musicians to the technical accuracy of a voice floating effortlessly over layers of treated sound.

They could bellyache all they liked – because McCartney left even *Arc Of A Diver* swallowing dust by sweeping straight to the top on both sides of the Atlantic. It was a kick up the backside for John Lennon too, who grinned at his own vexation when hearing himself humming 'Coming Up' when turning a thoughtful steering wheel. Next, a personal assistant was ordered to bring him a copy of *McCartney II*. That it was such a vast improvement on the "garbage"[3] of *Back To The Egg*, reawoke in John the old striving for one-upmanship, and was among factors that spurred a return to the studio to make his first album since reuniting with Yoko in 1975 and becoming her reclusive "househusband".

The resulting husband-and-wife effort, *Double Fantasy*, could almost be filed under "Easy Listening", but its '(Just Like) Starting Over' sold well, and, of more personal import, Paul liked 'Beautiful Boy (Darling Boy)' – track seven, side one – enough to include it among his eight choices when a "castaway" on BBC Radio Four's *Desert Island Discs* in 1982.

This lullaby to the Lennons' only child – and the album from whence it came – had been bequeathed with a "beautiful sadness" because, on 8 December 1980, two months after his 40th birthday, John Lennon had been shot dead on a New York pavement by a "fan" who was Beatle-crazy in the most clinical sense. Like it was with President Kennedy and, in 1977, Elvis Presley, everyone remembers the moment they heard.

In Britain, where we'd been asleep, the morning papers told us nothing – though it seemed to be the only item of news on the radio. By the afternoon, estate agents were wondering who'd be doing the probate assessment; publishers were liaising with biographers; hack composers were working on tribute songs and record moguls were contemplating what tracks by Lennon or associated with him they were entitled to rush-release. Under the editorial lash, pressured denizens of the media cobbled together hasty obituaries and *Help!* was screened in place of scheduled prime-time programmes on BBC1.

Accosted by a television camera crew and a stick-mike thrust at his mouth, Paul, almost at a loss for words, had uttered "It's a drag" and mentioned that he would carry on as intended with a day's work at a studio desk. On the printed page the next day, it seemed too blithely fatalistic, but McCartney was a shaken and downcast man, feeling his anguish all the more sharply for assuming that there'd always be another chance for him and John to talk, face each other with guitars in an arena of armchairs and continue to bridge the self-created abyss that, in recent years, they had become more and more willing to cross. What with Wings in abeyance and John back in circulation again, the notion of Lennon–McCartney – as opposed to Lennon and McCartney – hadn't been completely out of the question.

John's death was both an end and a beginning, simultaneously the most public last gasp and the ricochet of a starting pistol for a qualified rebirth of the Swinging Sixties. Financially, that turbulent decade's principal icons reaped indirect benefits from the tragedy through, say, increases in the already vast amounts of money being poured – mostly by American and Japanese visitors – into the English Tourist Board's coffers for twice-daily guided Beatle tours round London and Liverpool to such golgothas as the Abbey Road zebra crossing and 20 Forthlin Road, which the National Trust was to purchase as a building of historic interest.

Similar tourist facilities were in force in Hamburg – though some old haunts were recognisable only by their names. The Kaiserkeller, for example, was thriving as a transvestite hang-out, but the Top Ten had long gone – as had some of the old faces such as Star-Club proprietor Manfred Weissleder and, also taken a few months before Lennon's slaying, Bert Kaempfert, who had suffered a fatal coronary when on holiday in Spain.

Horst Fascher was still very much at large as an eminence at a Star-Club with a facade just like the old one, but located away from a Grosse Freiheit that was less open-minded about human frailty and the temptations of the flesh as it had been before its brothels were put under government licence, turning their employees into what could be described technically as civil servants with all the attendant by-the-book correctitude.

However embarrassed the mention of its red-light districts in official guidebooks, Hamburg was now displaying pride in its cradling of The Beatles via honorific plaques on significant Reeperbahn walls, and a statue of John Lennon that was unveiled by Fascher, whose affinity to the slain Beatle's birthplace had been strengthened by an espousal to the daughter of Merseybeat musician Faron of Faron's Flamingos, and the launching of their son into life with the name "Rory" – as in "Rory Storm". Horst would be conquering the desolation of the baby's cot death in 1992 when, less than a year later, hell's magnet pulled him down again when a daughter by his next wife died from a heart condition despite surgery by specialists flown in from New York by his old mate, Paul McCartney.

By then, Horst had become a wanted guest at the huge "Beatle Conventions" that are still annual events in cities throughout the globe. For many attending these celebrations – including John Lennon's killer – The Beatles became a craving, almost a religion. Beyond just fitting a few extra shelves to accommodate more accumulated records and memorabilia, and combing thinning hair in a Moptop, certain fans have been known to make a start on the canons of unconnected acts simply because they recorded on the same labels as The Beatles, and holiday in a different foreign country every year just to seek out and buy up Beatle discs issued with an alien label and matrix number, and, possibly, an additional second of reverberation on the closing major sixth of 'She Loves You'.

Certainly, an element of posthumous Beatlemania helped propel 'All Those Years Ago', a vinyl salaam to Lennon by George Harrison, high up international Top 20s. A further incentive for buyers was the superimposed presence of McCartney and Wings, such as they were, who'd added their bits when the unmixed tape arrived from George's Oxfordshire mansion.

For three months, on and off, Paul and the others had been at George Martin's studio complex on Montserrat, in the distant Carribean, working on 18 tracks from which to pick and choose for *Tug Of War*, an album that turned out to be the follow-up to *McCartney II* rather than the now-disintegrating Wings's *Back To The Egg*.

"It was really like going back to Abbey Road," surmised Martin while work was in progress. "We've been working very closely on trying not just to get the songs done, but the ideas behind the songs as well, so that we're playing about with sound, trying to create something new. We've got lots of different instruments on the thing. We used Paddy Maloney of The Chieftains [on uilleann pipes and tin whistle] on one track, and pan-pipes on another."[4]

Steve Holly and Laurence Juber had had nothing to do as Paul called on more renowned if disparate helpmates such as Eric Stewart of 10cc, rockabilly legend Carl Perkins, drummer Dave Mattacks, in and out of Fairport Convention since 1969, and Stanley Clarke, every jazz-rock clever-dick's notion of bass-playing splendour. The sessions were notable too for an artistic reunion with not only George Martin as producer, but also Ringo Starr, fresh from *Stop And Smell The Roses*, an LP with a more pronounced "famous cast of thousands" approach.

To this, Paul had donated the title track and catchy 'Attention', but had decided to cling onto another composition, 'Take It Away', considering that "I didn't think was very Ringo"[5]. Instead, it was the opening track and the fourth of no less than six singles from *Tug Of War* – which went the chartbusting way of *McCartney II*, when released in April 1982. Among other highlights were 'Here Today' – a more piquant tribute to Lennon than singalong 'All Those Years Ago' – and 1982's 'Ebony And Ivory', a duet with Stevie Wonder, which, issued on 45, was another double-first in Britain and North America.

For those who derive deep and lasting pleasure from studying chart statistics, one characteristic of the 1980s was a contagious rash of teaming-ups, some of them very unlikely – none more so than that of Johnnie Ray-era singer Rosemary Clooney and psychotic Los Angeles busker Wild Man Fischer with 1986's 'It's A Hard Business'.

Three years earlier, Cliff Richard had managed a Top Ten strike with Phil Everly. Not raising eyebrows either were alliances by Kenny Rogers and Tammy Wynette, and Queen and David Bowie, but also scrambling up Top Tens in the 1980s would be a Christmas 45 by David Bowie and Bing Crosby, and a Number One reprise of Gene Pitney's 'Something's Gotten Hold Of My Heart' by Pitney himself and crypto-punk vocalist Marc Almond. We Britons had been stunned too to notice gnarled Joe Cocker at Number One in the States with 'Up Where We Belong' and fresh-faced C&W star Jennifer Warnes, not to mention Suzi Quatro and Reg Presley's revamp of 'Wild Thing' for the disco floor; Dave Dee's second 'Zabadak!' with Klaus und Klaus, a German comedy duo – and Van Morrison recording an entire album with The Chieftains, leading ambassadors of Irish folk music.

Morrison and Cliff Richard climbed sufficiently high in the Top 40 to warrant a *Top Of The Pops* slot in December 1989; Van – on the show for the first time since 'Here Comes The Night' with Them – trading perspicatory lines with tall and tanned and young and lovely Cliff. The boy from Hertfordshire was lovely, granted, but Van, to whom nature had been as harsh as it had to Joe Cocker, stood his ground without looking out of place on the televisual flagship of the mainstream pop he thought he'd left behind long ago.

Paul McCartney, however, enjoyed a ten-year singles chart run from 1980 as rich as any thus far – though, after 'Ebony And Ivory' and 'Take It Away', 'Tug Of War' struggled wretchedly to Number 53 in Britain and nowhere in the Hot 100. However, the final 45 of 1982, 'The Girl Is Mine' cracked the UK Top Ten without effort, and nearly went all the way in the USA.

Whereas the 'Ebony And Ivory' liaison had been instigated by Paul, he himself had been solicited by Michael Jackson who, like Wonder, was a former Tamla-Motown child star. Now chronologically adult, he had been in the throes of recording the celebrated *Thriller* in Los Angeles. Paul was among several well-known guest musicians, and his cameo as jovial voice-of-experience to Michael's cheeky young shaver on 'The Girl Is Mine' was the radio-friendly antithesis of Hammer House Of Horror mainstay Vincent Price's as the more agreeable title song's undead, blood-lusting lurker-in-the-night with a rap – about "grizzly ghouls", "hounds of hell" and so forth – that dissolves into maniacal chuckling.

If Price received a fee for his services, McCartney was paid in kind when Jackson pitched in on 'Say Say Say' from 1983's *Pipes of Peace*, Paul's third post-Wings album. It also contained a title track that would be its maker's commercial apotheosis in Britain during the 1980s as 'Mull Of Kintyre' had been in the previous decade. A Yuletide Number One that lingered in the Top 50 for three months, it was helped on its way by a video that re-enacted the mythical and sociable seasonal encounter in No Man's Land between British and German soldiers in World War I. Nevertheless, as George Harrison's 'Isn't It A Pity' – when covered by Dana, a pretty colleen from Londonderry – had been aligned to the Troubles in Ulster, so 'Pipes Of Peace' was to the siting of US cruise missiles on Greenham Common RAF base and the arrival of women with camping equipment from all walks of life to stage a passive protest that continued into the 1990s. While she did not participate, Linda McCartney never failed to send her sisters-in-spirit an annual Christmas hamper from Harrods.

Outside the Knightsbridge department store on the very December day that 'Pipes Of Peace' made its chart debut, an IRA bomb killed six and maimed many more. No one wrote a song about that.

Yeah, well...the previous month, the critics had laid into the album. Surely *Melody Maker* had mistaken *Pipes Of Peace* for *Double Fantasy*, calling it "congratulatory self-righteous" and "slushy"[6] – while the *NME* weighed in with "a tired, dull and empty collection of quasi-funk and gooey rock arrangements"[7]. In retrospect, some of the tracks were rather in-one-ear-and-out-the-other, but, on the whole, it was pleasant enough, even if the stand-out numbers were its two singles.

The first of these, 'Say Say Say', Michael Jackson's returning of the *Thriller* favour, had suffered poor reviews too, but the public thought otherwise, and it shifted millions. It helped that Jackson was still basking in the afterglow of *Thriller* to the degree that even a video about the making of the Grammy-winning album precipitated stampedes into the megastores the minute their glass doors opened.

George Harrison judged *The Making Of Michael Jackson's Thriller* "the squarest thing I've ever seen," adding, "It was a bit off the way Michael bought up our old catalogue when he knew Paul was also bidding. He was supposed to be Paul's mate."[8]

The Beatles portfolio was to become Jackson's property for a down payment of nearly £31 million ($50 million), more than McCartney could afford, when ATV, its previous publishers, were open to offers for this and other bodies of work in 1986. Until then, the ex-Beatle and the superstar 16 years his junior had, indeed, been "mates", renting and watching cartoons like *Dumbo* and *Bambi* whenever Paul visited Michael's Never Never Land ranch in California. When sampling the McCartney's hospitality in Sussex, Jackson had tagged along when the family were invited to lunch by Adam Faith on his farm near Tunbridge Wells. Michael spent much of the time kicking a football about with the children, but over coffee, he'd asked his host, then writer of a weekly financial column, "Faith In The City", in a national newspaper, about how he should invest the fortunes he was earning. Faith suggested music publishing. "The rest is history," chuckled Adam, "Paul says I'm responsible for Jackson buying the rights to The Beatles' music, and then selling them on. He'd snatched them from under Paul's nose."[9]

Neither was McCartney best pleased about how 1984's self-financed and feature-length *Give My Regards To Broad Street* film was received. The initial shard of inspiration for this "musical fantasy drama" had cut him more than two years earlier during an otherwise tedious stop-start drive into rush-hour London. With a screenplay by Paul himself, the interlocking theme was a world-class pop star's search for missing master tapes for an album. This was riddled with *Magical Mystery Tour*-ish sketches in locations ranging from a churchyard to an expensive reconstruction of New Brighton's grand Tower Brighton – which had crumbled in a haze of powdered plaster in 1970. There were also musical interludes of which the majority were refashionings of Beatles and Wings favourites – though 'No More Lonely Nights', an opus fresh off the assembly-line, was the attendant hit single.

Ringo Starr would have nothing to do with the resuscitations of 'Eleanor Rigby', 'The Long And Winding Road' *et al*, but was amenable to providing a romantic undercurrent via his on-screen courtship of his real-life second wife, Barbara, who played "this gorgeous girl reporter from a music paper. Falling in love with your own wife isn't as easy as it looks."[10] Paul also doled out parts to Linda, George Martin and more recent familiars such as Tracey Ullman, a comedy actress who was to take a couple of pot-shots at the charts – and Welsh guitarist Dave Edmunds, who'd been more convincing as the monosyllabic "Alex" in *Stardust*, a 1973 sex-drugs-and-rock 'n' roll flick that was as imbued with tough realism as *Give My Regards To Broad Street* wasn't.

Throughout the six months of shooting, Paul stayed worries about the consequence as director Andros Eraminondas – no, I'd never heard of him either – guided and tempered his endlessly inventive paymaster's designations that, to outsiders, seemed as rash as a good half of *Magical Mystery Tour* had been. Nevertheless, throughout the interminable running of each celluloid mile, McCartney had been impressive for his learned recommendations about rhythm and pacing.

Yet, determined not to like it, certain reviewers looked on jadedly as flash-bulbs floodlit McCartney's anxious entrances to its several premières. While exchanging smirks at each other's cleverness, it was the bane of such people's existence that they had to write about a comparative amateur who was doing something they couldn't do. Paul was such an obvious sitting duck that they felt entitled to claim they'd lost the thread of the plot through scenes they felt should have been rigorously scissored, not laugh at things meant to be funny, snigger during "serious" parts and play safe by concluding that *Give My Regards To Broad Street* was an egocentric caper with precedents in, say, 1969's obscurer and even more self-indulgent *Can Hieronymous Merkin Ever Forgive Mercy Humppe And Find True Happiness*, the brain-child of Anthony Newley, an inverse of McCartney in that he was an actor who had become a singing composer.

*Variety*, the *Bible* and *Yellow Pages* of the latest cinema releases, shoved aside *Give My Regards To Broad Street* as "characterless, bloodless and pointless"[11]. As they always were, journals local to the towns where it was distributed were kinder, albeit while homing in less on the storyline than the spectacular visual effects that enhanced what was not so much in the tradition of *A Hard Day's Night* – or even *Magical Mystery Tour* in the end – as *Pop Gear, Just For You* and other of those conveyor-belt mid-1960s B-features of diversified and mimed pop ephemera connected by vacuous narrative. That was fine by me, though I preferred McCartney's more bite-sized videos for his singles, especially when he adhered to straightforward synchronisation with a musical performance, rather than project himself – or others – into dramatic situations.

The latter was to be the case with 'Only Love Remains', the principal ballad on his next album, *Press To Play*, which was centred on two elderly actors playing some dingy couple still in love after maybe half a century of wedlock: Darby and Joan who used to be Jack and Jill.

Three years before, McCartney had addressed himself to Jack, Jill and other infant video-watchers with *Rupert And The Frog Song*, 25 minutes dominated by one of the *Daily Express* cartoon character's adventures with voiceovers by sit-com shellbacks Windsor Davis and June Whitfield plus Paul himself, who'd owned the film rights to the checked-trousered bruin since 1970.

He gave *Rupert And The Frog Song* the best possible chance by ensuring it was second-billed to *Give My Regards To Broad Street*, and being a talking head, buoyant with sentiment, on the earlier Channel Four documentary, *The Rupert Bear Story*. Just as Paul's first solo album had beaten *Sentimental Journey* in the battle for chart placings in 1970, so it was in microcosm 14 years on when *Rupert And The Frog Song* defied all comers when both it and the lumped-together episodes of *Thomas The Tank Engine And Friends* – narrated by Ringo – were among BAFTA nominees as 1985's "Best Animated Short Film". Proving what traditionalists toddlers are, it also topped the video charts the previous Christmas. Into the bargain, the soundtrack's principal composition, 'We All Stand Together', sung by the animated frogs, had been high in the UK Top Ten.

Was there no end to this man's talent? He popped up again at Wembley Stadium that summer, emoting a gremlin-ridden 'Let It Be' to his own piano-playing as satellite-linked Live Aid approached its climax. Then he joined the assembled cast for a finale in which he and Pete Townshend bore organiser Bob Geldof on their shoulders.

Geldof was to be knighted for his charitable efforts. Another milestone along rock's road to respectability was the heir to the throne's Prince's Trust Tenth Birthday Gala in June 1986. Paul gave 'em 'I Saw Her Standing There' and 'Long Tall Sally' prior to closing the show by leading an omnes fortissimo 'Get Back'. A handshake from Prince Charles afterwards had less personal significance to McCartney than the fact that he'd just completed his first formal appearance in an indoor venue since Wings's last flap at Hammersmith Odeon in 1979.

If his main spot had been as nostalgic in its way as Gerry And The Pacemakers on the chicken-in-a-basket trail, in terms of audience response, he'd held his own amid Me-generation entertainers like Bryan Adams, Paul Young and, with their whizz-kid singing bass player, Level 42, not to mention Tina Turner, Eric Clapton, the ubiquitous Elton John and all the other old stagers.

Like them, he couldn't take Top 40 exploits for granted anymore, but *Press To Play* hovered round the middle of most international Top 30s, and the singles made token showings in some charts, even drippy 'Only Love Remains' after it filled Paul's entire slot on 1986's *Royal Variety Command Performance*.

He had better luck both critically and commercially – in Britain certainly – with 1987's *All The Best*, his second reassemblage of selected Wings and solo items – including the hitherto-unreleased 'Waterspout' and, of more resonance, 'Once Upon A Long Ago', the UK Top Ten single that was launched a week after the album.

Before the month was out, a similar package, Matt Monro's *By Request* – with a brief tribute by Paul in its accompanying booklet – was in the shops too. Following its use in the soundtrack of *Good Morning Vietnam* that same year, Them's 'Baby Please Don't Go' leapt out of the small screen with a voiceover extolling the virtues of a new make of Peugeot. It would have been foolish not to have put it out as a CD single. Monro, McCartney and Them were the tip of a huge iceberg. With repackaging factories in full production by then, it made as much sense for Monro, Van Morrison – and McCartney when he got round to it again – to include in onstage set-list hits maybe more than 30 years old as well as excerpts from the most recent album.

As commodity began to assume more absolute sway over creativity, the history of pop would be seized upon as an avenue for shifting records beyond simply getting information about compilations inserted in retailer catalogues. Saturation television commercials could hoick up sales from tens of thousands to a quarter of a million a year in the UK alone. In 1987, Steve Winwood's *Chronicles* would see action in the Christmas charts against *All The Best* and other "best of" and "greatest hits" offerings by Van Morrison, George Harrison and Bryan Ferry.

No matter how it was tarted up – as a 12in megamix or pressed on polkadot vinyl – the pop single had become a loss leader by then, a throwaway incentive for adults to buy an album on one of these new-fangled compact discs – on which you could almost make out the dandruff falling from George Harrison's hair on 'My Sweet Lord'. Teenagers, you see were no longer pop's most courted customers in the late 1980s, having been outmanoeuvred by their Swinging Sixties parents. Young marrieds too had sated their appetites for novelty, going no further than buying documentary exhumations of, say, a ragged gospel singalong from 1956 by the "Million Dollar Quartet" of Jerry Lee Lewis, Johnny Cash, Carl Perkins and Elvis Presley – or *Alive She Cried*, a concert by The Doors, which had spent weeks in the UK Top 40 in 1983.

These triumphs of repackaging were to be gilded by younger artists making practical acknowledgement of the lasting influence of old campaigners by contributing to tribute albums of elaborations – and just plain copies – of chosen examples from the portfolios of Syd Barrett, Captain Beefheart, Peter Green and like unforgotten heroes. Most of these were unsolicited, and The Beatles had no control whatsoever over 1988's *Sgt Pepper Knew My Father* on which several new acts depped for the Lonely Hearts Club Band – with Billy Bragg's 'She's Leaving Home' and Wet Wet Wet's 'With A Little Help From My Friends' as its chart-topping double A-side.

There'd be more fleeting *Top Of The Pops* visitations – either on video or in the chicken-necked flesh – with their latest releases by such spring chickens as The Rolling Stones, The Kinks and, a week before his sudden death in 1989, Roy Orbison. Cliff Richard too had shown that he wasn't all *Summer Holiday* and 'Congratulations' by revamping his musical aspirations and, with the aid of sprightlier minds than EMI house producer Norrie Paramor's, arriving in the late 1980s more popular than ever. Indeed, his 'Mistletoe And Wine', out in time for the festive season, was 1988's biggest-selling British single.

As the millennium crept closer, Paul McCartney would also score to a diminishing degree, not so much with songs he could have written in his sleep, but through a combination of stubbornly treading steep and rugged pathways and maintaining a lingering hip sensibility, often justifying the words of John McNally of The Searchers: "You don't have to be young to make good records."[12]

Even on "Sounds Of The Sixties" nights in the most dismal working men's club, The Searchers, The Troggs, Dave Berry and those of corresponding vintage would lure a strikingly young crowd by counterpoising contemporary offerings with the old showstoppers. After disappearing for years, neither was it laughable for others who'd travelled an unquiet journey to middle life to embark on sell-out trans-continental tours as did Paul Simon, Fleetwood Mac, The Grateful Dead, Leonard Cohen – and, after a decade away, Paul McCartney.

# 17  "Don't Get Around Much Anymore"

"We used to play the same kind of music, American R&B, and we're both from the North. We have the same accent, the same sense of humour."

– *Eric Stewart*[1]

As her distant step-brother readied himself for what amounted to his first tour outside the context of a group, the roar of the crowd seemed far away as Ruth McCartney toiled as a jobbing songwriter. Living in New South Wales in the early 1980s, she teamed up with vocalist John Farnham. Her confidence boosted when their 'New Blood' for Tina Cross reached the Australian Top 20 and Ruth relocated to Los Angeles to better ply her wares before more prestigious customers – among them Randy Crawford for whom she co-wrote 'Cigarette In The Rain', a hit in Scandinavia, South Africa and Italy as well as *Billboard*'s R&B chart.

Paul too had found a compatible collaborator. A telephone call had instigated a link-up with one who he thought initially might be, if not a Lennon, at least another Denny Laine.

Present on guitar and backing vocals in *Tug Of War* and *Pipes Of Peace*, Eric Stewart had also been evident in the videos to the singles 'Take it Away' and 'So Bad', and in *Give My Regards To Broad Street*. He was a Mancunian who'd been almost as much the chief public image of Wayne Fontana And The Mindbenders as Wayne himself. After Fontana and the group went their separate ways in 1965, each blaming the other for declining chart fortunes, the first face you were drawn to in most Mindbinders publicity photographs was that of Eric, lead singer on their first – and most far-reaching – single, 'A Groovy Kind Of Love'. He was also the acephalous outfit's chief creative pivot, though before calling it a day at the Liverpool Empire, on 20 November 1968, this final line-up included Graham Gouldman, one of the great enigmas of British beat: composer of Top 20 strikes for The Yardbirds, Hollies, Herman's Hermits, Dave Berry, Wayne Fontana and Jeff Beck, home and abroad, but unable to get anywhere with his own combo, The Mockingbirds.

While The Mindbenders were no more, Gouldman and Stewart remained business partners. Graham's composing royalties and Eric's solitary hit, 'Neanderthal Man', as one of Hotlegs with ex-Mockingbirds, Kevin Godley and Lol Creme, amassed sufficient capital for the expansion of their Strawberry Studio project, then humbly situated about a Stockport hi-fi shop. Among their clients was Mike McCartney for 1974's *McGear* LP, and it was during these sessions that Stewart and Mike's brother spoke for the first time since The Beatles and Wayne Fontana *et al* had brushed against each other in some backstage corridor in nineteen-sixty-forget-about-it.

Strawberry had already produced a world-class act in 10cc, ie Eric, Graham, Lol and Kevin. Signed to Jonathan King's UK label, the four had had their first chart-topper with 1973's 'Rubber Bullets', a story-in-song of an ill-advised dance at the local county gaol that led to an uprising so beyond control that the governor sent for fire-armed reinforcements. Like its Top Ten predecessor, 'Donna', 'Rubber Bullets' was, even with sociological implications and lines like "it's a shame those slugs ain't real" and "blood will flow to set you free", a borderline comedy disc with neo-"baby" lead singing and deep "fool" bass second vocal.

The laughs came harder in such as 1976's 'I'm Mandy Fly Me' – in which the first-person narrator ended up in the drink via the nosediving of a passenger jet. The charming titular air hostess not only saves him, but seems to walk on the waves to render the kiss of life "just like the girl in Dr No" on top of providing – no, anticipating – every comfort during the flight. Unconscious, he is picked up by the coastguard, but of Mandy, there is no sign. Studying her face on the airline's travel poster shortly afterwards he debates whether it had all been a crazy dream, but, if it had, how come he lived to tell the tale?

As Stewart slung in rhymes, chord changes and 'I'm Mandy Fly Me'-esque twists to the plot as he and McCartney had pieced together possibilities for what became *Press To Play*, the latter considered that he might have procured a Lennon rather than a Laine after all as their liaison first blossomed with 'Stranglehold'. Co-writer of five further selected tracks, an educated guess says that Eric stuck his oar in most obviously in lines like "I think we skip the preamble" and "I'll be happy to lay low, inevitably bound" from 'Stranglehold' or "Ears twitch like a dog breaking eggs in a dish" in 'However Absurd' plus references in 'Move Over Busker' to Mae West and "Nell Gwyn and her oranges" and further instances of a lyricism more peculiar to the wordier 10cc than Wings.

Musically, *Press To Play* was proficient but not adventurous. Many of the lodged conventions of songwriting methodology since the beat boom were, however, thrust aside when McCartney next bonded with Elvis Costello, one of the most successful post-pub rock ambassadors to get anywhere in North America. A series of inspired publicity stunts – and Costello's borrowing of Roy Orbison's horn-rimmed and uncommunicative stage persona – had assisted the passage of his first album, 1977's *My Aim Is True*, and early singles into the UK charts. Backed by The Attractions, he touched a commercial zenith in 1979 with *Armed Forces* as his biggest US seller, and its 'Oliver's Army' spin-off at a domestic Number Two.

For such a prolific and "covered" songwriter, it was perhaps odd that he had since returned to the UK singles Top Ten only with items penned by others, ie Sam And Dave's 'I Can't Stand Up For

Falling Down' (from 1980's *Get Happy*) and 'A Good Year For The Roses', a C&W morosity from the following year's *Almost Blue*. Both were examples of Costello's frequent ventures into unexpected musical areas. A more extreme one was to be 1993's *The Juliet Letters* with The Brodsky Quartet – for which he reverted to his given name, Declan McManus.

One of McManus–Costello's finest recent songs had been 1988's 'The Comedians' for role model Roy Orbison in which the Big O conducted himself with shocked dignity in the teeth of a dirty trick at a funfair whereby he was left dangling all night at the top of a ferris wheel by its operator. The latter's donkey-jacketed virility had, apparently, bewitched Roy's grounded harpy of a girlfriend: "not just that you're never coming back to me/It's just the bitter way that I was told."

Five years earlier, Costello's 'Shipbuilding', penned with guitarist Clive Langer, had been a UK Top 30 entry for Robert Wyatt. In it, an unemployed shipwright longs for the dockyards to open, even though he deplores the purpose of the war vessels – destined for Mrs Thatcher's self-glorifying Falklands conflict – that form his livelihood. Written with Wyatt's "ordinary geezer" voice in mind, it was, said Langer, "the saddest, most brilliant thing I've ever been involved with"[2].

That 33-year-old Costello had finished his formal education in Liverpool – and spent many previous school holidays with relations there – may have lent an element to 'Shipbuilding' that might have been absent had he been similarly connected to Basingstoke or Market Harborough. Elvis was of Irish stock too – another plus point for McCartney, who, a few months earlier, had sent a wreath shaped like a Celtic cross to the funeral of Eamonn Andrews, genial Dublin-born host of both *This Is Your Life* and the children's hour evergreen, *Crackerjack*.

In common with Paul too, Elvis's father was a musician – though, unlike Jim McCartney, Ross McManus had gone fully professional, even gaining a recording deal both as singer with Joe

Loss and his Orchestra and in his own right, albeit with such as an LP of Elvis Presley hits for the Golden Guinea budget label.

Offering hip credibility too, Costello was just what unfashionable McCartney needed, and, after perhaps initial slight misgivings, the two buckled down to "writing a bunch of really good songs," smiled Elvis. "A couple have stuck around in my repertoire, 'So Like Candy' and 'That Day Is Done', which is one that I'm fond of. It was great working with him. Of course it was. I was thrilled."[3]

Five hours a day in a room above Paul's studio in Sussex resulted in 'Back On My Feet' – the B-side of 'Once Upon A Long Ago' – and then items for Paul's *Flowers In The Dirt* and Elvis's *Spike*, albums with respective spin-off singles of which Costello's 'Veronica' figured in the US Hot 100 and the British Top 40.

As it had been when John and Paul had been working together, "his voice is so high so I would end up below him," observed Elvis, "which is a relationship he was familiar with."[3] Moreover, the general thrust of the McCartney–McManus output was the tempering of an abrasive edge with attractive tunes. 'My Brave Face' – a man's bitter freedom from his woman – just about reached the UK Top 20 for Paul – with follow-up 'This One' touching exactly the same apogee – Number 18 – but barely troubling the Hot 100 where 'My Brave Face' had got a look in at Number 25.

These so-so market volleys were incidental to *Flowers In The Dirt* returning McCartney to the top of all manner of album lists, and the ten months of the global tour (including six nights in Tokyo where all had been forgiven) earning an award from a US financial journal as the highest grossing such excursion of 1990 – with a stop in Rio de Janeiro breaking the world attendance record for a pop concert with a paying audience.

Spanning nearly every familiar trackway of Paul's career from 'Twenty Flight Rock' of Quarry Men vintage to 'My Brave Face', he was backed by quite a motley crew consisting of Linda, guitarist

Robbie McIntosh – who'd quit The Pretenders during sessions for a 1986 album – keyboard player and former PE teacher Paul Wickens, drummer Chris Whitten – who'd been with Wickens in a group led by self-styled "pagan rock 'n' roller" Julian Cope – and general factotum Hamish Stuart, founder member of The Average White Band.[4] They were a workmanlike and horn-laden Scottish soul outfit whose focus on the North American market had paid off with a US Number One, 'Pick Up The Pieces', in 1974 and further hits until disbandment in 1982, and Stuart's subsequent earning of credits on albums by, amongst others, Chaka Khan, Melissa Manchester and Adam Faith's managerial and production client, Leo Sayer, and as creator of hit songs for such as Diana Ross and The Temptations.

Stuart picked guitar very prettily on quasi-traditional 'All My Trials', an in-concert single captured in Milan – apparently, the only occasion it was performed by McCartney during this tour, apart from plugs on various TV magazines. In 1989, the number also known as 'All My Sorrows' was – like George Harrison's contemporaneous revival of another skiffle weepie, 'Nobody's Child' – a throwback to days when it slowed things down for The Quarry Men in ping-pong youth clubs, with mordant verses about "you know you're daddy is bound to die" and "carefree lovers down country lanes/Don't know my grief, can't feel my pain". How could Paul have been aware then that the most meaningful phrase for him was to be "my love has gone, left me behind", a parting not from choice, but at death's behest?

McCartney had confessed to Barry Miles that a chord change in 'I'll Get You', B-side of 1963's 'She Loves You', had been purloined from Joan Baez's treatment of 'All My Trials'. From time immemorial, more direct plundering of music in the public domain has been an intermittent ploy of British pop. One potent advantage is that publishers can cream off royalties. Well, who else ought to get them? God? Such mercenary rewards were frequently deserved. In 1963, there was an imaginative rocking-up of the Cornish Floral

Dance by The Eagles, a Bristolian beat group, and the Liverpool children's play rhyme "Johnny Todd" had been transformed most effectively by the late Fritz Spiegl into the theme tune for BBC television's *Z-Cars*. 1970 brought Traffic's daring version of "John Barleycorn" – thought more "authentic" than that of Steeleye Span. In its wake came the likes of the Nashville Teens's spooky 'Widecombe Fair' and Alan Price's 'Trimdon Grange Explosion', written in 1892 as a "whip-around" ditty to gather collections for victims of a County Durham mining disaster.

As well as filling one side of a single, Paul's 'All My Trials' utilised time on *Tripping The Light Fantastic*, a triple-album that was the quaint vinyl souvenir of the round-the-world expedition. Another by-product was the limited-edition *Unplugged: The Official Bootleg* – the sort of thing everyone-who-was-anyone was doing then – from one of the tour's post-scripts – an acoustic recital after the ticket-holders shuffled in from the February chill to the relatively downhome ambience of Limehouse Studios amid London's dockland wharfs. Some would see themselves in a consequent *MTV* broadcast, the first one to be issued on a record.

Nevertheless, no matter how endearing McCartney's wheezing mouth-organ – perhaps his first and most subtle attempt to checkmate the departed John's every artistic move – is on 'That Would Be Something' or how right-on his 'Ebony And Ivory' from behind the electric piano, the loudest ovations throughout these latest rounds of public displays would always be for the many unrevised Beatles selections. Audiences also clapped hard for Paul's olde tyme rock 'n' roll flings – which, in 1989 and 1990, paid homage to Fats Domino as well as Eddie Cochran.

Both Cochran's 'Twenty Flight Rock' and Domino's 'Ain't That A Shame' had just been recorded by Paul[5] among items of similar vintage for *Choba B CCCP* (translated as "Back In The USSR"), an initially Russia-only album of favourite non-originals dating from between Hitler's invasion of the Soviet Republic in 1941 and The Beatles' final season at the Star-Club in his defeated Germany.

From a pool of suitably rough-and-ready musicians, whether Nick Garvey from The Motors or Mick Green of a Pirates reconstituted without Johnny Kidd – and tracks ranging from 'Don't Get Around Much Anymore' (recorded in 1942 by co-writer Duke Ellington) to 1962's 'Bring It On Home To Me' from the catalogue of Sam Cooke, *Choba B CCCP* came out just before the Berlin Wall came down in 1989, and Checkpoint Charlie was rebuilt as a glass-towered conference centre. Perhaps McCartney had recognised that the impending opening up of the eastern bloc – East Germany, the Ukraine, Czechoslovakia and other previously *verboten* regions – would present a new world of possibilities. Few samples of western pop on disc had ever filtered beyond a Berlin where the partitioning of the Fatherland into two distinct cultures and political agendas was never more piquant; the flamboyance of the western Federal Republic contrasting like the Earth to the Moon with the grey Communist utilitarianism beyond the Wall.

With the establishment of a McDonald's fast-food outlet off Red Square not far away, it seemed an expedient exercise to fire a commercial boardside directly at consumers hitherto deprived of music from the very morning of post-war pop. Just as The Beatles' versions of 'Twist And Shout', 'Long Tall Sally', 'Money' *et al* were the only versions for anyone whose *entrée* to pop had been 'Please Please Me', so McCartney's would be of 13 set-works from the annals of classic rock for Russian record buyers until they came upon the originals – and, in the late 1980s, there seemed fat chance of that for a while. Besides, as David Bowie, Bryan Ferry, The Hollies – and John Lennon – were a handful of the many who'd indulged in entire albums of oldies already, why shouldn't Paul?

If nothing else, Paul sounded as if he enjoyed revisiting them. Worth mentioning here are Nick Garvey's memories of both his hand in *Choba B CCCP* and his impressions of its prime mover: "I went to a rehearsal place in Woolwich where Macca ran through and recorded several things with me on bass, him on guitar, Mickey Gallagher on piano and Terry Williams on drums. Linda was there too, but she didn't join in.

"Macca does have this ability to switch into performance mode. It was remarkable to watch it happen – the big smile, the whole thing... He was playing to us! He sang as if it was no trouble at all, though he could be a bit fey. He played too like it was easy as hell, and he knew exactly what he wanted from us, even if it was easy to get the impression that he likes to be in control, and that there's nobody around him to tell him if he's wrong. After all, he hadn't had the opportunity to live in the real world for over 30 years. He couldn't walk down the street because people bother him.

"Overall, I was knocked out by him. It was a lot of fun too. We did 'She's A Woman', all sorts of things. About three months later, I was called down to his studio in Sussex for a second day of recording. I noticed his old Hofner bass in there, with a set-list still stuck on the side. He himself proudly pointed out Bill Black's double-bass on 'Heartbreak Hotel' in the corner, and invited me to have a go on it.

"The line-up was like it was in Woolwich, but with Henry Spinetti – who I'd never met before then – on drums. We did all these old rock 'n' roll songs, most of them in one take with live vocals. There were just a few overdubs for backing vocals. Only three tracks I was on were used, but I got three hundred quid.

"The album was put out in a brown paper bag in Russia, and I thought that was that. However, it generated a certain amount of interest in the rest of the world, and about a year later it was released outside Russia. I wasn't expecting more money as I'd already received a session fee – so it was a real shock when a letter arrived explaining all this. The cheque inside had fallen to the carpet, and I imagined that it was for another 300 quid [$500] so I nearly had a heart attack when it was for £5,000 [$8,000]!"

Paul's reward for his generosity was meagre in hard financial terms in Russia itself, not because *Choba B CCCP* was a flop, far from it, but because – as he realised would be the case – the lump sum (with no performance royalties) he was paid was in roubles that could only be spent within the USSR. Yet he did his duty by the album by agreeing to a live phone-in (with attendant interpreter) on the BBC's Russian Service during a programme with a title that means "Granny's Chest". It was gratifying that more than 1,000 rang, but these were boiled down to 14 – at a cost of approximately £9 ($15) per minute – one of whom was a seven-year-old schoolgirl.

*A Hard Day's Night* came to Warsaw, and there'd been talk in 1966 of The Beatles crossing the Iron Curtain in person, but they had never been seen on a Russian stage, unlike so many British pop entertainers – including Paul in May 2003 – who have done so since 1989.

Ruth McCartney has been among them too. Pop is a business more riddled than most with chances-in-a-million, chaos theory and seeming trivialities that change everything. Dave Berry attributed his success in continental Europe to an arbitrary gesture with a cigarette butt someone had thrown onstage during his cobra-like act in a televised song festival in Belgium. On the other side of the same coin, PJ Proby's fall from grace was precipitated by his trousers splitting from knee to crotch during a second house at Luton Ritz. Brian Epstein turning up when a support group is valiantly over-running while backstage staff are trying to sober up the main attraction or a radio disc jockey flipping his lid over the B-side of a record and spinning it into the charts – perhaps a variable as unforeseen caused Ruth's self-penned debut album, *I Will Always Remember You*, to follow the footsteps of *Choba B CCCP* by climbing to Number One in *Komsomolkaya Pravda*, the closest you'd get in the USSR to *Record Retailer*.

Paul could wait until he felt like going there, but Ruth couldn't afford to keep the customers waiting, even though all proceeds from her trips to Russia had to be donated to charity until the rouble became an exchangeable currency. Nonetheless, she was well placed to recoup more than golden memories after the fall of communism via a lengthy trek that, in spring 1994, was to embrace reaches of Siberia so remote that they could only be reached by helicopter. When she landed in Salekhard, a fishing town within the Arctic Circle, the electricity turbines were so underpowered that there was no running water for the entire four days she was scheduled to work there – but that, as they often say, is showbusiness.

While Ruth brought the aura of a fresh sensation to Russia, Paul had dyed his greying hair black, having chosen not to go gently into that good night. At least most of it was still on his head – and so was George Harrison's, who, despite swearing that his 1982 album, *Gone Troppo*, had been his last, had pulled an unexpected stroke five years later with million-selling *Cloud Nine* and its singles – which included a US Number One, his first since 'Give Me Love'. Moreover, George's years away from the public at large had turned him too into the latest pop news – particularly now that he'd shaved off a scrappy middle-aged beard – for those young enough never to have heard much of him before.

A major factor in the reactivation of George's pop career was *Cloud Nine* producer Jeff Lynne, once leader of The Electric Light Orchestra, but now with a reputation for steering other faded stars back into the spotlight, notably Roy Orbison, one fifth of The Traveling Wilburys – an impermanent skiffle-like "supergroup" with George, Jeff, Bob Dylan and Tom Petty.

After the ill-starred Roy's fatal heart attack in December 1988, there was much speculation as to who would be his Wilbury replacement. In view of George's comment that "I'd join a band with John Lennon any day, but I wouldn't join a band with Paul McCartney", his "original mate in The Beatles"[6] wasn't in the running. Yet Paul expressed an unreciprocated wish to team up with George Harrison on the grounds that "George has been writing with Jeff Lynne; I've been writing with Elvis, so it's natural for me to want to write with George."[7] Well, it had been a long time since 'In Spite Of All The Danger'.

If there was yet no creative reunion, there were still companionable evenings in a bar or around a dining table – jokey reviling of each other like close friends do whenever they reminisce about the old days as Paul had done for a wider world on *Press To Play*'s 'Good Times Coming' with what I interpret as a veiled reference to two Institute schoolboys deciding on the spur of the moment to hitch-hike across Wales in the lost sunshine of 1958.

These days, it was common knowledge that Paul was prone to disguised nostalgic walkabouts on Merseyside, so much so that one had been mentioned in 1985's ITV sit-com, *The Brothers McGregor*. Apparently, Paul had dropped in at a club called the Blue Cockatoo, formerly the Coconut, for old times' sake. "That was where John Lennon first met Paul McCartney," Cyril McGregor, its resident singer, assured his solicitor. "Asked him for a dance. Used to be bloody dark in the Coconut."[8]

How delightful it was for the former Beatle to mingle anonymously among shoppers in a Wavertree precinct; in a pub garden on the Cheshire plain or browsing in a second-hand bookshop up Parliament Street. Unmolested by autograph hunters and worse, he was conducting himself as if he was a nobody, mooching about beneath an untroubled suburban sky. With the same blithe fatalism, he also chanced being seen by day in London too – pavement-tramping around St John's Wood, Chalk Farm and Ladbroke Grove; in a second-class train carriage to Waterloo; knocking back a quiet lunchtime pint somewhere in Soho; thumbing through scuffed wares in Notting Hill's Record And Tape Exchange; eating in a Camden Town café or taking the air in Regent's Park.

Back in Liverpool, he'd once surprised Tony Crane and Billy Kinsley of a still-functional Merseybeats by walking in on a session at their Amadeus studio in Everton. Luckily, it wasn't one for 'Heaven', a 1991 single by Kinsley and Pete Best.

Out on the streets again, Paul noticed that a Cavern had been reconstructed down Mathew Street next to Cavern Walks shopping mall. On the now-busy thoroughfare's opposite side stood the John

Lennon pub and, halfway up a wall, an Arthur Dooley statue of a madonna-like figure – "Mother Liverpool" – with a plaque beneath reading "Four Lads Who Shook The World", and one of them, like, flying away with wings. Get it?

Civic pride in The Beatles had been emphasised further in 1982 by naming four streets on a housing estate after each of the four most famous members – Paul McCartney Way, Ringo Starr Drive and so forth – in spite of one sniffy burgher's opposition "in the light of what went on in Hamburg and their use of filthy language."[9]

While *Backbeat* – a silver screen perspective on John, Paul, George and Pete in Hamburg – loomed on the horizon, "Beatle conventions" had been fixtures in cities throughout the world for years. Frequent attractions – especially when each August's Merseybeatle festival was on – at both the new Cavern in Mathew Street and the more authentic one in the Beatles museum on Albert Dock were groups whose *raison d'être* was re-enacting some phase of The Beatles' career from the enlistment of Ringo to the end of the Swinging Sixties. Others of their ilk paid homage to solely one Beatle as did Band On The Run, Hari Georgeson, Starrtime and the short-lived Working Class Heroes. By the mid-1990s, there'd be nigh on 200 such tribute bands in Britain alone, virtually all of them encumbered with a right-handed "Paul". The most accurate copycats were – and still are – The Bootleg Beatles, formed from the cast of the West End musical, *Beatlemania*.

While it was said that he procured one of the "Pauls" as a stand-in for a video shoot, McCartney was to raise an objection that, in *Backbeat*, "John" rather than his character sang 'Long Tall Sally', and seemed bemused generally that anyone should make a living impersonating The Beatles.

# 18 "Come Together"

> "If it moves, I can score it."
>
> – Carl Davis[1]

There are some entertainers who regard touring as absolute hell, but Paul McCartney isn't one of them. Within weeks of winding down from his turn-of-the-decade circuit of the planet, he was thinking aloud about doing it all again. Though it wasn't to happen until 1993, he ordered the wheels to crank into motion.

As expected, the next expedition was to be on hold until it could be tied in with an album and plethora of singles, and, when it was actually in motion, *Paul Is Live* (as opposed to *Paul Is Dead*), an in-concert package in time for Christmas. These products were to be in as many formats as the traffic would allow – 7- and 12in vinyl, cassette, picture sleeves, gatefold sleeves, CD, remixes and with or without posters, postcards, tour itinerary and bonus tracks. Such were the hidden costs for the truly dedicated, whether there from the beginning or *Flowers In The Dirt* latecomers, for whom every new McCartney release remains a special event.

The 1993 album, *Off The Ground*, was, however, less special than usual. It was telegraphed by 'Hope Of Deliverance', an instance of blinded-by-science production almost-but-not-quite smothering a mediocre song that died a death, even with Paul, Linda and the boys in the band miming it on *Top Of The Pops*. Though Liverpool poet Adrian Mitchell had been requested to give it and the rest of the *Off The Ground* libretto a once-over, 'Hope Of Deliverance' was a fair indication of what was to come in a collection that was unfettered by the objectivity of an Eric Stewart or Elvis Costello, apart from the latter's 'Mistress And Maid' – which sounded like a *Flowers In The Dirt* leftover – and a 'Lovers That Never Were' that was enjoyable enough, but not up to Costello's reading on his own *Mighty Like A Rose* in 1991.

Paul's animal rights protest number, 'Looking For Changes', was all very worthy too in its speaking up for the voiceless, but, both musically and lyrically, it was one that could have been shelved without much hardship. Yet 'Biker Like An Icon', the third single, did not bely Paul's description of it as "a good little rocky song"[2], though meaning did not take precedent over phonetics.

Perhaps the worst trauma an artist can suffer is a dream coming true. When you're as close as anyone can be to a pain-free existence, maybe there's not much left to say. Your dream became reality, and the feeling you had when you were young and struggling somehow becomes the new dream – more far-fetched than becoming rich and famous had ever been.

With no blues getting bluer, *Off The Ground* was the product of a satisfied mind. Polished and mostly unobjectionable, it was never expected to be astounding – by marginal McCartney enthusiasts anyway – but it sufficed because skillful arrangements and technological advances can help conceal ordinary-sounding songs in need of editing. It nudged the Top 20 in the USA where Beatlemania was always more virulent than anywhere else, and those afflicted bought Paul's records out of habit to complete the set like *Buffalo Bill* annuals. Over here, too many didn't want to like *Off The Ground*, especially during a period when Elvis Costello wasn't cool either, having strayed too far with *The Juliet Letters* from the punk rocker he'd never been.

Who remembered a time when either Costello or McCartney had been called a "genius"? Once upon a long ago, they might have possessed it, but the party line now was that it was soon exhausted. What's a genius anyway? Among the many blessed with that dubious accolade are Horst "A Walk In The Black Forest" Jankowski, Phil Spector, dart-throwing Jocky Wilson and the late Screaming Lord Sutch.

Never mind. As it had been in 1989, the press could slag off Paul's records; latter-day punks could denigrate him as one more bourgeois liberal with inert conservative tendencies and hippies disregard him as a fully paid-up subscriber to what Neil in BBC TV's *The Young Ones* sit-com called "the Breadhead Conspiracy", but there he was again, running through his best-loved songs for the people who loved them – and him – best of all in Melbourne Cricket Ground, Louisiana Superdome, Munich's Olympiahalle and further packed-out stadia designed originally for championship sport.

This time round, there were more Beatles numbers than ever from a portfolio that bulged with more crowd-pleasers than could be crammed into any evening with Paul McCartney, but ticket-holders understood, and were sad rather than angry if he didn't do their favourite. They'd seen it all before anyhow – him pop-eyed at the central microphone with a guitar or seated on a stage-left podium at a piano, the cynosure of perhaps a 100,000 eyes and maybe four sweaty spotlights. Having a high old time up there, he accommodated appropriate gestures and facial expressions as well as off-mike mouthings and momentary eye contacts that probably meant nothing, but made the heart of the recipient – or someone who imagined he or she was – feel like it would burst through its rib-cage.

As always, the mood was light, friendly, but what would have happened had the main set ended with politely brief clapping instead of the foot-stomping and howling approval that brought Paul back on for the encores of 'Band On The Run', 'I Saw Her Standing There' and, finally, everyone blasting up chorus after da-da chorus of 'Hey Jude'?

At last, he'd made a peace between his past and present situation. For form's sake, he stuck in tracks from whatever current album the onlookers may have heard or wouldn't ever hear between the timeless hits. Yet, however slickly predictable his stage show was becoming, he would prove to have much in common in his way with David Bowie, Jeff Beck, Van Morrison and other advocates of the artistic virtues of sweating over something new while Elton John, Phil Collins, Stevie Wonder and like Swinging Sixties contemporaries continued cranking out increasingly more run-of-the-mill albums.

Paul got into the swing of keeping you guessing what he'll be up to next by paying close attention to what made his now-teenage children and their friends groove nowadays. He could relate to much of what he heard, conspicuously that which had grown from a resurgence of unadulterated psychedelia in the 1980s. With Mood Six and Doctor And The Medics showing the way, such as The Sleep Creatures, The Magic Mushroom Band, Green Telescope, Palace Of Light, The Beautiful People, The Suns Of Arqa and Astralasia also garnered a piece of media action then. Their stock-in-trade was "head music for the feet", whereby disco rhythms were married to synthesizer arpeggio, instrumental meanderings, perfunctory and abstract lyrics and evidence of painstaking investigation of early Pink Floyd and Jimi Hendrix as well as The Soft Machine, Hawkwind, Caravan, Magma, Gong, Van Der Graf Generator and other victims of the same passion.

In the bowels of Reading's Paradise, The Fridge in Brixton and Deptford's Crypt, the proceedings were familiar to those aged hippies snapping their fingers within, if not to the majority of attendees who'd been little more than psychedelic twinkles in their fathers' eyes in 1967. As it had been in the *IT* launch and the Fourteen Hour Technicolor Dream, strobes flickered and ectoplasmic *son et lumière* was projected onto the walls as the bands played on and on and on for cavorters with eyes like catherine wheels. Modern trimmings included programmed accelerations of tempo as the night progressed, and, consequently, more dancing than trancing. "Psychedelic music flowered in the 1960s but it is a timeless thing," observed Garry Moonboot of The Magic Mushroom Band. "I love the whole genre because it incorporated so many different styles. Adding that funky beat to it gets a whole new thing going."

When the New Psychedelia was fused with revived interest in modern jazz, "acid jazz" was the result. More symptomatic of the growing bond between the dance floor and a crossover from reality to a wild dream via LSD and its "Ecstasy" descendant were trance, ambient jazz, ambient techno, ambient-pop, hardcore, acid-house, hip-hip, trip-hop, jungle, ragga and further sub-divisions. You had to be sharp to spot the shades of difference, and out-of-touch journalists tended to lump all of them together as "the Modern Dance" after it surfaced in mainstream pop through the chartbusting efforts of The Art Of Noise, The Prodigy, The Shamen, The Orb and The Cocteau Twins, and in rehashes of anthems from LSD's high summer such as Atom Heart's synthesized unearthing of Donovan's 'Sunshine Superman' or The Magic Mushroom Band's alarming reprise of Hendrix's 'Are You Experienced' with quotes from 'Third Stone From The Sun', and Garry Moonboot's wife punctuating her singing with sensual moans.

Exemplifying the form's original material is Astralasia's 'Sul-E-Stomp', a much-requested fixture at the crowded "raves" that brightened Saturday nights in the most unlikely locations. It started almost as a traditional Irish reel before an abrupt segue into a section of more typical fare, ratifying their Swordfish's comment: "There tends to be a mixture of all sorts of culture within our music. We might throw something from Australia in with something from India and try and cross all the cultures over. It's never directed at one vein."

While it is tempting to rationalise the Modern Dance as bearing the same "new broom" parallel as punk had to stadium rock, it was undercut with far greater respect for pop's elder statesmen. A special guest on The Magic Mushroom Band's *Spaced Out* in 1992 was Van Der Graaf Generator's David Jackson on woodwinds. The favour was returned when The Magic Mushroom Band assisted on Jackson's *Tonewall Stands*.

Fleetwood Mac founder Peter Green would be involved likewise in a remake of 'Albatross' in collaboration with Chris Coco, Brighton club disc jockey and mainstay of Coco-Steel-and-Lovebomb, an amalgam of "acid house" persuasion – though the new 'Albatross' was more ambient-techno. Then, in 1995, there was Screaming Lord Sutch's 'I'm Still Raving', another assisted exposition of the Modern Dance that "at over 140bpm [beats per minute]", it says here, "really 'kicks' and will get any club moving." The following year, Eric Clapton – as "X-sample" – had a go at trip-hop with producer and keyboard player Simon Climie, issuing a "bland, colourless album"[3], *Retail Therapy*, as TDF.

More profitable had been Duane Eddy's and Tom Jones's respective returns to the Top 20 via link-ups with The Art Of Noise, electro-pop innovators whose very name was taken from a tract written in 1913 by "industrial music" precursor Luigi Russolo, whose "line note" system of notation is still used by electronic composers today.

Before the group was formed, their Anne Dudley had been hired by Paul McCartney as a string arranger – and it was through her that he was introduced to Martin "Youth" Glover, who had had a prominent hand in an Art Of Noise remix album, 1990's *The Ambient Collection*. Before that, he'd plucked bass in Killing Joke, a post-punk outfit who went in for Searing Indictments of Society. Martin next struck out on his own as a respected Modern Dance producer. Among his clients was The Orb until a disagreement centred on finance in 1993 – which was when Glover became the enabler of Paul McCartney groping his way through a first and foremost essay as a Modern Dance exponent.

Perhaps just in case they looked back in anger at it, McCartney and Glover hid themselves beneath a pseudonym – The Firemen – but the fusion of "downtempo house" and a vague strata of dub-reggae heard on 1994's *Strawberries Oceans Ships Forest* and

1998's more freeform and slow-moving ambient-techno of *Rushes* certainly induced a near-trance-like effect in me – and I wouldn't recommend using either album as in-car entertainment. Maybe not "going anywhere" was almost the intention. With titles like 'Transpiritual Stomp', 'Pure Trance' and 'Fluid', it was almost the music at any given moment that counted instead of rather non-directional individual pieces – and individual players, unless you're a Beatles–McCartney completist.

Antecedents in Paul's body of work are discernable, I suppose, in the aural junk-sculpture of tape-loops that was the instrumental interlude of 'Tomorrow Never Knows' – and the yet-unissued 'Carnival Of Light' for that 1967 "happening" at London's Roundhouse (and my own feeling now is that it was probably meant to be experienced only on that night at that event).

Good old-fashioned guitars reared up among the synthesizers and samples in *Rushes*, and the overall effect was considered tame and old-fashioned by Orb and Youth fans, but if you like, say, Enigma (who superimposed Gregorian chant upon the grid of the Modern Dance) and *The Moon and the Melodies* (a merger of The Cocteau Twins and New Age composer Harold Budd) or maybe Brian Eno and Robert Fripp's *No Pussyfooting* and what David Bowie called his "dreamy stuff" on *Low* and *Heroes*, you'll probably half-like Youth and McCartney's efforts. Otherwise, it's aural wallpaper that you buy with the same discrimination as you would a few kilograms of spuds from the greengrocers.

Nevertheless, it demonstrated that Fab Macca dug the latest sounds – just as *Liverpool Oratorio* had his appreciation of classical music. As Martin Glover was to be the catalyst for The Fireman business, so Paul had leant on Carl Davis, Brooklyn-born and known chiefly as the classically trained composer of television incidental music and film scores, for this maiden venture into what he'd been brought up to regard as highbrow nonsense: "When symphonies came on the radio, my family just went, 'Oh bloody hell!' and switched the station."[4] However, he'd treasured aspirations of symphonic persuasion since penning the soundtrack of *The Family Way*, a 1966 celluloid farce starring Hayley Mills – and it had been Paul, rather than John, George or Ringo, who was photographed, baton in hand, in front of the orchestra during the session for apocalyptic 'A Day In The Life' on *Sgt Pepper*. "Mozart was a pop star of his day," he opined. "Had he been around, he would probably have been in The Beatles on keyboards."[5]

McCartney had first stumbled upon Carl Davis in 1988 via an engrossing feature about him in some "serious" music journal or other. They had a mutual friend in Carla Lane, who, like the McCartneys, had put her celebrity at the disposal of the animal rights movement. Carla, see, was the writer of Liverpool-centred television sit-coms *The Liver Birds* and *Bread*. The latter starred Jean Boht, wife of Davis – with whom Lane had collaborated on a musical drama, *Pilgrim's Progress*. Paul and Linda sent Carl a good-luck message, one of many that papered the walls of his dressing room when he conducted the Royal Liverpool Philharmonic Orchestra at the première. Noticing the McCartneys' note during the *après*-concert party, it occurred to the Orchestra's general manager, Brian Pidgeon, that Davis ought to explore the possibilities about a similar, if more newsworthy, collusion, even if economic potential might outweigh artistic merit, to climax the Liverpool Phil's forthcoming 150th anniversary concerts.

Not long afterwards, Carl's car engine duly died outside a McCartney house party in Sussex. Small-talk didn't become big-talk on that occasion, but Paul rang afterwards, and, during consequent hundreds of hours in each other's workrooms, he stood over Carl at the piano and vice-versa. They fielded all outside interference as one or other paced up and down the carpet, bedevilled by a half-forgotten but brilliant idea that might have jerked him from a velvet-blue oblivion in the still of the previous night. As the oratorio ripened, a companionship beyond a practised but detached professional relationship grew from the liaison of methodical Carl steeped in the formal do's and don'ts of the classical tradition, and the non-sight-reading *parvenu*, six years his junior, with the stylistic clichés and habits ingrained since he'd positioned yet uncalloused fingers to shape that E-chord on six taut strings when he was 14.

After the job had been done, there was a hiccup when Paul insisted that it be officially titled *Paul McCartney's Liverpool Oratorio*, but Carl, if affronted, caved in – as long as he was still paid as per contract, even though McCartney's sleeve notes to the attendant album read "I made the music and someone else wrote it down."

"It's something I have had to learn to live with,"[5] grumped Davis on the subject.

It might have been belt-and-braces self-defence on Paul's part: "It surprised me that some people who knew me quite well asked if I'd written the words and Carl the music," he glowered years later. "I had to explain that I could compose music but was unable to notate it. To me, music is something more magical than simply a series of black dots on a page."[6]

The sidelining of his co-writer was hardly a *Phantom Of The Opera* situation, was it? Yes, and if "world première" meant "last performance", it might be to the put-upon Carl's advantage to be its *éminence grise* rather than anything more resplendent.

As he kneaded the 90-minute work into shape for the big night – at Liverpool's Anglican Cathedral on Friday 28 June 1991 – Davis was not so humble that he couldn't put forward proposals for leading vocal roles. The most illustrious of those who accepted them was Dame Kiri Te Kanawa, a Maori soprano who'd cantillated an aria for millions at Prince Charles's televised wedding ten years earlier. Nonetheless, she was the down-to-earth antithesis of the stock tantrum-throwing primadonna of operatic legend. Furthermore, she'd been keen on The Beatles during her New Zealand girlhood and throughout a four-year scholarship from 1966 at the London Opera Centre.

For all the bel canto purity of Te Kanawa, Sally Burgess, Willard White and the other principal soloists – as well as the cathedral choir – Davis and McCartney elected not to temper the local accent germane to a libretto that, as it often is with first novels too, contained a pronounced measure of autobiography: a wartime genesis; quoting the Liverpool Institute motto in the opening line[7]; 'Headmaster's Song' to the memory of Jack Edwards – Institute headteacher in Paul's day; the death of a parent and "the frail magic of family life"[6]. Into this cauldron, Paul stirred in fictional ingredients such as the central character's birth in the midst of an air raid; his wife being the main bread-winner; his correlated inadequacy driving him to drink and a road accident that nearly causes the pregnant woman to lose the baby before they all live happily ever after.

Within the interlocking eight movements, *leitmotifs*, "second subjects" and all that – less Igor Stravinsky than Miklos Rozsa (or Carl Davis) – were pleasant tunes sufficiently self-contained to be divorced from the oratorio. McCartney thought so too, and authorised the issue of the first of two singles, 'The World You're Coming Into' coupled with 'Tres Conejos', a not altogether relevant number about a Spanish lesson at school. These and other *Liverpool Oratorio* songs might have suited Paul's untrained baritone too, and been capable of shoe-horning, without much adjustment, onto one of his pop albums. Certainly, they were more to do with the Edwardian light operas of Edward German and Gilbert and Sullivan than, say, Schoenberg's *Pierrot Lunaire* – with its complete suspension of tonality – or Edgard Varèse's *Nocturnal* – chromatic menace beneath Dadaist babble and seemingly random phrases from Anais Nin's *House Of Incest*.

*Music* magazine opined, however, that even the most melodic excerpts from *Liverpool Oratorio* "fell short of the standards set in his finest pop tunes," and suggested that McCartney had "yet to find a distinct 'classical' voice."[6] Nonetheless, while agreeing that it didn't break any barricades, the verdict from other classical organs, if foreseeably condescending and not rabidly enthusiastic, was that *Liverpool Oratorio* was pretty good for a bloke from the unsophisticated world of pop, albeit a multi-millionaire with the services of Carl Davis at his command, and a renown that had obliged him to sign autographs for 200 choirboys after the final rehearsal.

While reaching a lowly 177 in *Billboard*'s pop chart, the album displaced Italian tenor Luciano Pavarotti from the top of the classical list, performing similarly in Britain.

Critical and market response was heartening enough for Paul and Carl to put together *Liverpool Suite* – a nine-minute sequence of the most memorable bits – to follow in its immediate wake, and concert promoters across the continents to underwrite over 100 further performances of the oratorio to date.

Although McCartney didn't thus reinvent himself – as Andrew Lloyd Webber had done – as a sort of nuclear age Sir Arthur Sullivan by juggling milkman-friendly catchiness and Handel-like choral works, *Liverpool Oratorio* was instrumental in narrowing the gap between highbrow and lowbrow, "real" singing and "pop" caterwauling, 'La Donna E Mobile' and 'Long Tall Sally'. With chart strikes for Kiri Te Kanawa and Pavarotti pending, no one was to bat an eyelid when the *Sunday Times* revealed in 1996 that Van Morrison had written music for *Lord Of The Dance*, a multi-media show retelling Celtic folk tales, and centred on high-tech displays of step-dancing that was threatening to eclipse the fêted *Riverdance*.

Of sporadic antecedents, John McCormack – the Pavarotti *du jour* – at the height of his pre-war fame had given a quayside concert of popular ballads for Liverpool-Irish dockers during their lunch hour. More pertinent to this discussion, the University of Ulster had recognised the province's boffin-at-the-high-school-hop by conferring upon the former lead vocalist of Them an honorary doctorate of letters during the summer of 1992. With tasselled cap on his head, and sober grey suit, tie and white shirt covered by the approved red gown, 47-year-old George Ivan Morrison looked the complete antithesis of a hip-shakin' pop demigod – but then maybe he always had.

Bob Dylan's inauguration as an *ex officio* don of Princetown University over 20 years earlier had been a sign that academia had ceased distancing itself from pop – which was soon to begin its infiltration of school curricula. It was remarkable that, unlike film, jazz and other disciplines pertaining to the Coca-Cola century just gone, it had taken until then for higher education to take seriously music that has been recorded for the masses since before the death of Victoria. Nevertheless, by the 1980s, postgraduate research had been encouraged to the extent that the University of Liverpool opened Britain's first Institute of Popular Music – with Mike McCartney among those in its working party. Was it not entirely fitting that a self-contained faculty to centralise existing work should have originated in the birthplace of The Beatles?

The same could be said of the Liverpool Institute of Performing Arts – LIPA – a notion that had come to Paul McCartney shortly before his old secondary school closed in the mid-1980s, and "this wonderful building, which was built in 1825, was becoming derelict"[1]. There was something unstable about Liverpool at that time. Festering unrest amongst the youth in the most depressed districts had exploded during the swimming heat of 1981's summer. From Toxteth and the Dingle, the reek of burning had seeped as far as the city centre, where, for two nights, shops were looted with supermarket trolleys, and torched with petrol bombs.

"After the riots, various people suggested to me that I could help by taking the kids off the streets in some way," recalled Paul in 1994. "Four years ago, I announced the plan to build LIPA, and we started fund-raising. I put in some money to get it going, and we got a lot of help from different people."[1]

It was to be, he said, "like the school in the TV series, *Fame*"[1] in that talented youngsters could be primed for greener pastures via courses that included an artistic conditioning process that, time permitting, might involve songwriting tutorials by none other than the very founder himself – "but I won't be telling the kids how to do it because I think that it is part of my skill that I don't know exactly how to write a song, and the minute I do know how to do it, I'm finished. So I would want to explain that I don't agree that there is an accepted method of writing a song."[1] Perhaps echoing his experiments with Martin "Youth" Glover, he stressed that "the excitement for me would be if I could learn while they are learning."[1]

It was also going to be tenable to receive LIPA training as a road manager, a lighting engineer, a video producer, an A & R executive, a choreographer... but what couldn't be taught was the "bad" attitude necessary before a career in pop became an acceptable option to parents. When McCartney wasn't much older than his students, in dreary middle-class homes in the provinces – where the distance to Swinging London was measurable in decades as much as miles – for a boy to express a desire to make his way in pop was almost the precise equivalent of a girl seeking a post as a stripper. It would preface years of incomprehension, lamentation, deprivation, uproar, assault and oppressive domestic "atmospheres".

As a result, those who'd been psychologically damaged – as I was – by such persecution from so-called loved ones were much more liberal when, as former Mods, Rockers and hippies, they became parents themselves; buying MIDI equipment for 16th birthday presents for children who could con grants out of the government to form a group – even if, in the same defeated economic climate, record companies were no longer chucking blank cheques about as they did after the wheels of the universe came together for The Beatles in 1962 and The Sex Pistols a quarter of a century later.

Regardless, the Institute was to enroll its first students for 1996's spring term in between the preceding media hoo-hah that always went with the McCartney territory and the official unveiling of its plaque by the Queen – who'd been among those who'd dipped into her purse for LIPA – in June.

Though his sojourn at the Liverpool Institute was ignominious, George Harrison's loyalty to the old grey stones (and to McCartney) was strong enough for him to reach for his chequebook on LIPA's behalf too. He had also been amenable to joining with Paul and Ringo in 1994 for the compilation of *Anthology*, a vast Beatles retrospective that would embrace eventually nine albums (in sets of three), a lengthy television documentary – later available on video and DVD – and a group autobiography in the form of edited transcripts of taped reminiscences. "There were one or two bits of tension," smiled Paul, "I had one or two ideas George didn't like."[1] One of these was the project's working title, *The Long And Winding Road*, because it was after one of McCartney's songs. Ringo too blew hot and cold with Paul: "It's a good month and a bad month, just like a family."[9]

Since John's passing, there'd been no successor to him as self-appointed Beatles *paterfamilias* – who'd, purportedly, chastised George for the "incest"[10] of a brief affair in 1972 with Ringo's first wife – but Yoko had remained to the group roughly what the embarrassing "Fergie", the Duchess of York, is to the Windsors. There was no love lost between her and McCartney, who she perceived then as the Salieri to her late husband's Mozart. Yet she and Paul had shared a conciliatory hug at a Rock 'N' Roll Hall Of Fame award ceremony, and she'd spent a weekend that seemed more like a fortnight at the McCartneys when being courted for her co-operation on *Anthology*. Her stay was notable for a session at Paul's home studio in which he, Linda and the children accompanied seven minutes of Aunt Yoko's screech-singing of a one-line lyric called 'Hiroshima Sky Is Always Blue'.

Paul insisted that there was no ulterior motive, that he liked the track, and agreed with Yoko that it was "the result of our reconciliation after 20 years of bitterness and feuding."[9] Before the weather vane of rapprochement lurched back to the old thinly veiled antagonism, Yoko donated stark voice-piano tapes of Lennon compositions for McCartney, Harrison and Starr to use as they thought fit.

Isn't it marvellous what they can do nowadays? Only four years before one of John's demos, 'Free As A Bird', had taken shape as near as dammit to a new Beatles single, there'd been a hit remake of Nat "King" Cole's 'Unforgettable' as a duet by layering his and daughter Natalie's singing over a state-of-the-art facsimile of Nat's original 1951 backing track.

With Jeff Lynne as executive producer, 'Free As A Bird' was likewise doctored with a slide guitar passage from Harrison, Starr's trademark "pudding" tom-toms and McCartney emoting a freshly composed "bridge" as a sparkling contrast to John's downbeat verses. The effect was not unlike an inverse of 'We Can Work It Out'. Yet 'Free As A Bird' stalled in second place in Britain's Christmas list when up against *bête noire* Michael Jackson's 'Earth Song' and an easy-listening overhaul of Oasis's 'Wonderwall' by The Mike Flowers Pops. The Beatles' follow-up, 'Real Love', made the Top Ten more grudgingly, dogged as it was by exclusion from Radio One's playlist of the Modern Dance, twee boy bands and Britpop – ie mostly guitar-bass-drums acts that, like brand-leaders Oasis, borrowed melodies and lyrical ideas from the golden age of British beat.

Who could not empathise with Paul, Ringo and George's mingled dismay and elation when the million-selling *Anthology* albums demonstrated that almost-but-not-quite reaching the top in the UK singles chart was but a surface manifestation of enduring interest in The Beatles that made even their out-takes a joy forever?

The book was a bestseller too; its high retail price mitigated by a weight comparable to that of a paving slab. As for the content, we would like the impossible: videos of the Woolton fête engagement when John met Paul; a rehearsal around August 1962 when the group was about to rid itself of Pete Best; to be a fly on the wall in a dressing room just before *Sunday Night At The London Palladium* or to sample with our own sensory organs Paul's feelings about Yoko's intrusion on The Beatles.

Instead, we got Ringo, George and Paul – and John from media archives – providing not so much new twists in the plot as details about the food they ate, the clothes they wore, the stimulants they sampled, the violence they faced, the hairstyles they adopted – oh, and the music they played – information that the most obsessed Beatlemaniac wouldn't find too insignificant to be less than totally fascinating. McCartney's ruminations, however, were marred by an irritating conversational tic in his over-use of the word "little" – "little guitar", "little studio", "little club in Hamburg", "great little period" (at least twice) ad nauseam. He probably doesn't realise he's doing it.

Events since *Anthology* have demonstrated that it was far from the last word on The Beatles. Not a month passes without another few books adding – like this one – to the millions of words chronicling and analysing some aspect or other of their history. Bootlegs have continued unabated too with their manufacturers intrigued most recently by the emergence in Holland of further hitherto-unissued unforgiving minutes from the *Let It Be* era.

Thus The Beatles endure after the apparent levelling out of Britpop from its mid-1990s apogee. While it was going strongest, the biters were bitten on *Sixties Sing Nineties*, an intriguing 1998 collection in which hits by callow apprentices were given the masters' touch – and delivered with more guts that the originals in the cases of Dave Dee's crack at 'Don't Look Back In Anger' by Oasis, and the circle remaining unbroken with the Wet Wet Wet arrangement of 'Love Is All Around' by composer Reg Presley.

As he had with the Modern Dance, Paul McCartney, well into his 50s, masticated a chunk of Britpop too by combining with 37-year-old Paul Weller – who'd been dating daughter Mary of late – and, more to the point, Noel Gallagher, leader of Oasis, on an Abbey Road reworking of 'Come Together' for *Help!* a 1995 "various artists" album to raise funds to alleviate the war in Bosnia's aftermath of homelessness, lack of sanitation, disease and starvation. Symbolising three generations of pop aristocracy, the trio – naming themselves The Smokin' Mojo Filters – were *Help!*'s star turn, and, almost as a matter of course, 'Come Together' was its loss-leader of a single.

# 19 "My Dark Hour"

"I'd not have had a day again to equal this, would I?"
*– Sean Connery as Robin Hood*[1]

Just as "history" nowadays means mannered costume dramas in six weekly two-hour episodes on television, so "classical music" for many people is what you hear when put on hold to speak to a British Gas sales advisor. When Paul McCartney was young, it oozed in a similar fashion from the BBC Light Programme under the batons of Mantovani, Edmundo Ros, Geraldo and bandleaders of their hue. From *Music While You Work*, it was a short step to Reader's Digest's mail-order record wing with titles like "Music For Reading", "Music For Dining" and "Music For A Solemn Occasion" in its catalogue. 1963 brought *The Quiet Hour* spent with Patience Strong reading verse over holy organ Bach, "offering comfort and solace sorely needed in this hurrying, worrying world."[2]

Such sounds didn't require focus and being able to think, "Yes, that's interesting". There was nothing constructive you could say about it. It was just there, either slushy with strings or inconsequentially plink-plonk, these reductions to musak of *Tales Of Hoffman*, the *Lone Ranger* theme, Ravel's *Bolero*, Handel's *Largo et al*.

Occupying an area bordered by Elgar, Vaughan Williams and Britten, Sir William Walton's lighter pieces might have figured on the Light Programme playlist as well, particularly those written for the "talkies" to suit the conservative demands of Hollywood and Ealing. Walton was responsible too for *Fanfare For Brass* for EMI's celebration of its first 50 years in business, but, for the label's centenary in 1997, Paul McCartney came up with *Standing Stone*, a sonic monument to the very late Ivan Vaughan, the school friend through whom Paul had been introduced to The Quarry Men.

It took the form of a symphonic poem in a traditional division of four movements that the *Music* periodical reckoned "represented a significant leap forward in style and substance, the persuasive outcome of almost four years labour."[3]

Paul had figured out the basic pattern on piano, and drawn a sung narrative from verse he'd written that, addressing both Celtic myths and his Irish ancestry, was his perspective on the Earth's creation, the origins of life and the particular history of an "everyman"-type character named First Person Singular, whose life's journey is a quest for – as you don't need me to tell you – True Love.

While this musical and lyrical bedrock was all his, Paul didn't complete *Standing Stone* entirely on his own. Among helpmates were classical saxophonist and arranger John Harle and composer David Matthews, most vital as a trouble-shooter for McCartney's electronic keyboard, computer and composition software. "We're more or less contemporaries," smiled David, "and I'm a great Beatles fan. Sometimes I regret that I didn't take up the guitar.

"The orchestration he'd created on the computer wouldn't work in real life, and he wanted advice on practical matters, such as the doubling of instruments and balance. I wanted him in every case to make up his mind about what he wanted and not suggest things to him. The difference between what Paul produced on the computer and the finished piece is quite small, but I hope I helped to turn it into a polished work."[3]

To assist with harmonising the four-part chorale that would carry the libretto, Paul called upon the older Richard Rodney Bennett, a composer and concert pianist forever on BBC Radio Three, who'd studied under Pierre Boulez, himself a former pupil of Messiaen and Varèse. Bennett, however, wasn't to inscribe any more of a stylistic signature on the work than David Matthews because McCartney had made it clear from the start "that I wanted *Standing Stone* to be my piece. They understood exactly what I meant, so they kept out of the way while guiding and helping me whenever necessary."[3]

Nearer the beginning, he'd wheeled in jazz keyboard virtuoso Steve Lodder, who, said Paul, "was able to help me keep the flow of ideas by playing back any material I'd written and changing its order. When I finally had its shape, I began to talk with John Harle, who gave me some advice on the overall structure. He would say what he felt about a section and I'd go away for two weeks and work on it – which was a bit like having school homework to do. It was good to have a second opinion on what worked and what didn't. I wanted something to sustain the audience's interest – and mine – since, unlike Beethoven, I was unable to take a theme and develop it in a symphonic way. Whereas other people have been studying classical music for 30 or 40 years, I've seen this stuff only in passing – so I've heard a French horn, liked its sound and used it in a Beatles song like 'For No One'. Also, I used piccolo trumpet in 'Penny Lane' after I'd heard Bach's *Brandenburg Concerto* on television. With *Standing Stone*, I began to put things together in a way I'd never done before."[3]

His mood was one of quiet confidence when settling into a seat for the 300-piece London Symphony Orchestra and Chorus's première of *Standing Stone* at the Royal Albert Hall on 14 October 1997. Pockets of the audience behaved as if it was a rock concert, though they remained silent and not visibly fidgeting during the 75 minutes of grandiloquent music that finished with "love is the oldest secret of the universe" from the choir, prefacing some ticket-holders' exclaimed "yeah!" that set off a standing ovation.

Overnight, the press gathered its thoughts. The reviews weren't scathing, but *Standing Stone* wasn't an especially palpable hit either, now that the novelty of Paul McCartney, classical composer, had faded. Nevertheless, it was received more favourably at New York's Carnegie Hall the following month in a performance that was broadcast to nigh on 400 radio stations across the whole sub-continent. Of later recitals, the most far-reaching was that on British television one Christmas morning when the nation was midway between the children's pre-dawn ripping open of the presents and the Queen's Speech.

The morning after 14 October 1997, however, the critics had tended to overlook the McCartney pieces that had prefaced the main event at the Albert Hall. These were the seven movements of *A Leaf* and another orchestrated piece *Spiral* – for piano – as well as *Stately Horn* for a horn ensemble, and *Inebriation* from The Brodsky Quartet.

Now that he'd acquired a taste for it, Paul would be knocking out more of the same, most recently *Ecce Cor Meum* – "behold my heart" – an oratorio dedicated to Linda, that was the centrepiece of the first concert given at Magdalen College, Oxford's new chapel in November 2001.

Listening to that of McCartney's classical output issued thus far on disc – which includes the 'Andante' from *Standing Stone* as a single – adjectives like "restrained", "shimmering", "caressing" and "atmospheric" occurred to me, and a lot of it has, indeed, a reposeful daintiness that's just, well, nice. The aftertaste is not so much British Gas Showroom as music commensurate with meditation – as implied in *Standing Stone*'s 'Trance' section – improvised dance and other self-improving activities, but heard too in advertisements for mineral water and credit cards as well as in travelogues, painting studios, hip dental surgeries, health food stores, massage parlours and what used to be known as "head shops".

While they adhered to classical form, *Liverpool Concerto, A Leaf, Ecce Cor Meum et al* are avenues of "classical music" effect rather than "classical music" in absolute terms. Maybe the phrase I'm looking for is "New Age" – or, alternatively, "New Instrumental" or "Adult Contemporary Music" – predating the Modern Dance as the only wave of essentially instrumental music to have reached a mass public since jazz-rock in the mid-1970s. Rather than East Of Eden or The Art Of Noise, it connects more with Terry Riley, John Tavener, Morton Subotnik, arch-minimalist Philip Glass, Stomu Yamash'ta – "the Samurai of Sound" – and other "serious" composer-performers who were promoted almost as rock stars by such as CBS, Apple, Island, World Pacific and Elektra subsidiary, Nonesuch.

McCartney need feel no shame either in an affinity to fellow 1960s pop veterans who resurfaced as denizens of New Age. The mainstay of Stairway (probably the best-loved British New Age outfit) is actually Jim McCarty of The Yardbirds – who also penned *Medicine Dance*, a *Standing Stone*-esque opus minus the vocals and orchestral backwash, for a bash in capacious St James's Church off London's Piccadilly in 1993.

Rod Argent of The Zombies – whose trademark was a minor key contradiction of enjoyable melancholy – Eddie Hardin (Steve Winwood's replacement in The Spencer Davis Group) and ex-Georgie Fame sideman Ray Russell are but a few more old stagers who were also reborn as New Age executants – though offerings by both ex-Monkee Mike Nesmith and Todd Rundren never left the runway, perhaps because a perverse public was not prepared to disconnect them from previous incarnations.

If McCartney elects to persist courting the "classical" rather than New Age market, he needs to accept that he'll probably always be a tyro in comparison to someone like Scott Walker, now a kind of Roger Irrelevant of pop, whose infrequent albums are mostly an intellectual rather than aesthetic experience. To arrangements that range in density from everything but the proverbial kitchen sink to a subdued ghostliness, the artist – not *artiste* – seems at times to dart randomly from section to indissoluble section welded to tunes that verge on the atonal, encapsulating fragments of

Schoenberg, Penderecki and composers of that "difficult" persuasion – with only drums and electric bass placing the ilk of *Tilt* and *Pola X* even remotely in the realms of pop.

A more impossible yardstick for McCartney is the late Frank Zappa, perhaps the greatest North American composer of the 20th century or, indeed, any other era. That's not to say he was perfect; his 'Uncle Meat', for instance, was lifted directly from Milhaud's 'Un Homme Et Son Désir', and he lost me when he drifted from the incisive aural imbroglios of the 1960s to the lavatorial *humor* of his post-Mothers of Invention period.

Nevertheless, even the most crass lyrics were supported by complex and frequently beautiful music – and, like Mozart in his final years too, Frank ceased springing for the commercial jugular, and negotiated a complete artistic recovery as a "serious" composer by reconciling severe dissonance and clashing time signatures with serene, lushly orchestrated melody ("electric chamber music", he called it) with a transcendental edge and injection of outright craziness that you won't detect in *Standing Stone*, *Spiral* and all the rest of them. Today, you'll hear Zappa in the "Promenade Concerts" – as you might, for reasons other than musical quality, hear our own dear Paul McCartney one day.

Paul hadn't been so out of his depth – far from it – with 1995's *Oobu Joobu*, a radio series for the same US company that had networked the self-explanatory *Lost Lennon Tapes*. That *Oobu Joobu*'s title was derived from a surreal and burlesque 1908 play by Alfred Jarry may have caused some anticipatory trepidation in listeners, but it was simply eleven one-hour shows (plus a bumper 12th edition) of harmless family fun with records, jingles, funny stories, celebrity interviews, comedy sketches, previously unbroadcasted Beatles and Wings tapes, you get the drift.

There were also what might have been categorised in a more sexist age, "women's features" – mainly recipes – by Linda. The children, however, made only incidental contributions at most. Advisedly, they'd been so removed from direct public gaze that, as teenagers, they were able to walk around Rye and Campbeltown not unnoticed exactly, but without inviting too much comment.

Paul and Linda had instilled into Heather, Mary, Stella and James what ought to be admired about achievement by effort. Taking this to heart, Heather had pulled pints in a local pub, one of several menial jobs that she had held down prior to becoming a potter whose work came to be exhibited as far afield as Tokyo and Sydney.

As talented and as renowned in her way, Mary had followed her mother's footsteps, discovering words like "gate", "field" and "aperture" as applied to the camera as well as the versatility of delayed-action shutters, and what could be done to a negative when, in a darkroom at MPL offices, she began developing and printing her own films. Vocationally, she touched a zenith of sorts in 2000 when commissioned to snap the official photographs of Prime Minister Tony Blair's newborn son Leo. Just over a year earlier, Mary herself had given birth – to her father's first grandchild, Arthur, seven months after her marriage to film director and television producer, Alistair Donald.

Of all the McCartney daughters, however, Stella has thrust her head highest above the parapet. Her surname helped open a door to a flourishing career in fashion design after learning what she could *in situ* as runaround to Parisian couturier Christian La Croix. A chip off the old paternal block, Stella dismissed many preconceptions and introduced fresh ones when studying at Central St Martin's Design School in London, where, at the fashion parade for her "finals", Stella's creations were modelled to a soundtrack by the "proudest dad in the world"[4].

McCartney *père* was prominent too among onlookers at Stella's consequent shows when she landed a lucrative post as head designer at a leading Paris fashion house a mere 18 months after finishing at St Martin's, and was on the way to her first self-made million. This prompted inevitable it's-not-how-good-you-are-it's-who-you-know mutterings, but Stella had a natural flair for cutting the cloth, and, if she had been given any extra pushes up the ladder, the world of glamour benefitted as much as she did.

Stella was said to have crafted her own wedding dress for when she tied the knot with Alistair Willis, former publisher of the "style" magazine, *Wallpaper*, on New Year's Day 2003.

So far, Stella's brother's principal brush with fame – if that is the word – has been when he made headlines in September 1993 after the coastguard was called out by his very worried parents. This had followed James's disappearance from view when bodysurfing in the sea near Rye. Two years later, a misadventure on land left him with a broken ankle when the Land Rover he was driving overturned along a rutted track. In oblique mitigation, however, his co-writing and strumming the chords to 'Back In The Sunshine', a 2001 album track by his father, suggests that the accident-prone young man is turning into an adept guitarist and composer.

James's mishaps had been among few domestic hiccoughs in the mid-1990s, a "great little period" that Paul would remember not only for what happened at the end, but also for the contentment that had preceded it. Nothing was ever the same afterwards.

Lightning struck slowly. In December 1995, Linda recovered from an ostensibly successful operation to remove a lump from her breast. Yet within weeks, she had every appearance of being seriously ill, and was prescribed chemotherapy. That held the spread of what was obviously cancer at arm's length, but X-rays were to reveal malignant cells forming a shadow on her liver.

The ghastly secret became known to a media that noted Linda's absence when Paul was driven to Buckingham Palace on 11 March 1997. As Prime Minister John Major had done on the apparent behalf of Eric Clapton MBE, Van Morrison OBE and Sir Cliff Richard, so his more with-it successor, Tony Blair, a self-styled "guy", had advised the Queen to invest the showbusiness legend as responsible for 'I Saw Her Standing There' as *Liverpool Oratorio* with a knighthood – for "services to music". As it had been when

The Beatles were awarded their contentious MBE's 30 years earlier,
Paul was pleased, accepting the greater honour, he promised, "on
behalf of the people of Liverpool and the other Beatles."[5]

"A spokesperson" was to inform the *Sunday Times* that "he
is very down to earth about being a knight. He doesn't use the
title. None of his friends call him Sir Paul. The only time he gets
called that is when he is in restaurants or on airplanes."[6]
Nevertheless, like Sir Cliff Richard and Sir Elton John, he sealed
his status as pillar of the Establishment by paying £3,500 ($5,600)
to the College of Arms for the coat of arms that, since the reign of
Richard III, anyone considered a gentleman was supposed to keep
handy in case he was required to fight for the monarch. On Sir
Paul's, the principal symbols are a guitar and a Liver Bird – with
beak open as if singing. The design also embraces four shapes
resembling beetles, two circles representing records, and the title
of the Magdalen College oratorio, *Ecce Cor Meum*.

The guitar signified what was still his principal source of income,
and to that end, *Flaming Pie*, his first non-concert album for nearly
half a decade, materialised two months after the visit to the Queen.
Unlike *Ecce Cor Meum*, it wasn't meant to be taken especially
seriously. "I called up a bunch of friends and family and we just
got on and did it," he chortled. "And we had fun. Hopefully, you'll
hear that in the songs."[7]

Those that did bought *Flaming Pie* in sufficient quantity to ease
it up to a domestic Number One and to Number Two in the Hot
100. This – and a nomination for a Grammy – flew in the face of
dejecting critiques ("woeful stuff"[8], "rock 'n' roll with its teeth in
a glass of water by its bedside"[9]) for an album that conveyed a
likeably downhome, sofa-ed ambience, even if most of the 14 songs
*per se* weren't much more than sometimes tipsy musings written
on holiday or as the conclusion of just messing about. All were by
Paul alone apart from 'Really Love You' – born of a jam with
Ringo while a tape operator was fixing something or other – and
blues-inflected 'Used To Be Bad' with Steve Miller, whose 1969

single, 'My Dark Hour', had had McCartney on drums and bass. He renewed his professional acquaintance with Paul when his studio in Idaho hosted the bulk of the *Flaming Pie* sessions. "Bulk" is a crucial word here because Steve at 52 had put on weight alarmingly – as marked by a *Top Of The Pops* interlocutor who, damn his impudence, referred to Miller as a "porker" when a 1990 re-release of 'The Joker' topped the UK charts, thanks to its use in an ITV commercial.

Steve warranted a mention in *Many Years From Now*, Paul's authorised biography by Barry Miles. While this tome deals essentially with events up to and including the dissolution of The Beatles, it serves as an intriguing companion to this one, containing as it does more weighing of experience and estimation of motive than you'd expect in a pop life story freighted too with both unfamiliar anecdotes and the old yarns related from the subject's point of view.

He was kind about Jane Asher – from whom "I learned a lot and she introduced me to a lot of things"[10]. Married now to cartoonist Gerald Scarfe, Jane had put her acting career on hold owing to family commitments and those connected with her on-going presidency of the National Autistic Society. However, she had returned to television drama in the 1980s with such as *Love Is Old Love Is New* – a series centred on a couple who wished time had stopped in the 1960s, and containing a generous helping of Beatles songs – and most recently in a resurgent *Crossroads*. In March 2003, she narrated *The Real Cliff Richard*, a Channel Four documentary about the ageing Bachelor Boy.

Jane's aptitude as a home-maker had manifested itself in Jane Asher's *Calendar Of Cakes, Silent Nights For You And Your Baby, The Best Of Good Living* and similar domestic self-help tomes. When mass-produced, her cakes filled shelves in one supermarket chain, but even the most "creative" journalist couldn't make out that they were in competition with Linda McCartney's more savoury merchandise.

Linda was dying by inches. Nonetheless, amid gathering infirmity and awash with medications, she was filling what remained of her life with compiling another cookbook; developing enough film for two more photography exhibitions and battling on courageously with a solo album. More a hospital orderly than passionate *inamorato* now, Paul tried to blow sparks of optimism but resigned himself with wearied amazement that she was still clinging on as he helped attend to her day-long needs.

The flame was low on the evening of Thursday 16 April 1998, and 56-year-old Linda Louise McCartney was gone by the grey of morning. Following a hasty cremation, Paul announced the tragedy, having first endorsed an entirely fictional report that she'd died in California rather than on an Arizona ranch she and Paul had bought in 1979. Without this precaution, today's death bed would have become tomorrow's lapping sea of faces and camera lenses.

The ashes were transported back to England where the family were to mourn Linda publicly at a service of remembrance in central London, complete with celebrity eulogies and readings, someone leading her two Shetland ponies up the aisle, a bagpiper blowing 'Mull Of Kintyre' and renderings by The Brodsky Quartet of McCartney compositions pertinent to Linda. Paul himself was to sing a finale of 'All My Loving' with Elvis Costello during star-studded "Here, There And Everywhere: A Concert For Linda" at the Albert Hall nearly a year to the day after her passing.

Over in California, Eric Burdon had "had no idea how sick Linda had become. The last time I'd seen her was when she and her beloved Paul visited backstage after one of my shows at London's Hammersmith Theatre. Those two were perfect together, woven tight like a many-coloured Shetland sweater."[11]

At a memorial concert in the Sunken Gardens in Santa Barbara – where the press had first been led to believe Linda had died – Eric gave 'em 'The Long And Winding Road' and delivered an insightful oration, abridged thus: "She told me quite seriously that, to become a photographer, one should carry one's camera at all times – just like a soldier carries his weapon – because the action is all around you. She was one of the girls who became one of the boys by becoming a woman upon the road. Go, Linda, go."

# 20 *"She Said Yeah"*

"It would have been very easy for Paul McCartney to have retired years ago, but there's this old die-hard thing in him that still has so much music to make."

– *Rod Stewart*[1]

Predictably, there were rumours of a lady friend within months of Linda's funeral. Paparazzi squeezed sleazy mileage from naming one or two candidates, but there was no evidence to substantiate a new romance until late in 1999 when Paul was seen in public with a blonde from Tyne-and-Wear named Heather Mills, whose artificial leg was of no more account than an earring or a headband. Nothing could distract from the firm-breasted profile and timorously pretty but deceptively commanding face.

Heather had never lacked male attention, though the first major instance of it was at primary school when she and a classmate were kidnapped by a Mr Morris, their swimming instructor. They were held for three days before their escape and Mr Morris's subsequent suicide.

Life *chez* Mills in Washington, County Durham, wasn't happy either. Heather's father, an ex-paratrooper, would "yell, throw things and belt Mum over the head," she recalled. "It didn't matter if we [Heather, brother Shane and sister Fiona] were there or not. Sometimes, I really believed he was going to murder her."[2] Her spouse's rages so overwhelmed Mrs Mills that, when her elder daughter was nine, an affair with a TV actor – from *Crossroads* of all programmes – who'd been in a play at Newcastle Theatre

Royal, was the trigger for her upping and leaving for London with him. With the initial enthusiasm children often have for onerous household tasks, Heather slipped into the maternal role thus thrust upon her, feeding herself, Shane and Fiona on a miserly weekly budget supplemented with shoplifting.

Inevitably, Heather's schooling suffered, and was unofficially over when her father's shady business dealings led him to being gaoled for two years. The children went to live with a mother they scarcely knew now in Clapham. So rancorously alien was the new situation that 13-year-old Heather ran away to find eventual under-age employment with a travelling funfair. After the friend with whom she shared a caravan died an early death through drug abuse, the glamour of dodgems, candy-floss and shooting galleries palled, and Heather gravitated to London's South Bank to dwell with other vagrants in cardboard-boxed squalor.

She endured this for four months – it was left for others to imagine that it was constant dirt; perpetual mental arithmetic to eke out a few pence; chill from the misty river penetrating clothes that she would uncrumple after a sleepless night; washing in public-convenience hand basins and seeing fellow down-and-outs face down in a puddle of their own vomit.

Not far from her mother's was an off-licence owned by a kindly couple who got wind of Heather's plight, and invited her to move in with them. A local jeweller took her on part-time, but, when accused falsely of pilfering from the stock, she felt she had nothing to lose by actually doing so. Her illicit sale of a quantity of gold chains came home to roost, and an appearance in juvenile court terminated with a stern lecture from a magistrate who placed Heather on probation.

Her 16 years, therefore, hadn't been quiet ones, but, despite – or because of – the distressing odds, she was to emerge from her teens astoundingly self-confident and purposeful. Quite the astute business woman too, she was the brains behind several small if profitable business enterprises. Moreover, the hardships of her first two decades hadn't taken their toll on the good looks that had enabled her to win a *Daily Mirror* "Dream Girl" contest and land jobs as a presenter on *Wish You Were Here, That's Esther* and other television magazine programmes.

It all came tumbling down, however, on 8 August 1993 when Heather was on a Kensington street and in the way of a police motorcycle, which was hurrying to a false alarm. To the agitated oscillations of an ambulance siren, she was hastened to the nearest hospital where surgeons failed to reconnect her severed foot. More of the leg was amputated – fortunately, below the knee – during a lengthy operation.

This might have been the final scene in a 15-act tragedy, but, with her customary and extraordinary resilience, Heather Mills conquered desolation by anchoring herself to the notion that, one way or another, she'd emerge, if not entirely intact, then with hardened mettle. At least she could afford – especially with the out-of-court settlement by Scotland Yard – the thousands of pounds required for a shapely silicone limb with a flexible foot.

She also inaugurated the Heather Mills Trust, a charity for those who had become limbless in global theatres of war, having become horribly aware that "to lose a limb is also to lose your self-worth, your masculinity or femininity. The women no longer feel marriageable, though I saw at least 20 girls among the amputees (in Cambodia) who would have made super models."[2] Her tireless fund-raising was to involve a 1999 Heather Mills single entitled 'Voice' – with a lyric about a disabled girl – and spell-binding slots on chat shows where she provoked shocked laughter by rolling up her trousers and even removing her false leg. Up in the control room, where the producer barked excited instructions to the camera operators, it was fantastic television.

It also had the desired effect of drawing attention to a campaign that was to earn Heather a Nobel Peace Prize nomination and further formal recognitions for her work. Famous enough to warrant a frank-and-unashamed autobiography[3], she was a host at one such ceremony at London's plush Dorchester Hotel on 20 May 1999. Her future husband was there too, clutching the Linda McCartney Award For Animal Welfare he was to give to the founder of *Viva*, an associated movement.

Taking a benevolent interest in Heather's activities, Paul McCartney was to write out a huge cheque for the trust, and contribute guitar and backing vocals to 'Voice'. Then one thing led to another and, after she'd accepted an invitation to a bonfire party at Rye, she and Paul saw in the millenium together and set tongues a-wagging further with a joint ten-day holiday in the West Indies. His name now linked with hers in high society gossip columns, the 59-year-old widower seemed as fondly in love as he could be with a beautiful girlfriend a quarter of a century his junior. That she was a divorcée like Linda – and a veteran of three broken engagements – didn't ruffle him. After all, he'd hardly lived like a monk since the onset of puberty. "What we want most of all at the moment," he outlined to *Hello!*, "is a private life. It's very early days for us, and it's a wait-and-see situation."[2]

Nobody was getting any younger, but the gloom that had followed Linda's final illness had deferred the breezy vitality that had been Matt Monro's when contemplating settling cosily into old age on the consolidated fruits of his success – particularly when there was an unexpected godsend in the rise of *Heartbreakers*, a 1980 Monro compilation, to Number Five in the album chart. Unhappily, retirement was not on the cards for Matt. In 1984, he bid an unknowing farewell to the concert platform with a 'Softly As I Leave You' finale. Just over a year later, he was under the scalpel for an attempted liver transplant when a cancerous growth was uncovered. He was discharged, but returned within two days to die quietly on 7 February 1985.

His doctors blamed his smoking, a habit that George Harrison gave up when the cancer that was to take him too was first diagnosed. After *Cloud Nine* had burst, George had gone to ground again; his only significant return to media focus being inadvertent when he was half-killed in his own home by a knife-wielding paranoid schizophrenic.

Paul had long been concerned about physical attack. Homicidal fanatics were an occupational hazard. In 1971, one such "fan" had jumped onstage at London's Rainbow Theatre and hurled Frank Zappa into the pit, confining him to a wheelchair for almost a year. Not long after John Lennon's slaying, the newly inaugurated President Reagan had taken a bullet from a deranged man trying to impress a Hollywood actor he admired. Two months later, something similar happened to the Pope.

Twenty years after these last two incidents, discreet bodyguards were always around whenever Paul McCartney made formal appearances. One such public venture, however, was made with uncharacteristic stealth.

It concerned his interests in fine art. Even when his studies for A-level Art were far behind him, idle hours on this long-haul flight or in that dressing room had often been occupied with doodling in pencil or felt-tip. A selection of these were included in *Paul McCartney: Composer Artist*, published in 1981.[4]

At home and on holiday, he would unwind too in two- and three-dimensions by painting in oils and doing sculpture, sometimes using driftwood smoothed by decades beneath either the English Channel or the Irish Sea. Most of his efforts were OK, nothing brilliant, but he had those with which he was particularly pleased printed up in a small hardback book for private use, presenting copies to friends.

Other pop stars, however, did not hide such light under a bushel. To some acclaim, Ronnie Wood, now a Rolling Stone, began showing his paintings in the late 1980s during one of progressively longer breaks in the group's touring schedule – while former Kink Pete Quaife – now Peter Kinnes – did likewise in Canada in 1994. His hangings included some autobiographical illustrations such as *Baked Beans*, showing a hand removing a housefly from a plate of the same ("People think we always ate in fancy restaurants. We didn't. All we had time for was beans-on-toast"[5]). Another picture depicts a stern-looking hotel receptionist registering the group members.

An ex-Beatle decided to go public with a Paul McCartney art exhibition at the Kunstforum Lyz Gallery in Hamburg on 30 April 1999. Three years later, he risked displaying "The Art Of Paul McCartney" at the Walker in Liverpool – which was also curating some Turners in an adjacent gallery. This was perhaps unfortunate in its inviting of comparisons between the distinguished Victorian "colour poet" and one who wouldn't be there if not for the Fab Four's long shadow.

While one expert deemed Paul's efforts to be "more interesting than I thought" and another in the same newspaper reckoned they had "promise", a third critic turned his nose up at "wholly talentless daubs. Perhaps endless adulation has made McCartney deaf to the voice of criticism."[6]

Maybe the Beatles' fairy-tale had rendered this particular scribe as deaf to the voice of approbation. Either way, McCartney was in a no-win situation – unless he'd exhibited his art pseudononymously like Pete Quaife. If you'd seen his work like that in a gallery near you, what would you think? Without such objectivity, pop stardom has invested McCartney's hands-on involvement with a similar poignancy to that of such as Bob Dylan, the Prince of Wales, Syd Barrett, Captain Beefheart, David Bowie, The Who's John Entwistle and – yes – John Lennon and Stuart Sutcliffe: goods bought principally as investments for their historical and curiosity value. In fairness, however, Beefheart – as Don Van Vliet – has had over 30 art exhibitions around the world since 1982 when he elected to devote himself to painting. Most buyers were unfamiliar with his pop past.

Yet little intimates that because Paul McCartney was so fully occupied with his musical career, he was a regrettable loss to the world of fine art. As a figure in time's fabric, his period as a Beatle will remain central to most considerations of him.

He'd harked back to the years prior to the 'Love Me Do' countdown with 1999's *Run Devil Run*, a quasi-*Choba B CCCP* album, but with three originals in the same vein. Anyone with the confidence to slot these in without jarring the stylistic flow of such as 'All Shook Up', 'Brown-Eyed Handsome Man' and 'Blue Jean Bop' deserved attention. Give him further credit, Paul's go at Larry Williams's 'She Said Yeah' was almost on a par with The Rolling Stones' 1965 revival, itself as redefining as The Beatles' 'Long Tall Sally' had been to the Little Richard blueprint. Paul's 'She Said Yeah' certainly made a 1964 crack at it by The Animals seem thuggish. Likewise, he improved (though there wasn't much competition) on one of *Run Devil Run*'s comparative obscurities, 'No Other Baby' from Dickie Bishop and his Sidekicks, a sub-Donegan skiffle outfit, but better known – in the USA at least – via a cover by Peter and Gordon's chief competitors in North America, Chad and Jeremy.

The most significant plug for *Run Devil Run* was an end-of-the-century bash at the replica Cavern along Mathew Street to a capacity raffle-winning crowd – including a chap who'd changed his name by deed-poll to "John Lennon" – but with a webcast audience of over three million. Rather than be accompanied by an existing group – as Jeff Beck had been by The Big Town Playboys for 1993's *Crazy Legs*, a Gene Vincent tribute album – Paul pulled together an all-star line-up of Deep Purple drummer Ian Paice, Pink Floyd guitarist Dave Gilmour (who was to also augment The Pretty Things when they resurrected *SF Sorrow* at the Royal Festival Hall in 2002), 1975 one-hit-wonder Pete Wingfield on keyboards and Mick Green, whose dazzling lead-rhythm guitar technique still enlivened a Pirates that had survived pub-rock's fall from favour, and when he was moonlighting in Van Morrison's backing band.

From McCartney's own portfolio, the set contained only 'I Saw Her Standing There' and two of his three compositions on *Driving Rain*. Otherwise, it was wall-to-wall classic rock for 50 minutes that, if you listened dispassionately, sounded fine in a dated sort of way to a dated sort of person.

His fans loved it – just as Ian Dury's did several months later through the release of *Brand New Boots And Panties*. Once described with vague accuracy in the *Daily Express* as "a sort of dirty old man of punk", Dury had spat out in Oi! Oi! Cockney his perspectives on London's seedy-flash low-life; his casually amusing discoveries taking form as musical-literary wit. His death from cancer on 27 March 2000 made the *Six O' Clock News* on BBC1, and the track-by-track exaltation of his most famous album, *Brand New Boots And Panties*, was earmarked for release as near as was feasible to the first anniversary. Backed by Dury's old combo, The Blockheads, McCartney's 'I'm Partial To Your Abracadabra' was as creditable as, say, Robbie Williams's 'Sweet Gene Vincent' or Shane McGowan's 'Plaistow Patricia' whilst swallowing dust behind Madness's 'My Old Man' and a startling re-arrangement of 'Clever Trevor' by Wreckless Eric: "I made it my own rather than doing a kind of karaoke version with The Blockheads playing it just like they used to. I wasn't up for that. I worked hard on that track – so much so that I got a production credit."

Paul had more of a creative role in an album taped after Martin "Youth" Glover reared up again as the producer of Super Furry Animals, formed in Cardiff in the mid-1990s as an amalgam of the Modern Dance, Britpop and olde tyme progressive rock. Like Mary Hopkin before them, they'd become enormous in that area of Welsh pop in which the likes of of Tom Jones, Amen Corner, Dave Edmunds, Man and Catatonia are incidental to acts that sing exclusively in Welsh. Unlike Y Tebot Piws, Edward H Dafis, Y Trwynau Coch and other esteemed predecessors, however, Super Furry Animals did not remain indifferent to the English-speaking market.

The spirit of 1995, therefore, faced the ghost of 1962 at an *NME* awards evening in February 2000. The two factions chatted amiably enough and, through the agency of Glover, McCartney and Super Furry Animals collaborated on *Liverpool Sound Collage*, which was to be up for a Grammy – as 2001's "Best Alternative Musical Album". It had been intended in the first instance as a sort of hi-tech "Carnival Of Light" for "About Collage", an exhibition at the Tate Liverpool by Peter Blake, whose pop-associated pursuits had not ended with his montage for the *Sgt Pepper* front cover.

Neither had Paul's non-pop dabblings with "The Art Of Paul McCartney", though he was on firmer ground with 2001's *Blackbird Singing*, a collection of over 100 poems interspersed with lyrics from some of his songs – dedicated to his and the late Linda's children. As it was with the Walker and his pictures, you wonder if Faber and Faber would have published the manuscript had it been submitted anonymously. "Most artists and musicians are trapped by their own vanity," sneered Billy Childish, himself an artist and musician, "I just don't know how he could allow them to publish his lyrics as poetry, apart from being a foolish big-head. It just says to me that he can't have much regard for himself. I can't believe he would allow himself to be made to look so stupid. Either he is stupid or he doesn't mind looking stupid. I guess either one lets him off the hook."[7]

This was the viewpoint of one who also regarded *The Beatles Live At The Star-Club In Hamburg, Germany 1962* as "their finest album" after the doctoring of the atrocious sound quality of two or so hours on the boards with the newly recruited Ringo, immortalised on Kingsize Taylor's domestic tape recorder. Paul joined forces with George and Ringo in an attempt to nip its release on CD in the bud, but a less onorous professional duty was that by *Driving Rain*, a McCartney solo album that was as freshly state-of-the-art as *The Beatles Live At The Star-Club* wasn't. Sticking mainly to singing and playing bass, he picked 15 of 22 items dashed off in a fortnight with a guitar-keyboards-drums trio of Los Angeles session players whose keeping of expensive pace with him was leavened by technical precision deferring to spontaneity. "We didn't fuss about it," he shrugged. "I'd show them a song, and we'd start doing it."[8]

These songs included 'Back In The Sunshine' (the one co-written by James), ten-minute 'Rinse The Raindrops' – and 'From A Lover To A Friend', the only A-side. It lasted a fortnight in the domestic Top 50, and proceeds were donated to the families of New York's fire service who perished in the aftershock of the terrorist attacks on the World Trade Center.

Just as the previous century had started not on New Years's Day 1900, but 22 January 1901 when Queen Victoria, the personification of an age, shuffled off this mortal coil, so the third millenium began on 11 September 2001 with the collapse of the Twin Towers and its stirring up of further of mankind's destructive instincts and contemptuous treatment of its own minority groups.

That's a generalisation. A lot of people think war is wrong. I mean, like, people get killed, y'know. And how has pop reacted to this? The easiest option, especially in the mid-1960s, was with one-size-fits-all protest songs – 'Where Have All The Flowers Gone?', 'Eve Of Destruction', 'Give Peace A Chance' and so on. The least lyrically complex were sung *en masse* on Ban The Bomb marches, student sit-ins and anti-war demonstrations – though strains of The Kinks's 'Every Mother's Son' were heard outside the White House during the Vietnam moratorium.

It didn't affect decisions made already any more than Killing Joke's set at a CND rally in Trafalgar Square in 1980 – at which the singer introduced one musical comment-on-the-society-in-which-we-live with "I hope you realise that your efforts today are all quite futile."

Understanding this, Paul McCartney – who'd been present in New York when the hijacked aeroplanes tore into the World Trade Center – organised a benefit concert at Madison Square Garden with no political agenda other than raising money for the firefighters and other victims, and to show solidarity against terrorism. Naturally, he wrote a song about it.

As a raw composition, 'Freedom' was convoluted and over-declamatory, certainly nowhere as strong as other anthems on the same subject such as 'Universal Love' by Art "Ski" Halperin, the last "discovery" by the late John Hammond Senior, who'd also brought Billie Holliday and Bob Dylan to a wider world. 'Freedom' wasn't really very good at all, but that didn't matter in the context of the euphoric atmosphere on that October Saturday six weeks after "nine-eleven" – as epitomised in the inevitable video by a manic youth, risen from his seat and, with eyes rolling in his head, oblivious to everything but bawling the raucous refrain as Paul reprised chin-up 'Freedom' with Billy Idol, Destiny's Child, The Who, Bon Jovi, Mick Jagger, David Bowie and the rest of the artistes who'd done their bit on that night-of-nights.

We never see a man. We only see his art. I mean this most sincerely, friends. So how could we ever know if McCartney (once the man for whom "starvation in India doesn't worry me one bit. Not one iota, it doesn't, man"[8]) was seizing an unforeseeable but welcome opportunity to trumpet the November release *Driving Rain* – to which 'Freedom' had been tacked on as a bonus track – or was motivated by a simple desire to help?

He wasn't to perform 'Freedom' when, after assuring enquirers that "We are hoping to bring joy to the world, nothing else,"[9] he commenced putting action over debate with regard to what he was to call his "Back In The World" tour, subtitled "Driving USA" for the country in which it was to be an antidote, said many, to September the 11th as The Beatles' 1964 visit had been to President Kennedy's assassination.

Prior to setting off on this latest jaunt, however, there was something McCartney had to do that was as special in its way as the New York spectacular. On 29 November 2001, George Harrison, no longer able to permit himself the luxury of hope, lost his last and toughest battle. As they had for John Lennon, flags flew at half-mast in Liverpool where there was immediate talk of a concert for George as there'd been for Colin Manley, who'd gilded his fretboard skills with a grinning vibrancy in the ranks of The Remo Four. When he too had died of cancer in 1999, Colin was one of The Swinging Blue Jeans – and both they and surviving members of The Remo Four had been among the cast celebrating his life at the Philharmonic Hall.

George's memorial was to be at the Empire on what would have been his 59th birthday on 24 February 2002. Paul shared a few yarns with the audience and, at the very end, gave 'em a spirited 'Yesterday', just as John McCormack had sung 'Ave Maria' at the concluding Mass of 1932's Eucharistic Congress in Dublin's Phoenix Park.

On the more secular occasion at the Empire (and the one for Colin Manley) you should have been there – because, while no one could pretend that this is what it must have been like in the dear, dead days of Merseybeat, as an atmospheric and companionable evening, it was past objective criticism.

Paul paid homage to George again on more glittering events at the Albert Hall – and on 3 June 2002 at Elizabeth II's "Jubilee Concert" in the grounds of Buckingham Palace during a slot that began with a maiden stage performance of the *Abbey Road* vignette, 'Her Majesty' and reached a climax of sorts in a duet with Eric Clapton of George's 'While My Guitar Gently Weeps' from the "White Album".

Not seen in the televisual coverage was the final number, 'I Saw Her Standing There'. As its coda yet reverberated, Paul was thinking ahead to the following Monday when he was to marry Heather Mills – for whom he'd penned an eponymous song on *Driving Rain* – at a castle hired for that very purpose in the Irish republic.

As Charles Kingsley reminds us, "Love can make us fiends as well as angels." Paul's courtship of his Tyneside paramour had often floated into a choppy sea if stray scum-press paragraphs were to be believed about pre-nuptial agreements; violent quarrels that resonated along hotel corridors and opposition to the match from McCartney's daughters (who "loathed and feared" Heather, according to a *Daily Mail* tittle-tattler[10]). Nevertheless, Heather and Paul's was the fuss wedding of the year after the castle's elderly laird, unused to press encroachment, gave the game away.

Back from the honeymoon, the groom embarked on the second leg of what was now a wartime tour. He was able to charge the best part of £100 ($160) per ticket, more than The Rolling Stones, Cher, Madonna, Elton John, The Who, you name 'em. Most attendees were of, well, a certain age – as they were for a reformed Yes, a stadium-swelling act a little lower in *Pollstar*, the Californian market research company's tabulation of box-office draws. "It seems a lot of our original fans have become professional people," grinned their vocalist, Jon Anderson, "from doctors to astronauts; amazing but logical really."[11]

With this in mind, there was a greater preponderance of Beatles items – including a couple sung on disc by George and John – than ever before – to the extent that "Paul McCartney Sings The Beatles" drew the eye to a *Sunday Times* advertisement that chucked in three-star overnight accommodation on top of the concert when McCartney reached Manchester on 10 April 2003.

Wherever he could – on programmes or the spin-off "live" album – he ensured that composing credits read "McCartney–Lennon" like they had fleetingly before Parlophone and everyone else had made it the more alphabetically correct "Lennon–McCartney", even on the *Anthology*. Paul's attempt then to have it otherwise had been vetoed by John's volcanic widow, and reawoke a dispute that hasn't yet been resolved. You can understand Paul's attitude. On the basis of mostly song-by-song breakdowns by Lennon during one of his last interviews, BBC Radio Merseyside presenter Spencer Leigh figured out that, statistically, McCartney was responsible for approximately two-thirds of The Beatles' output of originals, including 'Yesterday' and 'Hey Jude'.

This was borne out by implication too in John's remarks to an aide in 1979: "Paul never stopped working. We'd finish one album, and I'd go off and get stoned, and forget about writing new stuff, but he'd start working on new material right away, and as soon as he'd got enough songs, he'd want to start recording again."[12] McCartney corroborated this 23 years later in a weighty press statement, fulminating too that "Late one night, I was in an empty bar, flicking through the pianist's music book when I came across '"Hey Jude" written by John Lennon'. At one point, Yoko earned more from 'Yesterday' than I did. It doesn't compute – especially when it's the only song that none of the [other] Beatles had anything to do with."

Was it ever thus? It would be pleasant to think that any number of black bluesmen with a lackadaisical regard for business, received if not royalties then acknowledgement due to them from white rock bands like Led Zeppelin, who rewrote Howlin' Wolf's 'How Many More Years' as 'How Many More Times'. More to the point, a typing error attributed a version of The Yardbirds' 'Shapes Of Things' on an album by The Jeff Beck Group to bass player Paul Samwell-Smith alone rather than drummer Jim McCarty and singer Keith Relf too. Then there was the case of The Animals' 'House Of The Rising Sun'. This joint overhaul of a traditional ballad topped international charts, but as there wasn't sufficient room on the single's label to print all five Animal names, only one was used – that of organist Alan Price, who'd had least to do with the arrangement of the song. The others were placated with the promise that it wouldn't make any difference to shares in the royalties, but insists drummer John Steel, "We never saw any of that money. Alan still earns on it today."

Just as Price was ostracised by the other Animals, so Yoko Ono wasn't invited to either Linda McCartney's memorial service in New York or, apparently, Paul's nine-eleven concert.

While McCartney remains bound to Ono by Beatles business, a woman with closer personal affinity to him has no direct communication whatsoever anymore. Nonetheless, Ruth McCartney cuts a familiar and appealing figure at US Beatles conventions where, if proud of her step-brother's standing as "the Walt Disney of love songs", she has no qualms about airing her views regarding his shortcomings.

While his name, unlike Ruth's, might not mean all that much to Beatles fans in the States, Cliff Bennett could, if he chooses, be a wanted guest at such festivals in Europe, thus accruing a secondary income to earnings on the Swinging Sixties circuit. As McCartney could have told him, a mere Great Voice wasn't enough to sustain contemporary interest. Indeed, a disillusioned Cliff had withdrawn from the music business altogether for many years, but nothing could stop him singing, and, come the 1980s, he'd been back with another Rebel Rousers at a Star-Club Rock 'n' Roll Jubilee with other faces from its pop yesteryears. As soulful as he ever was, the big man with the big voice had brushed aside the millennia since 1962 like so many matchsticks. As the century continued to die, time's winged chariot transported Cliff to Summer Sixties 1999, a weekend wallow in nostalgia at the capacious Brighton Centre with other of the kingdom's surviving entertainers from the decade that had ended with the disbandment of The Beatles. According to a random survey, Cliff and his latest Rebel Rousers stole the show.

Denny Laine did the same when making himself pleasant as one of two pop "personalities" at a charity record fair at the University of Northumbria in 1996. That, however, isn't saying much because the other one was me. This was during a series of one-nighters in the northeast starring Denny and his lone acoustic guitar and my solo turn that defied succinct description.

We became friends, but I couldn't help but feel a frequent sense of wonderment – as if both Denny and the situations in which we found ourselves weren't quite real. Admission was free at the Malt Shovel in Middlesbrough, where my act was interrupted by a woman who kept barging into the playing area and bawling into the microphone at irregular intervals until the landlord threw her out. With this problem removed, I went the distance. A small contingent had been with me all the way, but I only reached the rest during my big finish.

Predictably, Denny went down better by pandering admirably to assumed audience desires with 'Go Now', 'Say You Don't Mind', singalongs (including a 'Mull Of Kintyre' finale) from his decade in Wings, a couple of Dylan numbers, and a 'Blackbird' that would've given Paul McCartney pause for thought had he heard it. For me, however, his finest moment was the unreleased 'Ghost Of The Scrimshaw Carver', a self-penned sea shanty impressive for its instant familiarity.

Denny was also recipient of the most lionising afterwards, both at the Malt Shovel and the following evening at Newcastle's Archer where I still drew uproar from a mixed crowd ranging from undergraduates to "Sid the Sexist" types. Somehow it encapsulated my entire career as a stage performer. Outbreaks of barracking punctuated laughter and applause as I walked an artistic tightrope without a safety net – but with a malfunctioning PA system.

Midway, a strapping lass beckoned me to the lip of the stage to utter an eye-stretching but flattering proposition in my ear. She was probably having a laugh, but this put so much lead in my metaphorical pencil that I was cheered back on for an encore that I did not deliver owing to some hard case clambering up to inform the assembled populace that, to give his foul-mouthed insolence a polite translation, my music was not so good. I retaliated by enquiring off-mike, but loud enough for his mates to hear, about whether he was having trouble with his hormones.

After 'Mull Of Kintyre' just over an hour later, I was stunned when the idol that a provincial schoolboy had encountered in Carnaby Street in 1965 called me from the dressing room to duet with him on his encore, a medley of rock 'n' roll favourites. Twenty-four hours later, this honour was bestowed once more (and with interest) when, following a looser set in which Denny dredged up favourites from as far back as the pre-Moody Blues era, a more subdued recital at Dr Brown's in Huddersfield closed when Chris Kefford, once of The Move, resurfaced as the third member of what one wit present christened the "Beverley Brothers" for 'Roll

Over Beethoven', 'Baby Let's Play House', 'Whole Lotta Shakin'',
'Hound Dog' and so on and so on.

Hurtling home along the M1, I came to the conclusion that
Denny Laine still has everything it takes for another bite – albeit
a qualified one – at the cherry of pop stardom. Yet it had to be
said that *Reborn*, his new album that was pulsating from my car's
cassette player, wasn't quite the means of delivery from the
roughhouses where he and I had been working for most of that
week. Nothing screamed out as a potential single – no 'Say You
Don't Mind' or the 'Ghost Of The Scrimshaw Carver' showstopper
– but he was in fine voice, the playing was polished, the lyrics
erudite and the production lush.

For those very reasons, I found myself wishing, now and then,
for some musical dirt, something a bit crude, to capsize the cleverly
processed stratas of sound. This was exacerbated by arrangements
that hinged on a similar medium tempo that tended to make for
much of a muchness when listening to ten new all-original tracks.

Third from the end, 'Within Walls' (a blues and the only stylised
number present) was the most ear-catching the first time round
– with the preceding 'Fanfare' a close second. Perhaps you have
to get used to the overall drift of *Reborn*. Yet I didn't feel that
because greater effort was needed to "appreciate" individual
tracks that they are somehow "deeper" than anything more
instant. However, I'm glad I possess *Reborn* if only for its promise
of finer things to come.

The next time I saw Denny was in Eastbourne when he opened
the second half of *With A Little Help From Their Friends*, a Beatles
tribute show that you shouldn't have missed but probably did.
Partly because a heavy cold had weakened Laine's voice to a
tortured rasp, the night belonged to The Merseybeats, a working
band for over 30 years, and the most vibrant paradigm of the
Liverpool beat explosion that Joe Average is ever likely to encounter
these days. Ten years before, they were an intermission act in bingo
halls – the legs-eleven patter recommencing while the last cadence

of their encore was still fading – but their dogged pursuit of better things was rewarded in 1996 when they were voted Top Group in a readers' poll in *The Beat Goes On*, then the mouthpiece of the 1960s nostalgia scene. At Eastbourne, this confidence boost showed in The Merseybeats' own delight in being there – a feeling that infected the entire auditorium.

Bantering continuity by mainstays Tony Crane and Billy Kinsley supplemented an affectionate medley of favourites by The Searchers, Billy J *et al*, and Billy and Tony's own cache of lovelorn smashes with the original personnel – 'I Think Of You', 'Wishin' And Hopin'' and so forth. More recent releases like 'Poor Boy From Liverpool' and 1995's revival of Lennon and McCartney's (sorry, McCartney and Lennon's) 'I'll Get You' were received as ecstatically – though, during the latter, the counterpointed quotes from other Beatles items didn't quite come off as far as I was concerned.

Apart from a tendency to over-milk the audience, the effect had been similar at a "Mersey Reunion" tour where The Merseybeats were also required to back a turn by compère Mike McCartney who, if no Ken Dodd, struck a convivial note with 'Two Days Monday' – his Scaffold's debut 45 – during a protracted switchover. With The Merseybeats, he poured out the hits that had elicited little positive response from me when first heard but, at Guildford Civic Hall, I was as captivated as the rest by 'Thank U Very Much' and 'Liverpool Lou'. Even 'Lily The Pink' (with Tony and Billy singing the John Gorman and Roger McGough parts) was nearly tolerable.

Unsubstantiated backstage hearsay had it that Paul was going to roll in from Sussex to cheer on his brother and renew his acquaintance with The Merseybeats and, also on the bill, an entity called Mike Pender's Searchers.

To a more pragmatic purpose than mere socialising, he'd resurfaced in the life of John Duff Lowe, who, in 1981, had let it be known that he proposed selling the worn 'That'll Be The Day'–'In Spite Of All The Danger' relic to the highest bidder. "The acetate lay in my linen drawer for years," recollected John. "Though I played it to one or two people. Then I spoke to Sotheby's to see what it was worth. This got into the newspapers, and Paul immediately put out an injunction because it had an original song of his on it that had never been published.

"A letter from his solicitor's arrived, saying that he wanted to settle the matter amicably. Paul and I had a couple of telephone conversations. He suggested that I come up to London for a chat about the old days, but I said that we ought to get the business about the acetate out of the way first. He sent his business manager and solicitor to see me in Worcester – where I was working at the time. I handed it over, perfectly happy with the deal we agreed, and that was that."

One condition of this was that Lowe was forbidden from discussing – or performing – 'In Spite Of All The Danger' for five years. Furthermore, the mooted chat in London never took place, but John had a close encounter with his old colleague when he was among the 1,000-odd listening to Paul reading his *Blackbird Singing* poems at the annual Hay-on-Wye Literary Festival held over Whitsun in 2001. In the midst of one announcement, Paul directed the crowd's attention to Lowe, who took a bow and even signed autographs later when someone was searching him out in order to bring him to McCartney in the VIP area. However, the bird had flown by the time John was found.

All might not be lost because John Duff Lowe is now – some of the time anyway – in the same profession as McCartney. For a while, Lowe had combined membership of a latter-day Four Pennies with the relaunch of a Quarry Men and the interrelated promotion of their *Open For Engagements*, a 1994 album that most listeners found more *Sgt Pepper* than olde tyme skiffle, despite the inclusion of 'Twenty Flight Rock', 'Come Go With Me' and further items from the 1958 line-up's repertoire.

"Rod Davis came over from his home in Uxbridge to play rhythm guitar on the sessions," said John. "I wrote to Paul and

George asking if they'd like to be on it. Only Paul replied, saying that he couldn't do it, but wished us the best of luck.

"The guitarist and drummer are John Ozoroff and Charles Hart of The Four Pennies – Charles takes one lead vocal, John does the rest – and we have Richie Gould on bass from West Country 'yokel' band, The Carrot-Crunchers."

The flurry of activity continued with my audition to take over from a genial John Ozoroff as lead singer – but that's another story – and Lowe's negotiations for dates at "Beatlefests" in Los Angeles and Chicago, and a tour of Japan.

So far, there's been no follow-up to *Open For Engagements* – at least not by a Quarry Men containing John Duff Lowe – but another with a bit-part in McCartney's life story, Tony Sheridan, has been able to protract a prolific recording career that has included items of greater musical if not commercial worth than the tracks he punched out in three takes at most with John, Paul, George and Pete for Bert Kaempfert.

That Sheridan's journey to his sixth decade hadn't been peaceful became clear after he arrived from Germany for an appearance as one of the advertised "surprise legends" at a "Skiffle Party" in the 100 Club in London's West End on 5 March 1997. He reminded me vaguely of the "Max" character played by John Hurt in *Midnight Express*. His hair was as white as frost, but most of it was still on his scalp above a lined forehead – and, though it might have been a bit of a squeeze, his body looked as if it would still fit into the clothes he'd worn in 1960. Crucially, however, he rocked as hard as ever he did.

After a fashion, much the same is true of Gerry Marsden, omnipresent at all manner of high-profile nostalgia and variety revues such as 1990's Gerry's Christmas Cracker season at Birmingham Town Hall. Beyond Britain, an average of six months a year of international engagements has included spots as celebrity speaker at Beatles conventions such as a Beatlefest in Chicago where his recountings of what Paul McCartney said to Horst

Fascher at the Top Ten in 1961 was punctuated with songs on an acoustic six-string. It was through a suggestion by organiser Mark Lapidos that Gerry came to write his autobiography *You'll Never Walk Alone*[13] with another Beatlefest guest, the late Ray Coleman, former editor of *Melody Maker*.

In this thoroughly diverting account, The Beatles were conspicuous among fellow travellers in the journey that brought Marsden from suburban youth clubs to reliving his past glories in Britain, Australia, North America and everywhere else he's fondly remembered.

Record releases, however, have been sporadic, if often newsworthy. For all his criticism of 'Mull Of Kintyre' in 1977, Gerry selected it for 1985's *The Lennon–McCartney Songbook*. That this vinyl long-player was less Lennon–McCartney than Lennon and McCartney – especially sleeve-note writer McCartney – was the decision of producer Gordon Smith. "He approached me with the idea that I do an LP of John and Paul's numbers," elucidated Gerry. "I never sang any of their songs onstage. Conversely, they never sang mine, sod 'em, but I still liked their music. So I thought, 'Brilliant!'. Gordon sent me a list of the ones he'd like me to do, paid for everything, and I enjoyed the sessions."

That same year, Gerry was amongst principals of The Crowd, the aggregation that reached Number One with a money-raising re-hash of his 'You'll Never Walk Alone' for victims of the Herald Of Free Enterprise shipwreck.

A comparable disaster closer to home was to push Marsden, however unwillingly, to the fore again when Paul McCartney, Elvis Costello and other Liverpool-associated stars, past and present, joined him on 1989's overhaul of Gerry's hit 'Ferry 'Cross The Mersey' – a song that Paul, as he reiterated, had wished he'd written. This was in aid of the Hillsborough Disaster Fund after 95 ordinary people were crushed to death in a swollen stadium during a Liverpool soccer team away match.

After this second 'Ferry 'Cross The Mersey' slid from the charts, the next Britain at large saw of Gerry was in an edition of Channel

Four's *Brookside* soap opera as singing guitarist in a Liverpool "supergroup" with Ray Ennis of The Swinging Blue Jeans, ex-Remo Four bass player Don Andrew – and Pete Best.

Among Pete's most recent attempts to recover scrapings of his stolen inheritance is *Casbah Coffee Bar: Birthplace Of The Beatles*, an album with the teenage Paul McCartney in pride of place on the front cover. Nonetheless, the disc's real star was Billy Kinsley as producer, singer and general factotum in a studio assembly that also encompassed other local luminaries such as saxophonist Brian Jones from The Undertakers, Beryl Marsden – who should have represented Liverpool womanhood in the 1960s charts rather than a lesser talent like Cilla Black – and Roag Best, the youngest brother, as second drummer.

Content was chosen from items on the bar's original juke box – and so are most of the arrangements, though certain idiosyncrasies creep in such as the synthesized orchestral backwash that kicks off 'Red River Rock', the fade-in to 'Sea Cruise' and an inspired rethink of 'Sleepwalk' that invokes an ocean dawn from the quarterdeck, and stands head and shoulders above Paul's ragged effort during the 1974 session with John Lennon and his "lost weekend" cronies in California.

Yet the decades of technology that have passed since the Casbah opened in 1958 means that, overall, there wasn't as much grit as I'd have liked – but perhaps that's not the point for incorrigible old rockers with no other cards left to play. If nothing else, *Casbah Coffee Bar* sounds like it was fun to record, even if this particular brand of fun wasn't a thing that money can't buy.

What am I to bid for a review copy of *Produced By George Martin: Fifty Years In Recording*, a lavish box-set retrospective of six CDs? Relevant to this discussion are Martin's self-penned *Pepperland Suite*, a nutshelling of the incidental music to the *Yellow Submarine* movie, and acknowledgement that Paul was the Beatle with whom George had most artistic empathy via the presence of McCartney's contributions to *The Family Way* flick and the

*Thingamybob* sit-com. There are also four of his post-Beatles efforts on the two discs in this collection that celebrate the later work of the now-retired architect of discs by the showbusiness sensation that made more fortunes than have ever been known in the history of recorded sound.

# Epilogue
## *"Besame Mucho"*

"Why don't Paul McCartney and Ringo Starr step into the shoes of John Entwistle and Keith Moon to create the supergroup we've always wanted; say The Whotles or The Bho?"

*– GJ Kenna*[1]

He'd arrived at the gateway of the next century with more money than sense, and loaded with all manner of honours that he'd accepted with a becoming modesty. Like the other surviving Beatle – not to mention the two still living of the original Who – his prosperity and good works will be sustained into old age, and be subsidised less by new output than the tightly controlled repackagings of classics he'd recorded decades earlier.

Though he acquitted himself admirably onstage as the biggest box-office draw on the circuit in 2003, the days of instant Number Ones and even automatic Top 40 entries have long gone for Paul McCartney. Nevertheless, he's still happy to bask in the limelight of whatever hit records remain in him.

In the immediate wake of Elvis Presley's death in 1977, there was a swiftly deleted tribute single, 'The Greatest Star Of All' by a certain Skip Jackson in which steel guitars weep behind a sort of Illinois Cockney who declares in a flat tone that regrets that "one more great record to make it all complete" hadn't been forthcoming.

On his 50th birthday in 1992, Paul was overcome with similar sentiment, musing a little ruefully that "despite the successful songs I've written like 'Yesterday', 'Let It Be' and 'Hey Jude', I feel I just want to write one really good song. People say to me, 'What's left for you to do?' – but I still have a little [that word again!] bee in my bonnet telling me, 'Hang on. The best could be yet to come. You could write something which could be just incredible.' That keeps me going. Looking at things now, I don't seem to be over the hill."[2]

Nothing of 'Yesterday'–'Hey Jude' quality has come to him since – or maybe it has, but wasn't able to reach enough listeners because of a marketing climate and attitude much changed since The Beatles – and Wings – were around. As Gene Pitney has theorised, "You can't write a great Sixties song now and have it be successful."[3] When was the last time you heard the latest by Paul McCartney or Gene Pitney on Radio One? When was the last time you listened to Radio One? However much he might gainsay it, Paul's target group – like that for this biography – are those who don't buy rap, Britpop, boy bands, *Pop Idol* winners *et al*, whose appetite for novelty is satiated, and who only bother with singles during the Christmas "silly season".

Above all, 'From Me To You', 'Yesterday', 'Hello Goodbye' and 'Lady Madonna' aren't so much vibrations hanging in the air anymore as symbols of the Swinging Sixties – and McCartney has been prevented from soundtracking pop eras that have come after to anywhere near the same degree. While that watershed decade has been over for 40 years, the emotional rather than intrinsic significance of its music lingers, and new songs, however worthy, sung by a Beatle voice can leave a peculiar afterglow. In a parallel dimension, perhaps 'Only Love Remains' by The Beatles is the most covered composition of all time, while 1986's 'Yesterday' by Paul McCartney petered out at a domestic Number 34 before being consigned to the archives of oblivion.

In the real world, all most visitors to the Louvre want to see is the *Mona Lisa*, ignoring what might be essentially finer paintings along the corridors leading to it. Paul McCartney singing 'From

A Lover To A Friend' in concert is regarded as an artistic indulgence, an obligatory lull requiring a more subdued reaction than that for when 'Eleanor Rigby' or 'I Saw Her Standing There' makes everything all right again.

How, therefore, can he ever imagine that "the best could be yet to come'? Another impediment, of course, is that, though hair dye and a soft-focus lens rendered him an old-young creature gripping an electric guitar for the principal *Back In The World* publicity shot, BBC television cameras treated him less kindly in a recurring 2003 trailer for Radio Two – of a solo 'Band On The Run' in which: "He's playing every instrument ever invented," in the sarcastic over-estimation of veteran jazzman Stan Tracey, "and some that are about to be invented. He's mastered them all of course. It's rather touching."[4]

Yet, apart from *choba* jowls and *oobu-joobu* lips, McCartney showed his age here little more than Cliff Richard would have done. Like Richard, too, he remains an irregular chart contender – and an object of admiration by the most disparate people. "I don't think that music has an automatically high value because it's hard to listen to," pontificated modern classical composer Michael Nyman, "and a low value because it's easy to listen to. Give me a Beatles song any time."[5]

To heavy metallurgist and docu-soap personality Ozzy Osbourne, McCartney is "a hero. I met him on *The Howard Stern Show* in 2001, and there were photographs taken of me with him, and I wrote to him and asked if I could have one. He never got back to me and I was kind of disappointed. I mean, The Beatles were the reason I wanted to get into music. I wanted Paul to play on 'Dreamer' [from 2000's *Down To Earth* album], but he didn't want to do it. He said, 'I couldn't play it any better than the bass player that's already playing on there' – but that wasn't the point. The point was to have Paul McCartney playing bass on one of the most Beatle-esque songs I've ever written. He apologised to me and I told him to forget it. Just the fact that he'd sat down and listened to my song was enough for me."[6]

As the subject of sick-making stories of crapulous debauchery and bringing a press conference to a standstill by biting the head off a white dove – and swallowing it – Ozzy's seemingly permanent expression of dazed bafflement might have been been a true reflection of inner feelings when he was granted a one-song spot at the Queen's "Jubilee Concert". Paul McCartney, however, had accepted his longer sojourn on the boards – the last act on – as his due. The dean of British pop, he acknowledged acclaim for merely existing after a comic introduction by Dame Edna Everage.

The intensity of the ovations neither rose nor fell as he completed a polished set consisting of nothing but Beatles numbers. Only if he'd made a complete pig's ear of them, could viewers at home and in the palace grounds have said anything constructive beyond "That's Paul singing 'Her Majesty', 'Blackbird', 'While My Guitar Gently Weeps', 'Sgt Pepper's Lonely Hearts Club Band', 'The End'…"

Then the other acts walked back on and stood in respectful rows when joined by our gracious Queen with the Prince of Wales, who said a few well-chosen words before 'Hey Jude' and its joyous coda sung *ad infinitum* by all the big showbusiness names up there – Shirley Bassey, Tony Bennett, Cliff, Ozzy, Ray Davies, Brian Wilson, Steve Winwood, one of The Spice Girls, Rod Stewart, Tom Jones, you name 'em – and, at the centre of it all, Paul McCartney!

# Notes

In addition to my own correspondence and interviews, I have used the following sources, which I would like to credit:

## Prologue: 'Till There Was You'

1 *Sunday Times*, 11 January 2003

2 *The Paul McCartney Encyclopaedia* by B Harry (Virgin, 2002)

3 *Paul McCartney: The Songs He Was Singing* by J Blaney (Paper Jukebox, 2003)

4 *Paul McCartney: Many Years From Now* by B Miles (Vintage, 1998)

## Chapter 1: 'Que Sera Sera'

1 *Cry: The Johnnie Ray Story* by J Whiteside (Barricade, 1994)

2 *Singing Together* (BBC Publications, 1953)

3 *Who's Who In Popular Music In Britain* by S Tracy (World's Work, 1984)

4 *Daily Express*, 23 August 1955

5 *Melody Maker*, 17 September 1958

6 *The Life And Times Of Little Richard, The Quasar Of Rock* by C White (Harmony, 1984)

7 *The Facts About A Pop Group: Featuring Wings* by D Gelly (Whizzard, 1976)

8 *Buddy Holly: The Real Story* by E Amburn (Virgin, 1996)

9 *Backbeat: Die Stuart Sutcliffe Story* by A Clayson and P Sutcliffe (Bastei Lubbe, 1994), a translation of the original manuscript of *Backbeat – Stuart Sutcliffe: The Lost Beatle* by the same authors (Pan-Macmillan, 1994)

## Chapter 2: 'That'll Be The Day'

1. *Clint Eastwood: Film Maker* by D O'Brien (Batsford, 1996)

2 *Picturegoer*, 1 September 1956

3    Quoted in sleeve notes to *The Very Best Of Matt Monro* (Spectrum, 1997)

4    *Who's Who In Popular Music In Britain* by S Tracy (World's Work, 1984)

## Chapter 3: 'It's Now Or Never'

1.   *Backbeat: Die Stuart Sutcliffe Story* by A Clayson and P Sutcliffe (Bastei Lubbe, 1994), a translation of the original manuscript of *Backbeat – Stuart Sutcliffe: The Lost Beatle* by the same authors (Pan-Macmillan, 1994)

2.   *Bratby* by P Davies (Bakehouse, 2002)

3.   *The Times*, 24 September 1988

4.   *The Beat Goes On*, November 1992

5.   *New Musical Express*, 1 November 1957

6.   Quoted in sleeve notes to *The Very Best Of Matt Monro* (Spectrum, 1997)

7.   *Acts Of Faith* by A Faith (Bantam, 1996)

## Chapter 4: 'What'd I Say?'

1.   *Acker Bilk* by G Williams (Mayfair, 1960)

2.   *New Musical Express*, 19 August 1958

3.   *Melody Maker*, 11 March 1963

4.   *Let's All Go Down The Cavern* by S Leigh (Vermilion, 1984)

5.   BBC Radio Bedfordshire, 29 December 1985

6.   *Backbeat: Die Stuart Sutcliffe Story* by A Clayson and P Sutcliffe (Bastei Lubbe, 1994), a translation of the original manuscript of *Backbeat – Stuart Sutcliffe: The Lost Beatle* by the same authors (Pan-Macmillan, 1994)

7.   *Beatle!: The Pete Best Story* by P Best and P Doncaster (Plexus, 1985)

8.   *Music*, November 1997

9.   *Hamburg: The Cradle Of British Rock* by A Clayson (Sanctuary, 1997)

10.  US title: *Call Me Genius!*

11.  *The Times*, 24 November 1988

12.  A 1960 US Number One, and a UK Top 20 entry in 1961 for Maurice Williams And The Zodiacs

13.  *Good Day Sunshine*, November 1989

## Chapter 5: 'Over The Rainbow'

1.   *The Spinning Wheels: The Story Of A Melbourne Rhythm And Blues Band* by D Hirst (Park Fraser, 2002)

2    *Backbeat: Die Stuart Sutcliffe Story* by A Clayson and P Sutcliffe (Bastei Lubbe,

1994), a translation of the original manuscript of *Backbeat – Stuart Sutcliffe: The Lost Beatle* by the same authors (Pan-Macmillan, 1994)

3. *The Beat Goes On*, November 1999

4. *The Beat Goes On*, February 1991

## Chapter 6: 'Some Other Guy'

1. *John Lennon: Living On Borrowed Time* by F Seaman (Xanadu, 1991)

2. *Let's All Go Down The Cavern* by S Leigh (Vermilion, 1984)

3. *Brian Epstein: The Man Who Made The Beatles* by R Coleman (Viking, 1989)

4. Paul McCartney's sleeve notes to *The Lennon–McCartney Songbook* by Gerry Marsden (K-Tel, 1985)

5. *Midland Beat*, No 1, October 1963

6. *New Musical Express*, 8 January 1962

7. *The Life And Times of Little Richard, The Quasar Of Rock* by C White (Harmony, 1984)

8. *Backbeat: Die Stuart Sutcliffe Story* by A Clayson and P Sutcliffe (Bastei Lubbe, 1994), a translation of the original manuscript of *Backbeat – Stuart Sutcliffe: The Lost Beatle* by the same authors (Pan-Macmillan, 1994)

9. *Drummed Out! The Sacking Of Pete Best* by S Leigh (Northdown, 1998)

10. *Mersey Beat*, 10 March 1962

11. *Beatle!: The Pete Best Story* by P Best and P Doncaster (Plexus, 1985)

12. *Q*, June 1992

## Chapter 7: 'Don't You Dig This Kind Of Beat?'

1. *Midland Beat*, No 1, October 1963

2. *Midland Beat*, No 13, October 1964

## Chapter 8: 'Nobody I Know'

1. *Kink* by D Davies (Boxtree, 1996)

2. *Cry: The Johnnie Ray Story* by J Whiteside (Barricade, 1994)

3. *Behind The Song: The Stories of 100 Great Pop & Rock Classics* by M Heatley and S Leigh (Blandford, 1999)

4. *The "Playboy" Interviews With John Lennon and Yoko Ono* by D Sheff and G Barry Golson (New Enigsh Library, 1982)

5. On a poster for his appearance at Redhill Market Hall on 30 January 1964

6. *Nowhere To Run* by G Hirshey (Pan, 1984)

7. *The Facts About A Pop Group: Featuring Wings* by D Gelly (Whizzard, 1976)

8. *1,000 Days That Shook The World, Mojo Beatles Special*, October 2002

9. *Paul McCartney: Many Years From Now* by B Miles (Vintage, 1998)

10. However, Walsh's most renowned work was a portrait of the late Cuban *guerilléro*, Che Guevara. As a poster print, this became a fixture in student hostel rooms in the later 1960s.

11. They were to record several albums for RCA, tour with Led Zeppelin and be on the bill at 1969's Isle of Wight festival.

12. *TV Times*, 23 October 1965

13. *Thank U Very Much* by M McGear (Arthur Barker, 1981)

14. *Random Precision: Recording The Music Of Syd Barrett* by D Parker (Cherry Red, 2001)

## Chapter 9: 'I'm The Urban Spaceman'

1. *Loose Talk* by L Botts (*Rolling Stone*, 1980)

2. *Lost In The Woods: Syd Barrett And The Pink Floyd* by J Palacios (Boxtree, 1998)

3. *Playpower* by R Neville (Jonathan Cape, 1970)

4. *Scene At 6.30* (ITV, 4 March 1967)

5. *International Times*, 16–29 January 1967

6. *Which One's Cliff?* by C Richard (Coronet, 1977)

7. *The Process,* No 5, autumn 1968

8. *Paul McCartney: Many Years From Now* by B Miles (Vintage, 1998)

9. *Days In The Life: Voices From The English Underground, 1961–1971* by J Green (Heinemann, 1988)

10. *Lennon Remembers: The Rolling Stone Interviews,* ed J Wenner (Penguin, 1973)

11. Quoted in *Crazy Fingers* by A Carson (Carson, 1998)

12. *Record Collector,* No 285, May 2003

13. *The Playboy Interviews With John Lennon and Yoko Ono* by D Sheff and G Barry Golson (New English Library, 1982)

14. Quoted in *The Yardbirds* by A Clayson (Backbeat, 2002)

15. *Disc And Music Echo*, December 1965 (precise date obscured)

16. *1,000 Days Of Revolution, Mojo Beatles Special,* March 2003

## Chapter 10: 'Goodbye'

1. *The Love You Make: An Insider's Story Of The Beatles* by P Brown and S Gaines (Macmillan, 1983)

2. Quoted in *No Sleep Till Canvey Island: The Great Pub Rock Revolution* by W Birch (Virgin, 2000)

3. *Loose Talk* by L Botts (Rolling Stone, 1980)

4. Press release, 17 April 1970

5. *Stone Alone: The Story of a Rock' N' Roll Band* by B Wyman and R Coleman (Viking, 1990)

6. *Blue Melody: Tim Buckley Remembered* by L Underwood (Backbeat, 2002)

7. *Don't Let Me Be Misunderstood* by E Burdon and J Marshall Craig (Thunder's Mouth, 2001)

## Chapter 11: 'Wedding Bells'

1. *Who's Who In Popular Music In Britain* by S Tracy (World's Work, 1984)

2. *The Guardian*, 11 March 2003

## Chapter 12: 'Love Is Strange'

1. *The Facts About A Pop Group: Featuring Wings* by D Gelly (Whizzard, 1976)

2. Though publication was to be resumed in the 1980s.

3. *Paul McCartney: Many Years From Now* by B Miles (Vintage, 1998)

4. *Brass Bands* by AR Taylor (Granada, 1979)

5. *Chase The Fade* by A Nightingale (Blandford, 1981)

6. *Record Mirror*, 15 April 1971

7. *The John Lennon Encyclopaedia* by B Harry (Virgin, 2000)

8. *Paul McCartney* by A Hamilton (Hamish Hamilton, 1983)

9. *The Paul McCartney Encyclopaedia* by B Harry (Virgin, 2002)

10. *New Musical Express*, 27 May 1971

11. Quoted in *The Illustrated New Musical Express Encyclopaedia Of Rock,* ed N Logan and B Woffinden (Hamlyn, 1976)

12. *Let It Rock*, January 1973

13. *Irish Rock* by MJ Prendergast (O'Brien, 1987)

14. *Joe Cocker* by JP Bean (Omnibus, 1990)

15. *Don't Let Me Be Misunderstood* by E Burdon and J Marshall Craig (Thunder's Mouth, 2001)

## Chapter 13: 'Mary Had A Little Lamb'

1. *Don't Let Me Be Misunderstood* by E Burdon and J Marshall Craig (Thunder's Mouth, 2001)

2. *Times Educational Supplement*, 16 November 1986

3. *The Rolling Stone Record Guide,* ed D Marsh and J Swenson (Rolling Stone, 1979)

## Chapter 14: 'Crossroads'

1. *Melody Maker*, 17 May 1973

2. *Melody Maker*, 18 and 25 September 1973

3. *The Record Producers* by J Tobler and S Grundy (BBC, 1982)

4. *Nowhere To Run* by G Hirshey (Pan, 1984)

5. *The Paul McCartney Encyclopaedia* by B Harry (Virgin, 2002)

6. First issued as an A-side in 1977, and attributed to 'Suzy And The Red Stripes'

7. *Fab Four* (French fanzine), March 1991

8. *The Facts About A Pop Group: Featuring Wings* by D Gelly (Whizzard, 1976)

9. *Melody Maker*, 5 April 1976

10. *Rolling Stone*, 19 December 1974

11. Quoted in *Behind The Song: The Stories of 100 Great Pop & Rock Classics* by M Heatley and S Leigh (Blandford, 1998)

12. *Stardust: The Life And Times Of David Bowie* by T Zanetta and H Edwards (Michael Joseph, 1986)

13. Quoted in *John Lennon* by A Clayson (Sanctuary, 2003)

14. *The "Playboy" Interviews With John Lennon And Yoko Ono* by D Sheff (Playboy Press, 1981)

## Chapter 15: 'Japanese Tears'

1. *Behind The Song: The Stories of 100 Great Pop & Rock Classics* by M Heatley and S Leigh (Blandford, 1998)

2. *Sunday Mirror*, 12 November 1995.

3. *Top Of The Pops* by S Bracknell (Patrick Stevens, 1985)

4. *The Paul McCartney Encyclopaedia* by B Harry (Virgin, 2002)

5. *The Rolling Stone Record Guide,* ed D Marsh and J. Swenson (Rolling Stone, 1979)

6. *Rolling Stone*, 12 December 1979

7. *Chase The Fade* by A Nightingale (Blandford, 1981)

8. *The Sun*, 27 January 1980

9. *Japan Times*, 27 January 1980

## Chapter 16: 'Just Like Starting Over'

1. *New Musical Express*, 15 February 1963

2. *Hit Men* by F Dannen (Muller, 1990)

3. *John Lennon: Living On Borrowed Time* by F Seaman (Xanadu, 1991)

4. *The Record Producers* by J Tobler and S Grundy (BBC, 1982)

5. *Club Sandwich*, No 26, 1982

6. *Melody Maker*, 5 November 1983

7. *New Musical Express*, 6 November 1983

8. *Q*, January 1988

9. *Acts Of Faith* by A Faith (Bantam, 1996)

10. *Club Sandwich*, No 35, 1984

11. *Variety*, October 1984

12. *Sunday Times*, 5 May 1990

## Chapter 17: 'Don't Get Around Much Anymore'

1. *Beatles Unlimited*, March 1996

2. *Death Discs* by A Clayson (Sanctuary, 1997)

3. To Spencer Leigh

4. By coincidence, The Average White Band's original drummer was also called Robbie McIntosh.

5. As had Elvis Presley's post-army 'It's Now Or Never' for *The Last Temptation Of Elvis*, a charity compilation album.

6. *The Paul McCartney Encyclopaedia* by B Harry (Virgin, 2002)

7. *Q*, July 1989

8. *The Brothers McGregor* by A Wells (Grafton, 1985)

9. *Rolling Stone*, December 1981

## Chapter 18: 'Come Together'

1. *Gramophone*, July 1988

2. *The Paul McCartney Encyclopaedia* by B Harry (Virgin, 2002)

3. *All-Music Guide to Electronica,* ed V Bogdonov, C Woodstra, ST Erlewine and J Bush (Backbeat, 2001)

4. *Backbeat: Die Stuart Sutcliffe Story* by A Clayson and P Sutcliffe (Bastei Lubbe, 1994), a translation of the original manuscript of *Backbeat – Stuart Sutcliffe: The Lost Beatle* by the same authors (Pan-Macmillan, 1994)

5. *Classic FM*, August 1997

6. *Music*, November 1999

7. *"Non nobis solum sed toti mundo nati"* ("Not for ourselves alone but for the whole world were we born")

8. *Liverpool Oratorio* (Parlophone LDB 9911301, 1991)

9. *Sunday Mirror*, 23 July 1989

10. *The Sun*, 15 July 1980

## Chapter 19: 'My Dark Hour'

1. *Robin And Marion* (Columbia/Rastar Technicolor, 1976)

2. Sleeve notes for *The Quiet Hour* by Patience Strong (Saga STSOC 956, 1963)

3. *Music*, November 1997

4. *Daily Express*, 22 June 1995

5. *Daily Mail*, 1 January 1997

6. *Sunday Times*, 22 December 2002

7. *Daily Express*, 19 May 1997

8. *Independent On Sunday*, 10 May 1997

9. *The Times*, 9 May 1997

10. *Paul McCartney: Many Years From Now* by B Miles (Vintage, 1998)

11. *Don't Let Me Be Misunderstood* by E Burdon and J Marshall Craig (Thunder's Mouth, 2001)

## Chapter 20: 'She Said Yeah'

1. *Rod Stewart* by T Ewbank and S Hildred (Headline, 1991)

2. *Hello!* (date obscured)

3. *Out On A Limb* by H Mills and P Cockerill (Little, Brown, 1995)

4. By Pavilion

5. *Beat Merchants* by A Clayson (Cassell/Blandford, 1995)

6. *Daily Mail*, 24 May 2002

7. *Chatham's Burning* (Hangman, 2003)

8. Quoted in *Neil's Book Of The Dead* by N Planer and T Blacker (Pavilion, 1984)

9. *The Times*, 29 March 2003

10. *Daily Mail*, 11 June 2002

11. *Sunday Times*, 12 January 2003

12. *John Lennon: Living On Borrowed Time* by F Seaman (Xanadu, 1991)

13. *You'll Never Walk Alone* by G Marsden and R Coleman (Bloomsbury, 1993)

## Epilogue: 'Besame Mucho'

1. Reader's letter to *Viz*, September 2002

2. *The Paul McCartney Encyclopaedia* by B Harry (Virgin, 2002)

3. *The Guardian*, 14 May 2003

4. *The Guardian*, 11 April 2003

5. *The Guardian*, 8 January 2003

6. *Black Sabbath* by S Rosen (Sanctuary, 1996)

# Index

*Abbey Road* 135
Abbey Road
  The Beatles' first
   recording 84
  experimental sessions
   116–17
  The Beatles' last
   performance 134
  Wings at 161, 176
academia, and pop 238–9
"acid jazz" 232
Acquaye, Speedy 130, 191
*Aftermath* (The Rolling
  Stones) 101–2
Airforce 131
'Albatross' 233
album tie-ins 228
Aldershot, The Beatles in
  70–1
Alexandra Palace,
  Fourteen Hour
  Technicolor Dream 114
'All My Trials/Sorrows'
  220, 221
*All The Best* 212
'All Those Years Ago' 204
Almond, Marc 205–6
Amey, Ian "Tich" 72 (see
  also *Bostons, The*)
Anderson, Jon 201, 269
Andrew, Don 75, 278
Andrews, Chris 87
Andrews, Eamonn 218
animal rights, Paul's
  involvement in 198–9,
  229

Animals, The 129, 132,
  270
'Another Day' 116, 140
*Anthology* 241–3, 269
Antonioni, Michelangelo
  109, 112
Apple Corps 124–6,
  134–5
Apple Records 124, 126
Argent, Rod 249
Art Of Noise, The 232,
  233
Asher, Jane 105–6, 111,
  127–8, 254
Asher, Margaret 106
Asher, Peter 106–7, 111,
  112, 126
Aspinall, Neil 117
Astralasia 232
Atkins, Chet 171
Atom Heart 232
'Attention' 205
Attractions, The 217
avant-garde, The Beatles
  and 112–13, 115
Average White Band 220

'Baby's Request' 191
Bachelors, The 89–90,
  100–1
'Back In The Sunshine'
  266
'Back On My Feet' 219
*Back To The Egg* 190–1
"Back To The World"
  tour 267, 269

*Backbeat* 66, 227
Baez, Joan 220
Bainbridge, Beryl 48
Baker, Ginger 131, 142,
  167
Ball, Kenny 36
'Ballad Of John And
  Yoko' 134
ballads 52
  Paul as singer 52, 63–4
Balls 130–1
Bambi-Filmkunsstheater
  (Hamburg) 58, 60, 61
*Band On The Run* 166–8
'Band On The Run' 163,
  166–7
Banks, Bessie 93
Bates, Simon 186
Beach Boys, The 101
"Beat Generation" 45
"Beatle Conventions" 204,
  227
*Beatles Live At The Star-
  Club ...* 265
*Beatles Monthly* 136
Beatles, The
  reasons for success 54
  in Hamburg 56, 58–9,
   69, 78, 81, 83, 102–3,
   265
  first non-UK
   performance 58–9
  uniforms 58, 71, 77
  deported from
   Hamburg 61 popularity
   with Exis 63

choice of songs 65, 68
rock 'n' roll numbers
  67–8
debut at the Cavern 69
hostility to 71
use of songs from films
  and musicals 73 first
  recording 74
first Abbey Road session
  84
first LP 87
wholesomeness 90
at "NME Pollwinners'
  Concert" 94
instrumental
  augmentation 96 Paul's
  control of publicity 97
and soul music 99
and The Beach Boys
  101
tours 103–5
death threats 105
and avant-garde
  112–13, 115
concept albums 117–18
"hidden messages" in
  discs 117–18
and Apple Corps 124,
  125
business disagreements
  134–5
Paul's control of 134
Paul's resignation from
  138
continuing interest in
  140, 204, 243–4 formal
  dissolution 140 reunions
  180–2 obsession with
  204 portfolio bought by
  Jackson 208
tribute bands 227
Anthology 241–3
beatniks 44–5, 62
Beck, Jeff 98, 132, 191,
  231
Beefheart (Don Van Vliet)
  262
Bell, Maggie 170
Bennett, Cliff 37–8, 81,
  91–2, 99, 271
Bennett, Richard Rodney
  246–7

Berio, Luciano 112, 113,
  115
Berry, Dave 79, 177, 178,
  213, 224
Bertelmann, Fred 55
Best, Mona 50, 69, 76
Best, Pete 57, 58, 278
  autobiography 59
  character 63
  and Paul 70
  The Beatles haircut and
    71
  looks 76, 85
  and Sutcliffe's death
    83–4
  sacking from The
    Beatles 84–5
Best, Roag 278
Betterdays, The 72, 79
Bevan, Bev 60, 79
Big Three, The 68, 91
'Biker Like An Icon' 229
Bilk, Acker 36, 54, 194
Birmingham bands 79–80
Bishop, Dickie 263
Black, Cilla 99, 136
Black Dyke Mills Band
  137–8
black music 98–9
'Blackbird' 179
Blackbird Singing 265
Blackjacks, The 50, 57
Blair, Tony 251, 252
Blake, Peter 44, 152, 265
Blind Faith 125, 177
Blockheads, The 264
Blunstone, Colin 119,
  153
"Bobbies" 44, 89
bodyguards 261
Boht, Jean 235
Bomberg, David 44
Bonham, John 80, 191
Bonzo Dog Doo-Dah
  Band, The 122–3
Bootleg Beatles, The 227
Bostons, The 56, 136
Bowie, David 181, 205,
  231
Bragg, Billy 213
Bramlett, Bonnie 173
Branson, Richard 160

brass bands 137–8
Bratby, John 44
Britpop 242, 243
Britton, Geoff 169,
  172–3
Brodsky Quartet, The
  218, 248, 255
Bron, Gerry 123
Brookside (soap opera)
  278
Bruce, Jack 181
Bruce, Lenny 126
Buckley, Tim 128
Burdon, Eric 129, 132,
  152, 154, 255–6
Burroughs, William 45
Burton, Trevor 130–1
Byrne, Johnny 45, 46

'C Moon' 157, 175
Calvert, Eddie 23
Capitol Records 200
Carl Wayne And The
  Vikings 57
'Carnival Of Light' 115,
  234
Casbah (club) 50
Casbah Coffee Bar 278
Casey, Howie 175
Cavendish Avenue (Paul's
  London home) 107,
  134
Cavern 36, 69, 102
Cavern (new) 227, 263
'Cayenne' 43
CBS Records 200, 201
Chad and Jeremy 207,
  263
Chandler, Chas 129, 150
Chants, The 88
Chapman, Norman 51–2
Charles, Prince of Wales
  211, 283
Charles, Ray 45–6, 100
Chas McDevitt Skiffle
  Group 35
Chelsea Reach (pub) 165
Cherry, Ava 181
Chieftans, The 206
Childish, Billy 265
children's music 157,
  210–11

*Choba B CCCP* ('Back In The USSR') 221–2
Christie, John 171
Christmas singles 192
Clapton, Eric 115, 142, 191, 233
Clark, Dave 90, 107
Clarke, Allan 178
Clarke, Stanley 205
Clarke, Tony 146
"classical" music 234–8, 245–50
Clayson, Alan 271–3
Climie, Simon 233
Clooney, Rosemary 205
coat of arms, Paul's 253
Cochran, Eddie 49, 50, 221
Cocker, Joe 151, 206
Coco, Chris 233
Cocteau Twins, The 232
Cohen, Leonard 214
Coleman, Ray 277
Collins, Phil 231
'Come And Get It' 137
'Come Together' 135, 243–4
'Coming Up' 200–1
compositions by Paul with John Lennon 39, 49, 60, 73, 99
home studio 108
for brass band 137 with Elvis Costello 219
"classical" music 234–8, 245–50
techniques 60, 147, 175–6 (see also *recording techniques*)
(see also *songwriting partnership with John Lennon*)
concept albums 117
*Concerts for Bangla Desh* 179
Conteh, John 186
'Cook Of The House' 176
copyright
Paul's acquisitions 177, 200
of The Beatles portfolio 208

Cordell, Denny 92–3, 151, 152
Costello, Elvis (Declan McManus) 217–19, 229, 255
*Juliet Letters, The* 218, 229
'Country Dreamer' 159
Country Hams, The 171
Cox, Michael 43
Craine, Don 132
Crane, Tony 56, 226, 274
Crawford, Randy 215
Creme, Lol 216
Crickets, The 178
Crosby, Bing 95, 205
Cross, Tina 215
'Crossroads' 174
Crowd, The 277

Dana 207
dance hall music, 1940s and 1950s 20–1
Dark Horse label 167–8
Davies, Dave 95, 97, 132
Davis, Carl, and *Liverpool Oratorio* 234–7
Davis, Jesse Ed 182
Davis, Rod 275
Davis, Spencer 92, 99
Davis, Windsor 210
'Day In The Life, A' 235
'Daytime Nightime Suffering' 190
Dean, James, influence 29
Dee, Dave 56, 178, 206, 243
Delcardoes, The 68
Derry And The Seniors 58
Diplomats, The 79–80, 142
Doctor And The Medics 231
Dodd, Ken 52, 70
Domino, Fats 100, 221
Donald, Alistair 251
Donegan, Lonnie 34–5
Dooley, Arthur 82
Doors, The 213
Dorsey, Tony 173
*Double Fantasy* 202
Dowlands, The 88

Drifters, The 99–100
*Driving Rain* 265–6
drugs
Paul and 113–14, 164–5, 195–7
George and 133
music influenced by 232, (see also *"acid jazz"*)
Dudley, Anne 233
Dukes, The 187
Dunbar, Aynsley 168
Dunbar, John 111, 112
Duncan, Johnny 35
Dury, Ian
tribute album 264
Dylan, Bob 100, 147–8, 182, 225, 239

Eagles, The 220–1
East Gate Farm, Sussex 133–4, 159
Eastman and Eastman Inc 154
Eastman, John 154–5, 196
Eastman, Lee 134, 200
Eastman, Linda (see *McCartney, Linda*)
Easton, Eric 90
'Ebony And Ivory' 205
*Ecce Cor Meum* 248
Eddy, Duane 233
Edkins, John 102
Edmunds, Dave 209
Edward Middleditch 44
Edwars, Jack 237
Eire Apparent 150
'Eleanor Rigby' 115–16, 136–7
Electric Light Orchestra, The 131
Electric String Band, The 119–20
Elizabeth II, Queen 240–1, 268
Ellis, Royston 47
Empire Ballroom (venue of Wings launch) 148
English, Joe 173, 176, 183, 187
English Tourist Board 203
Ennis, Ray 278

Epstein, Brian 75–6
  and The Beatles 77, 78, 124
  musical tastes 77–8
  interest in Bennett 91
  as The Moody Blues' manager 118
  death 120
  Paul and 154
Eraminondas, Andros 209
Essex, David 186
Evans, Mal 97, 101
Evans, Mike 82
Everage, Dame Edna 283
Everly, Phil 205
existentialists 45
'Exis' 62–3

Faith, Adam 53, 62, 87, 171, 208
Faithfull, Marianne 96–7, 109
'Falling In Love Again' 73
Fame, Georgie 132
Family Way, The (film soundtrack) 235
Farlowe, Chris 96
Farnham, John 215
Fascher, Horst 60, 63, 203–4
Fenton, Shane 72
Ferry, Bryan 212
'Ferry 'Cross The Mersey' 277
films 121–2, 208–10
  songs from 73
Firemen, The 233
First Gear, The 99
Fischer, Wild Man 205
Flaming Pie 253–4
Fleetwood Mac 195, 197, 214
Flowers In The Dirt 219
Fontana, Wayne 132
Ford, Ricky 79
Foster, Neil 68
Fourmost, The 99
Frampton, Mary 199
Franklin, Bill 95
'Free As A Bird' 242
free open-air rock concerts 125

'Freedom' 267
Friswell, Paul 100
'From A Lover To A Friend' 266
'From Me To You' 89
'From The Bottom Of My Heart' (The Moody Blues) 94

Gallagher, Mickey 223
Gallagher, Noel 243–4
Garfunkel, Art 100–1
Garvey, Nick 12, 185, 222–3
Geldof, Bob 211
"genius" 229–30
Gentle, Johnny 50–1, 87
Germany
  rock 'n' roll 54–5
  and British pop 56
Gerry And The Pacemakers 49, 61, 68, 78, 89, 136
'Getting Closer' 191
Gibbons, Steve 130, 131
Gilmour, Dave 191, 263
'Girl Is Mine, The' 206
girls, Paul and 31–2, 52, 59, 76–7, 127–8
'Girls School' 189
'Give Ireland Back To The Irish' 156–7
'Give Me Love' (Harrison) 162–3
Give My Regards To Broad Street 208–9
Glass, Philip 249
Glitter, Gary 178, 192
Glover, Martin "Youth" 233–4, 264–5
'Go Now' 14, 93, 174
Godley, Kevin 216
Golden Crusaders 79
Good, Jack 43
'Good Times Coming' 226
'Goodnight Tonight' 190
Gordon, Noele 80, 174
Gorman, John 82
'Got To Get You Into My Life' 99
Gould, Richie 276

Goulden, "Wreckless" Eric 177, 264
Gouldman, Graham 216
"granny music" 135, 162
Grant, Eddy 201
Grant, Julie 93–4
Grateful Dead, The 214
Grease Band 151
Greaves, Derrick 44
Grech, Rick 142
Green, Mick 222, 263
Green, Peter 233
Greenham Common protest 207
Grosse Freiheit (Hamburg) 56, 61, 103
groups, finish solo careers 87
guitar playing, Paul's 40, 65, 67, 72
Gustafson, Johnny 69

haircuts (see pilzen kopf haircut)
Haley, Bill, And The Comets 21, 22, 30
Halperin, Art "Ski" 267
Hamburg 56, 59, 102, 203–4
  The Beatles in 56, 58–9, 69, 78, 81, 83, 102–3, 203–4, 265
Hamilton, James 93
Hamilton, Richard 44
Hammond, John Senior 267
Hancock, Tony 62–3
Hardin, Eddie 249
Harle, John 246, 247
Harrison, George
  in The Quarry Men 40–1, 42, 43, 47
  The Beatles haircut and 71
  and 'Yesterday' 97
  and the Maharishi 120
  Electronic Sounds 126
  police raid 133
  and end of The Beatles 135
  All Things Must Pass 140, 179

post-Beatles 140–1, 142, 146, 162–3, 179, 207, 225
record label 167–8
tribute to John Lennon 204
on Jackson 208
"best of" 212
*Cloud Nine* 225
reunion with Paul 225–6
and LIPA 241
and John Lennon's tapes 242
illness 260–1
knife attack on 260–1
death 267
memorial concert 268
Harry, Bill 76
Hart, Charles 276
Harvey, Alex 145
'Heart Of The Country' 159
Heather Mills Trust 259, 260
'Helen Wheels' 166
*Help!* (1995 album) 243–4
Hendrix, Jimi 114–15, 119–20, 150
Henri, Adrian 46, 82, 102
'Henry's Blues' 152–3
'Her Majesty' 268
'Here Today' 205
Hewison, Dwight 165
'Hey Jude' 99–100, 126, 136–7, 269–70, 283
'Hi Hi Hi' 157
Hill, Benny 130
Hines, Barry (see *Laine, Denny*)
hippies 109–10
'Hiroshima Sky Is Always Blue' 241
Hollies, The 99
Holly, Buddy 31, 104, 177–8
Paul and 177–9
*Holly Days* 178–9
Holly, Steve 190, 205
homes (see *Cavendish Avenue*; *East Gate Farm*; *Mull of Kintyre*)

Hope Hall (Everyman) cinema 27
'Hope Of Deliverance' 228–9
Hopkin, Mary 126, 151
Hopkins, John 110, 112
Horovitz, Michael 46
Hotlegs 216
'How Do You Sleep' 146
'However Absurd' 217
Humble Pie 177

'I Saw Her Standing There' 71, 73, 75, 268
*I Survive* 171
Ian And The Zodiacs 103
Ifield, Frank 86
'I'll Get You' 220
'I'm Mandy Fly Me' 216–17
'I'm Partial To Your Abracadabra 264
'I'm The Greatest' 180
'I'm The Urban Spaceman' (Bonzo Dog Doo-Dah Band) 122–3
'Imagine' 180
'In Spite Of All The Danger' 40, 274–5
Indica Gallery and Bookstore 111–12
Indra (Hamburg) 57, 58
*Inebriation* 248
Innes, Neil 122–3
instrumental playing
Paul as bass guitarist 40, 65, 67, 72
Paul as drummer 51–2
*International Times* 109–10, 111, 114
Ireland, showbands 149–50
Iron Door 36, 69
Isley Brothers, The 68, 73
'It's For You' 136
'I've Just Seen A Face' 179

Jacaranda coffee bar 27
Jackson, David 232–3
Jackson, Michael 98, 242
on Paul 167
collaborations with

Paul 206–8
*Thriller* 206, 207–8
buys Beatles portfolio 208
Jackson, Skip 280–1
Jagger, Mick 101–2, 128–9, 181
Jam Factory 173
James, Dick 96
James, Nicky 79
*James Paul Mcartney* 165
Jankowski, Horst 230
Japan 195, 219
jazz
Jim Mac's Jazz Band 18–19
traditional 36, 54
jazz-poetry fusions 46
and Exis 62–3
Jenkins, Barry 129
'Jet' 166
Jets, The 57
Jim Mac's Jazz Band 18–19
John, Elton 231
*John Lennon: Plastic Ono Band* 140, 145
Johnny And The Dominators 79
Johns, Glyn 135, 161–2
Jones, John Paul 191
Jones, Kenney 191
Jones, Paul 132
Jones, Rod 32, 46
Jones, Tom 233
Juber, Laurence 190, 205
Jubilee Concert (2002) 268, 283
'July 4' 171
'Junior's Farm' 171
Jurgens, Udo 55

Kaempfert, Bert 72–3, 74, 103, 203
Kaiserkeller (Hamburg) 57, 60, 203
Kaye Sisters, The 71
Keen, Speedy 170
Kefford, Chris 272–3
Kerouac, Jack 45
Kestrels, The 88
Keyes, Bobby 182

Kidd, Johnny 55–6, 104
Kierkegaard, Soren 45
King, Andrew 105, 106
King, Danny 80
Kinks, The 97
Kinnes, Peter (Pete Quaife)
    261–2
Kinsley, Billy 226, 274,
    278
Kirchherr, Astrid 62, 63,
    64, 83, 103
Klaus und Klaus 206
Klein, Allen 134–5, 138,
    139, 180
Koschmider, Bruno 58, 61
Kramer, Billy J 96
Kramer, Floyd 171–2

'Lady Madonna' 116
Laine, Denny (Brian
    Frederick Hines)
    early life 38, 79–80
    songwriting 80
    visit to Epstein 120
    in Balls group 130–1
    first contact with The
    Beatles 142–3
    in Wings 142, 143,
    164, 168, 169, 174,
    176
    on Paul 147
    solo albums 172, 197
    Holly Days 178–9
    and 'Mull Of Kintyre'
    189
    lasting popularity
    271–3
    Reborn 273, (see also
    Moody Blues, The)
Lane, Carla 235
Langer, Clive 218
Lapidos, Mark 277
Leaf, A 248
Lee, Peggy 171–2
Leigh, Spencer 84–5
Lennon, Cynthia (née
    Powell) 76–7, 129
Lennon, John
    character 33–4, 63
    education 33
    relationship with Paul
    33, 34, 47, 51, 134,

    145–6, 180–1, 182,
    201–2
    first meeting with Paul
    39
    songwriting partnership
    with Paul 39, 49, 60,
    68, 84, 100, 116, 136,
    269–70
    leaves Hamburg 62
    with Cynthia 76–7
    Little Richard on 82
    musical tastes 100
    and avant-garde 113
    and Paul's "death" 118
    and Yoko Ono 126–7,
    129, 134
    Plastic Ono Band 129,
    140, 145
    marriage to Yoko Ono
    133
    name change 134 post-
    Beatles numbers 140,
    163, 189–90
    comparison with Paul,
    post-Beatles 145
    on Wings 145–6
    support for Harrison
    180
    final meeting with Paul
    182–3
    death 202
    reactions to his death
    202–3
    donation of tapes by
    Yoko Ono 242
Lennon–McCartney
    Songbook, The 277
'Let 'Em In' 176
Let It Be 134, 135
'Let It Be' 211
'Let Me Roll It' 166
'Let's Love' 171–2
'Letting Go' 173–4
Lewis, Jerry Lee 46
'Listen To What The Man
    Said' 173
Litherland Town Hall,
    Beatles at 67
Little Richard 30–1, 46,
    81–2
    and Paul 82
Live Aid 211

'Live And Let Die' 166
Liverpool Institute 22, 193
Liverpool Institute of
    Performing Arts (LIPA)
    239–41
'Liverpool Lou' 171
Liverpool and Merseyside
    in 1950s 26–7 growing
    number of groups 68–9
    prominence 82, 102
    decline as pop Eldorado
    91
    Paul's return to 193–4,
    226–7
    The Beatles and 226–7
    riots 239
Liverpool Oratorio 234–8
Liverpool Scene, The 102
Liverpool Sound Collage
    265
Liverpool Suite 238
Liverpool University,
    Institute of Popular
    Music 239
Liverpool Beat 91
Lodder, Steve 247
Lodge, John 119
London Town 187–8, 189
'Lonely People' 174
'Long And Winding Road,
    The' 179, 255–6
'Long Tall Sally' 82
'Looking For Changes'
    229
'Love Me Do' 84, 85, 86
'Lovely Linda, The' 139
'Lovers That Never Were'
    229
Lowe, John Charles Duff
    24, 40, 41, 274–5
LSD 114
Lutton, Davy 168
Lynne, Jeff 225, 242

McCartney, Heather (step-
    daughter) 128, 250–1
McCartney, (James) Paul
    life
        Irish background 16
        birth 17
        schooling 22–6, 36
        first recording 74

move to London 106, 107
rumours of death 118
marriage to Linda 133
moves to Sussex home 133–4
moves into London home 134
first solo album 138–40
extradition from Japan 195
first grandchild 251
receives knighthood and coat of arms 252–3
art exhibitions 261–2
marriage to Heather 269

character
as performer 55–6, 65, 149, 165–6, 185–7, 192–3, 223, 230
as "sunny boy" of The Beatles 63
reverence for other singers 82, 95
business sense 154

interests
composition (see *compositions by Paul*)
musical 19–20, 22–3, 97–8, 100
visual arts 25, 43, 175, 261–2
contemporary and avant-garde ideas 45, 97–8, 112–13, 115
political issues 110–11, 156–7, 242–3, 266–7
in religions and mysticism 121
rural life 159–60
animal rights 198–9

McCartney, James (son) 186–7, 250–1, 252, 266
McCartney, Jim (father) 17, 51
musical interests 18–19, 35–6
'Walking In The Park With Eloise' 19, 149, 171
and Best 85
death 184
McCartney, Linda (née Eastman) 127, 128, 138
moves in with Paul 129
marries Paul 133
as musician 141, 142, 152, 153
as singer 176 vegetarian food company 199, 254
political sympathies 207
Paul's film 209
and *Oobu Joubu* 250
illness 252
death 255
memorial concerts 255–6
McCartney, Mary (daughter) 133, 250–1
McCartney, Mary (née Mohin, mother) 16, 17, 25
McCartney, (Peter) Michael (brother - later Mike McGear) 18, 72, 82–3, 106, 128, 165, 216, 274
McCartney, Ruth 120, 184–5, 198, 215, 270–1
Russian album and tour 224–5
McCartney, Stella 141–2, 250–2
*McCartney* 138–40, 144, 146
*McCartney II* 201
McCarty, Jim 249
McCormack, John 238
McCracken, Hugh 143

McCulloch, Jimmy 169–70, 172, 174, 183, 187
McCullogh, Henry 149–51, 152–3
in Wings 152
leaves Wings 167
McGear, Mike (see *McCartney, [Peter] Michael*)
McGough, Roger 46, 82
McIntosh, Robbie 220
McManus, Declan (Elvis Costello) 217–19, 229, 255
McManus, Ross 218–19
McMasters, Andy 185
McVay, Ray 148
*Magic Christian, The* 137, 170
Magic Christians, The 137
Magic Mushroom Band 231, 232–3
*Magical Mystery Tour* 121–2
Magritte, René 43, 175
Maharishi Mahesh Yogi 120–1
Maloney, Paddy 205
Manley, Colin 48, 69, 267–8
Mann, Manfred 132
Manor Studios 160–1
Marmalade 130
Marsden, Beryl 278
Marsden, Gerry 165, 188, 276–8
Marsh, Tony 89
Martin, George 52–3, 84, 105, 117, 166, 204–5, 278–9 influence on Beatles songs 85
in Paul's film 209
Marvin, Hank B 191
'Mary Had A Little Lamb' 157, 165
Mathis, Johnny 116
Mattacks, Dave 205
Matthews, David 246
'Maxwell's Silver Hammer' 135
Mayall, John 170

'Maybe I'm Amazed' 139
'Medicine Jar' 174
*Melody Maker*
    and Paul 146, 158,
    189, 207
    and Wings 166
    John and Paul in 180
Menuhin, Yehudi 115
*Mersey Beat* 75, 78, 85
Merseybeats, The 91, 226,
    273–4
Merseyside (see *Liverpool
    and Merseyside*)
Michell, Adrian 228–9
'Michelle' 100, 166
*Midland Beat* 79, 92
Miles, Barry 109, 111–12,
    125, 220 *Many Years
    From Now* 254
Millander, Colin 66
Miller, Jimmy 130, 131
Miller, Steve 253–4
"Million Dollar Quartet"
    213
Mills Brothers 191–2
Mills, Heather 257–60,
    268–9
    early life 257–8 meeting
    with Paul 260 marriage
    to Paul 269
Mindbenders 94, 132,
    215–16
Mingard, Mike 195
Miracles, The 68
'Mistress And Maid' 229
Mitchell, Mitch 168
Mockingbirds 216
"Modern Dance" 232–3
Monterey, International
    Pop Music Festival 115
Montez, Chris 89
*Monty Python's Flying
    Circus* 122
Mood Six 231
Moody Blues, The 92–4,
    118–19, 145
Moon, Keith 191
Moonboot, Garry 232
Moore, Tommy 48–9, 51
Moores, John 27–8
Morrison, Van 132, 206,
    212, 231, 238–9

Motors, The 185
Motown 98
'Move Over Busker' 217
Moynihan, Johnny 151
MPL Communications
    154, 177
Mud 177
Mull of Kintyre 107, 159
'Mull Of Kintyre' 188–9
Munro, Matt 37, 52–3,
    96, 97, 212, 260
*Music* (periodical) 237–8,
    246
musicals, songs from 73
'Must Do Something
    About That' 176
*My Bonnie* (EP) 75
'My Bonnie Lies Over The
    Ocean' 74, 75, 81
'My Brave Face' 219
'My Dark Hour' 253–4
'My Love' 157–8, 162–3

Nashville Teens 221
National Trust 203
Nesmith, Mike 249
New Age music 248–9
New York Philharmonic
    Orchestra players 143
Newby, Chas 67, 69
Newley, Anthony 210
Newman, Andy 170
Nigeria, recordings in 167
Nilsson, Harry 176, 181,
    182
*NME* Pollwinners'
    Concert (Wembley,
    1965) 94 on
    McCartneys 144, 207
    on 'dinosaur' acts 195
'No More Lonely Nights'
    209
'No Other Baby' 263
Northern Ireland,
    Troubles 156, 207
Nyman, Michael 282

Oasis 242, 243
'Ob-la-di Ob-la-da' 130
*Off The Ground* 228–9
*Oh Boy!* (TV series)
    29–30

'Old Siam Sir' 191
Oldham, Andrew Loog
    77, 90
'Once Upon A Long Ago'
    212
'Only Love Remains' 210,
    211, 281
Ono, Yoko 109–10, 114,
    126–7, 133, 134,
    241–2, 269, 270
    and The Beatles 129
    and Paul's extradition
    from Japan 195
*Oobu Joobu* 250
*Open For Engagements*
    275
Orb, The 232, 233
Orbison, Roy 52, 89, 141,
    218, 225
Orenstein, Harold 200
Oriental music, into pop
    music 97
Osbourne, Ozzy 282–3
'Over The Rainbow' 50,
    73
Overlanders, The 100
Owen, Alun 82
Ozoroff, John 276

Paice, Ian 263
Paolozzi, Eduardo 44
Parlophone 81
    The Beatles contract 84
    (see also *Martin,
    George*)
Parnes, Larry 49, 50, 78
Patrick, Bobby 91
Patten, Brian 46, 82
*Paul Is Live* 228
'Penny Lane' 116
People, The 150
Perkins, Carl 205
*Pet Sounds* (The Beach
    Boys) 101
Peter and Gordon 106–7,
    177
Petty, Norman 178
Petty, Tom 225
'Photograph' 163
Pickett, Wilson 136–7
Pidgeon, Brian 235
*pilzen kopf* haircut 62, 71

Pinder, Mike 94
Pink Floyd, The 109
*Pipes Of Peace* 207
'Pipes Of Peace' 207
Pitney, Gene 205–6
Plastic Ono Band, The 129, 140, 145
'Please Please Me' 86
poetry
  jazz-poetry fusions 46
  readings 46–7
  Paul's 265
Polydor Records 72, 81
Poole, Brian 132
Poor Souls, The 79
Pop Art 44
pop music
  polarisation 144–5
  changing audience 212–13
  pop single as loss leader 212
  copying of other writers' music 220–1
  academic respectability 238–9
  disapproval of 240 (see also *rock 'n' roll*)
Presley, Elvis 30, 52, 56, 73
Presley, Reg 206, 243
*Press To Play* 21, 210, 217, 225
Preston, Billy 81, 134
Price, Alan 132, 221, 270
Price, Vincent 206
Pride, Dickie 55
Prince's Trust Tenth Birthday Gala 211
Proby, PJ 224
Procul Harum 125
Prodigy, The 232
protest songs 266
psychedelic music, New Psychedelia 231–2
Putnam, Curly "Junior" 171

Quaife, Pete 261–2
Quarry Men, The 34, 38–47, 178, 220

Quatro, Suzy 206
Queen 205
Quiet Five, The 101
Quinn, Freddy 55, 83

radio music, 1940s 20
Raelettes, The 45
*Ram* 144, 146
"Ramon, Paul" 51
Rapid, Kerry 79
"raves" 232
Ray, Johnnie 95
*Ready Steady Go* 92
'Real Love' 242
'Really Love You' 253
Rebel Rousers (see *Bennett, Cliff*)
*Rebel, The* 62–3
record companies and The Beatles 89, 200, (see also *Apple*, *Polydor*)
recording techniques, using home studio 108, 138–9
  "live" 146
  control of 161–2
  with George Martin 204–5
*Red Rose Speedway* 161–2, 182
Reed, B Mitchell 93
Reeves, Jim 21, 104
Relf, Keith 132
Remo Four, The 48, 103, 268
*Revolver* 115–16
Rhone, Dorothy 59, 76–7
Richard, Cliff 55, 72, 111, 205, 206, 213
'Richard Cory' (Simon) 101, 174
Richards, Keith 90, 101–2, 178
Riley, Terry 249
'Rinse The Raindrops' 266
Rio de Janeiro concert 219
Roberts, Malcolm 36–7, 116
rock 'n' roll 21–2, 67–8
  Donegan on 34
  female performers 152
  (see also *pop music*)

Rockin' Berries, The 57, 92
Roe, Tommy 89
Rogers, Kenny 205
*Rolling Stone* 144, 145, 162
Rolling Stones, The image 90–1
  free open-air concerts 125
  and Linda 128–9
Roulettes, The 87
Roundhouse "happenings" 109, 115
*Run Devil Run* 263–4
Rundren, Todd 249
*Rupert And The Frog Song* 210–11
*Rushes* 234
Russell, Ray 249
Russia-only LP, Paul's 221–4
Russolo, Luigi 233

'Sally G' 171
Salzman, Harry 166
San Francisco, Summer of Love 114
Sartre, Jean-Paul 45
'Say Say Say' 206, 207–8
Scaffold 82–3, 102, 171
Schwartz, Brinsley 164
Searchers, The 102, 177
'Seaside Woman' 152, 168, 170
Secunda, Tony 92–3, 118, 130, 131, 142
See, Melvin (Linda's first husband) 129
'See My Friends' (Kinks) 97
Seiwell, Denny 143, 167
sexually explicit songs 157
*Sgt Pepper Knew My Father* 213
*Sgt Pepper's Lonely Hearts Club Band* 116–17
Shadows, The 43
Shamen, The 232
Shankar, Ravi 115
Shapiro, Helen 89

*Shaved Fish* 190
Shaw, Sandie 126
'She Said Yeah' 263
Sheridan, Tony 50, 54, 57, 72–4, 81, 91, 276
'Shipbuilding' 218
showbands, Ireland 149–50
'Silly Love Songs' 176
Silver Beatles, The 48–53
    as intellectuals 45, 49
    auditioned as backing group 50
Simon, Paul 100–1, 214
Simpson, Jim 56–7
sitar, in pop music 115
*Sixties Sing Nineties* 243
skiffle 34–5
Small Faces, The 187
Smith, Gordon 277
Smokin' Mojo Filters 244
'So Like Candy' 219
Soft Machine, The 109
'Something In The Air' 169–70
song lyrics, Paul's publication of 265
songwriting partnership with John Lennon 39, 49, 60, 116, 269–70
    reason for starting 68
    George Martin's first opinion 84
    differing tastes 100
    after The Beatles 136, (see also *compositions*)
'soul' music 68, 98–9
Spector, Phil 135, 230
Spiegl, Fritz 221
*Spike* 219
Spinetti, Henry 223
*Spiral* 248
'Spirits Of Ancient Egypt' 174
Stairway 249
*Standing Stone* 246–8
Stanshall, Vivian 123
Star-Club (Hamburg) 78, 81, 83, 203, 265
Starr, Barbara 209
Starr, Ringo
    as Best's replacement 84–5

on Best 85
and end of The Beatles 135
in *The Magic Christian* 137
post-Beatles 146, 159, 163, 176, 180
    collaborations with Paul 205, 209, 253
    narration 211
    and *Anthology* 241 and John Lennon's tapes 242
*Stately Horn* 248
Steel, John 270
Steele, Tommy 34
Steeleye Span 177
Stewart, Eric 205, 215–17
Stewart, Rod 139
Stigwood, Robert 142
Stockhausen, Karlheinz 113, 115
Stone The Crows 170, 172
*Stope And Smell The Roses* 205
Storm, Rory 68
'Stranglehold' 217
*Strawberries Oceans Ships Forest* 233–4
Strawberry Studio 216
Strong, Barrett 68, 98
Stuart, Hamish 220
Subotnik, Morton 249
success, problems of 229
'Sul-E-Stomp' 232
'Summertime' 73
'Sunday Bloody Sunday' 156
Super Furry Animals 264–5
Supremes, The 100
Sutch, Screaming Lord 55, 230, 233
Sutcliffe, Stuart
    as painter 43, 46, 60
    and John Lennon 47, 51
    in Hamburg 60, 61–2, 63, 69
    as musician 60, 64, 65–6, 69

onstage fight with Paul 66–7
leaves Beatles 69–70, 75
death 83–4
Sweeney's Men 150–1
Swingle Singers 188

T Rex 140, 142
'Take It Away' 205
'Takers, The 88
Tamla-Motown 98
Tavener, John 249
'Taxman' 98
Taylor, James 139
Taylor, Kingsize 68, 91, 102, 103, 265
Te Kanawa, Dame Kiri 236, 238
'Teddy Boy' 139
Teddy Boys 29
television commercials, songs used in 212
10cc 216
'That Day Is Done' 219
'That Would Be Something' 139
Them 101, 132, 212
'Thingummybob' 137
'This One' 219
Thomas, Ray 93
'Those Were The Days' 126
*Thrillington* 188
Thunderclap Newman 169–70
'Till There Was You' 73, 89
'Time To Hide' 176
'Tomorrow Never Knows' 115, 234
*Top Of The Pops* 186
Top Ten (Hamburg) 61, 70, 72, 203
touring, Paul and 152–3, 155–6, 164, 176, 219–20, 267, 269
Townsend, Rob 168
Townshend, Pete 115, 191
Tracey, Stan 282
*Trad Tavern* (TV series) 52
traditional jazz 36, 54

Traffic 221
Traveling Wilburys, The 225
Tremeloes, The 132
Trends, The 88
'Tres Conejos' 237
tribute albums 213
*Tripping The Light Fantastic* 221
Troggs, The 213
*Tug Of War* 204–5
'Tug Of War' 206
Twiggy 126
Twinkle 61
*Two Virgins* 127

Ugly's 130
Ullman, Tracey 209
underground culture 109–10
Undertakers, The 88
Underwood, Lee 128
uniforms
  The Silver Beatles 48
  The Beatles 58, 71, 77
  Laine And The Diplomats 80
United States, "British Invasion" of 101
*Unplugged: The Official Bootleg* 221
Untamed, The 99
'Used To Be Bad' 253, 254

Vanilla Fudge, The 116
*Variety*, on Paul's film 210
Vaughan, Frankie 29–30, 110
Vaughan, Ivan 246
vegetarianism 198–9
*Venus And Mars* 172–5
'Venus And Mars' 173–4
'Veronica' 219
Viceroys, The 79
Vincent, Gene 50, 81
Viscounts, The 87
visual arts, Paul and 25, 43, 175, 261–2
'Voice' 259, 260
Vollmer, Jurgen 63, 71

Walker Brothers 132

Walker, Scott 249–50
'Walking In The Park With Eloise' (Jim McCartney) 19, 149, 171
Waller, Gordon 106–7
Walsh, Sam 102
Walton, Sir William 245–6
Warnes, Jennifer 206
Warwick, Clint 118
'Waterspout' 212
Wayne, Carl 57
'We All Stand Together' 211
Weller, Paul 243
Wet Wet Wet 213, 243
'Whatever Gets You Through The Night' 163
'When I'm Sixty-Four' 116, 166
'When The Saints Go Marching In' 74
Whiskey, Nancy 35
White, Alan 131, 142
"White Album" 118, 127, 129, 135
Whitfield, June 210
Whitten, Chris 220
Wickens, Paul 220
*Wild Life* 146, 147, 148
Wilde, Marty 55, 177
Williams, Allan 47–8, 50, 57, 69
Williams, Angela (Paul's stepmother) 84, 120
Williams, Larry 263
Williams, Terry 223
Willis, Alistair 252
Wilson, Brian 101
Wilson, Jocky 230
Wingfield, Pete 263
Wings 142
  reason for name 141
  first album 146
  launch party 148
  tours 152–3, 155–6, 164, 176
  No 1 hits 163, 168, 189
  in Nigeria 167–8
  auditions for new

members 168–9
new members 168–9, 190
Nashville sessions 170–1
end of 183
in tribute to John Lennon 204
*Wings At The Speed Of Sound* 176
*Wings Greatest* 190
"Wings Over America" 179
'Wino Junkie' 176
Winwood, Steve 131, 201, 212
Wirtz, Mark 117
*With A Little Help From Their Friends* (tribute show) 273–4
*With The Beatles* 99
'Woman' 107
Wonder, Stevie 182, 205, 231
'Wonderful Christmastime' 192
Wood, Chris 131
Wood, Ronnie 261
Woodstock 151
Wooler, Bob 75
'Working Class Hero' (Lennon) 145
World Trade Center attacks 266
'World You're Coming Into, The' 237
Wyman, Astrid 128
Wynette, Tammy 205
Wynter, Mark 87

Yamash'ta, Stomu 249
Yardbirds, The 97, 98
'Yesterday' 96–7, 100, 166, 179, 269, 270, 281
*Young Americans* 181
'Your Mother Should Know' 121–2

Zappa, Frank 161, 250, 261
Zapple records 126